Multicultural Queer:
Australian Narratives

Multicultural Queer: Australian Narratives has been co-published as *Journal of Homosexuality,* Volume 36, Numbers 3/4 1999.

Multicultural Queer: Australian Narratives

Peter A. Jackson
Gerard Sullivan
Editors

Multicultural Queer: Australian Narratives, edited by Peter A. Jackson and Gerard Sullivan, was issued by The Haworth Press, Inc., under the same title, as special issues of Journal *of Homosexuality*, Volume 36, Numbers 3/4 1999, John P. DeCecco, Editor.

Harrington Park Press
An Imprint of
The Haworth Press, Inc.
New York • London

ISBN 1-56023-123-8

Published by

Harrington Park Press, 10 Alice Street, Binghamton, NY 13904-1580 USA

Harrington Park Press is an imprint of The Haworth Press, Inc., 10 Alice Street, Binghamton,
NY 13904-1580 USA

Multicultural Queer: Australian Narratives has been co-published
as *Journal of Homosexuality*, Volume 36, Numbers 3/4 1999.

The development, preparation, and publication of this work has been undertaken with great care.
However, the publisher, employees, editors, and agents of The Haworth Press and all imprints of The
Haworth Press, Inc., including The Haworth Medical Press® and Pharmaceutical Products Press®,
are not responsible for any errors contained herein or for consequences that may ensue from use of
materials or information contained in this work. Opinions expressed by the author(s) are not necessarily those of The Haworth Press, Inc.

The Haworth Press, Inc., 10 Alice Street, Binghamton, NY 13904-1580 USA

Cover design by Kent Chuang and Ray Howard.

Library of Congress Cataloging-in-Publication Data

Multicultural queer : Australian narratives / Peter A. Jackson, Gerard Sullivan, editors.
     p. cm.
    " . . . co-published simultaneously as Journal of homosexuality, volume 36, numbers 3/4 1999."
    Includes bibliographical references and index.
    ISBN 0-7890-0651-0 (alk. paper) ISBN 1-56023-123-8 (pbk. alk. paper)
    1. Minority gays–Australia. 2. Homosexuality–Australia. I. Jackson, Peter A. II. Sullivan,
Gerard. III. Journal of homosexuality.
HQ76.3.A8M85 1998
306.76'6'0994–dc21

                                     98-51298
                                      CIP

INDEXING & ABSTRACTING

Contributions to this publication are selectively indexed or abstracted in print, electronic, online, or CD-ROM version(s) of the reference tools and information services listed below. This list is current as of the copyright date of this publication. See the end of this section for additional notes.

- *Abstracts in Anthropology*
- *Abstracts of Research in Pastoral Care & Counseling*
- *Academic Abstracts/CD-ROM*
- *Academic Search: database of 2,000 selected academic serials, updated monthly*
- *Alternative Press Index*
- *Applied Social Sciences Index & Abstracts (ASSIA) (Online: ASSI via Data-Star) (CD-Rom: ASSIA Plus)*
- *Book Review Index*
- *Cambridge Scientific Abstracts*
- *CNPIEC Reference Guide: Chinese National Directory of Foreign Periodicals*
- *Contemporary Women's Issues*
- *Criminal Justice Abstracts*
- *Criminology, Penology and Police Science Abstracts*
- *Current Contents: Clinical Medicine/Life Sciences (CC: CM/LS) (weekly Table of Contents Service), and Social Science Citation Index. Articles also searchable through Social SciSearch, ISI's online database and in ISI's Research Alert current awareness service*
- *Digest of Neurology and Psychiatry*
- *EMBASE/Excerpta MedicaSecondary Publishing Division*
- *Expanded Academic Index*
- *Family Studies Database (online and CD/ROM)*

(continued)

- *Family Violence & Sexual Assault Bulletin*

- *Higher Education Abstracts*

- *HOMODOK/"Relevant" Bibliographic database, Documentation Centre for Gay & Lesbian Studies, University of Amsterdam (selective printed abstracts in "Homologie" and bibliographic computer databases covering cultural, historical, social and political aspects of gay & lesbian topics)*

- *IBZ International Bibliography of Periodical Literature*

- *Index to Periodical Articles Related to Law*

- *INTERNET ACCESS (& additional networks) Bulletin Board for Libraries ("BUBL") coverage of information resources on INTERNET, JANET, and other networks.*

- *Leeds Medical Information*

- *MasterFILE: updated database from EBSCO Publishing*

- *Mental Health Abstracts (online through DIALOG)*

- *MLA International Bibliography*

- *PASCAL*

- *Periodical Abstracts, Research I (general and basic reference indexing and abstracting data-base from University Microfilms International (UMI))*

- *Periodical Abstracts, Research II (broad coverage indexing and abstracting data-base from University Microfilms International (UMI))*

- *PsychNet*

- *Public Affairs Information Bulletin (PAIS)*

- *Religion Index One: Periodicals, the Index to Book Reviews in Religion, Religion Indexes: RIO/RIT/IBRR 1975- on CD/ROM*

- *Sage Family Studies Abstracts (SFSA)*

- *Social Planning/Policy & Development Abstracts (SOPODA)*

- *Social Sciences Index (from Volume 1 & continuing)*

(continued)

- *Social Science Source: coverage of 400 journals in the social sciences area; updated monthly*
- *Social Work Abstracts*
- *Sociological Abstracts (SA)*
- *Studies on Women Abstracts*
- *Violence and Abuse Abstracts: A Review of Current Literature on Interpersonal Violence (VAA)*

Book reviews are selectively excerpted by the Guide to Professional Literature of the Journal of Academic Librarianship.

Special Bibliographic Notes related to special journal issues (separates) and indexing/abstracting:

- indexing/abstracting services in this list will also cover material in any "separate" that is co-published simultaneously with Haworth's special thematic journal issue or DocuSerial. Indexing/abstracting usually covers material at the article/chapter level.
- monographic co-editions are intended for either non-subscribers or libraries which intend to purchase a second copy for their circulating collections.
- monographic co-editions are reported to all jobbers/wholesalers/approval plans. The source journal is listed as the "series" to assist the prevention of duplicate purchasing in the same manner utilized for books-in-series.
- to facilitate user/access services all indexing/abstracting services are encouraged to utilize the co-indexing entry note indicated at the bottom of the first page of each article/chapter/contribution.
- this is intended to assist a library user of any reference tool (whether print, electronic, online, or CD-ROM) to locate the monographic version if the library has purchased this version but not a subscription to the source journal.
- individual articles/chapters in any Haworth publication are also available through the Haworth Document Delivery Service (HDDS).

For Roger, from whom I learned about many of the issues in this book.

Gerard

ABOUT THE EDITORS

Peter A. Jackson, PhD, is a Research Fellow in Thai History in the Research School of Pacific and Asian Studies at Australian National University in Canberra. Fluent in spoken and written Thai, Dr. Jackson has conducted extensive research on gay and lesbian communities in Bangkok and nearby provinces. Dr. Jackson was a founding member of the Australian Gay and Lesbian Immigration Task Force and helped develop a Thai language curriculum in Australian high schools. His book, *Dear Uncle Go: Male Homosexuality in Thailand* (1995), was the first major study of male homoeroticism in Thailand. His other books include *Buddhism, Legitimation, and Conflict: The Political Functions of Urban Thai Buddhism* (1989), *The Intrinsic Quality of Skin* (1994), and the forthcoming book *Lady Boys, Tom Boys, Rent Boys: Male and Female Homosexualities in Contemporary Thailand* (The Haworth Press, Inc.).

Gerard Sullivan, PhD, is Senior Lecturer in the Department of Behavioral Sciences at the University of Sydney in Australia. His research interests in gay and lesbian studies include civil rights, health issues, and the social construction of homosexuality in different cultural contexts. A board member of the Australian Centre for Lesbian and Gay Research, Dr. Sullivan is also the co-editor of *Gays and Lesbians in Asia and the Pacific: Social and Human Services* (The Haworth Press, Inc., 1995) and the forthcoming book *Lady Boys, Tom Boys, Rent Boys: Male and Female Homosexualities in Contemporary Thailand* (The Haworth Press, Inc.).

CONTENTS

Acknowledgments

A former director of the Australian Centre for Lesbian and Gay Research at the University of Sydney, Robert Aldrich persuaded us to collaborate and organize a conference in 1995 on homosexuality and cultural differences, which led to the idea for this book. The project was supported in part by the Department of Behavioural Sciences and the Faculty of Health Sciences at the University of Sydney, the Sydney Gay and Lesbian Mardi Gras, and the AIDS branches of the Commonwealth Department of Human Services and Health, and New South Wales Department of Health. Gary Simes, Stephen Murray and Robert Aldrich provided bibliographic support, and Garry Wotherspoon, Clive Faro, Lily Rahim and Sally Tapscott gave helpful comments on parts of the draft. Tony Hassett, Stephanie Cooke and Inthira Padmindra provided administrative support for the project. In addition, Laureen Asato and Sabi Inderkum, Laurence Leong, and the Komori family provided assistance while Gerard was doing research for this book, as did staff at the Institute for the Study of Social Change at the University of California at Berkeley. Our thanks and appreciation to Kent Chuang and Ray Howard for the cover design, and to those photographed who include: Hinde Ena Burstin, Uma Kali Shakti, Annie Goldflam, Russell Goldflam, Kent Chuang, Pak Liu, and Nicholas Kokindis. We would also like to thank the many friends and informants who generously shared their experiences, feelings and ideas with us and who have shown us new worlds. The list is long and their generosity great. We thank them for their time, hospitality and support.

Gerard Sullivan
Peter A. Jackson

Foreword

When they think of Australia, many people outside the country still think of the infamous White Australia Policy, under which people of non-European ancestry were effectively prohibited from migrating to this country for the first six decades of the twentieth century. However, a racially non-discriminatory immigration policy was formulated in the early 1970s and, as a result, Australia is now a genuinely and thoroughly multicultural country: over 20 percent of the population was born overseas and a further 20 percent of the population has parents who were born abroad–a high proportion of whom are from non-English-speaking countries. In addition, anti-discrimination legislation now operates in most federal and state jurisdictions in Australia and this gives a measure of protection to people on the basis of several factors, including their ancestry and ethnicity, and in some areas on the basis of their sexual orientation. A process of reconciliation is also underway between immigrants and their descendants, on the one hand, and indigenous Australians, on the other.

Over the past 200 years, Australia has been host to successive waves of immigrants, both refugees and free settlers, many from war-torn countries, or areas which have experienced economic or political unrest. In addition to a constant stream of immigrants from the United Kingdom and New Zealand, traditionally the sources of most new residents, Australia has received large numbers of settlers from Southern and Eastern Europe following the conclusion of World War II, Lebanese in the 1970s, and more recently, Africans and residents of the former Yugoslavia. Australia is closer to Asia than any other Western country, sharing a common sea border with Indonesia, and it has a long history of providing humanitarian assistance to people in need in the Asian region. After the end of the Vietnam war in 1975, Australia became a haven for many refugees from Indo-china. These Asian refugees have been joined by free settlers from China, the Philippines, Malaysia, Hong Kong, Korea, and many other countries in the region. This process has changed the face of Australia, and over thirty percent of the populations of the major cities of Sydney and Melbourne are now overseas born.

The arrival of such large numbers of immigrants, especially when they come from cultures different from that of the host society, brings with it enormous social change. Local people must become accustomed to having others in their environment who speak different languages, practice different religions, eat different food, and who have different ways of thinking and relating to others. For people to live harmoniously in a context of cultural diversity they need to learn about ways different from those they grew up with; and to tolerate, accept and share resources with those who are different from themselves. This process necessarily takes some time and, as might be expected, there are pockets of resistance. Established residents who feel threatened or vulnerable rather than seeing opportunities in social change may not be very hospitable to newcomers; and immigrants, especially older ones, who find their new environment bewildering, dismaying or too challenging may be slow, or even unable, to adapt effectively to their new cultural context.

It is sometimes argued that Australian society has changed enormously in a relatively short period as it has come to accommodate people of diverse cultural backgrounds. Indeed, migration has led to many changes to the legal and educational systems, the provision of health, social and welfare services, as well as business and work practices. The multilingual character of official publications and government funding for radio and television broadcasting in Asian and European languages are some of the most visible changes. While this is all very encouraging, there is undoubtedly a considerable amount of work to be done before members of minority ethnic groups can fully participate, with a sense of equity, in the civic, economic, political and cultural domains of life in Australia.

I am very pleased indeed to have been invited to write a foreword to this insightful and much needed book, which I believe will contribute to the development of an even more inclusive Australian society. The articles in this book vividly illustrate how, in many ways, the lesbian and gay communities reflect the larger society of which they are part. Lesbian and gay members of ethnic minorities still sadly experience at times visible prejudice and discrimination when participating in gay and lesbian spaces in Australia's cities. Whilst overt discrimination is certainly less common than more subtle forms of social exclusion, such as those described by authors in this volume, pervasive stereotyping and marginalizing practices remain a formidable obstacle for individuals who are consciously aware of their ethnic minority status while struggling to come to terms with their homosexuality.

In this volume, the authors provide a comprehensive coverage of many important issues regarding the lesbian and gay experience of individuals from ethnic minorities. These include:

- culturally shaped attitudes towards homosexuality
- cultural variations in homosexual conceptualization, identity, and expression

- oscillation and attempts at mediation between membership of an ethnic group and the lesbian and gay community; and
- interaction (including partnerships) between lesbians and gay men of different cultural backgrounds.

This is not a book about "problems." It is a balanced account of both the positive and negative aspects of gay and lesbian life in a multicultural environment. I think it is important to emphasize the book's encompassing perspective. As a Vietnamese-born gay man living in Australia, I could resonate with several authors' autobiographical accounts, as well as relate them to the experiences of some of my clients. In this respect, health service providers will hopefully find this book informative as well as culturally enriching. Being a member of a minority group can cause enormous psychological strain and surviving double or triple minority status can be a most challenging experience even for those with extensive support networks. Unfortunately, many immigrants, and more so those who are refugees, often have to cope with very limited support, because of, among other reasons, separation from, and fragmentation of, the extended family network as well as language barriers and insufficient practical knowledge of local bureaucracies.

While the articles in this volume are mainly about Australia and for the most part deal with specific ethnic groups, their applicability is much broader than these parameters. One can find very similar situations in the United States, Canada and Britain, as well as in a number of European countries. Furthermore, while the descriptions of people's experiences in this book–and particularly those in the autobiographical accounts–are sometimes drawn from specific cultural examples, the processes of ostracization, alienation and exclusion (from one's family, ethnic group, or the gay and lesbian community) apply widely.

It would be very regrettable for leaders and members of ethnic communities to dismiss this book simply because it does not contain a chapter dealing with their specific cultural group. Homosexuality is universal, even if it takes somewhat different forms, or is driven underground because of societal condemnation. The subject of homosexuality generates so much anxiety and apprehension in Vietnamese culture as to remain an unspeakable taboo. Because we do not see it or are not familiar with it, or refuse to acknowledge it, does not mean that it does not exist. The denial of homosexuality has widespread and costly sequelae. Those who experience homosexual feelings are subjected to enormous stress from cognitive dissonance while their families either try to ignore their painful experiences, or in more desperate cases, attempt to cure their "affected" relatives through forced marriages. Ignoring homosexuality and cultural diversity does not make them go away, but rather leads to intolerable and damaging conflict within and between individuals. In many ways, this book applies as much to the Vietnamese, Swahili, Greek and other communities as it does to the Italian, Chinese, Jewish and other cultures who are specifically referred to here.

Finally I commend the authors and editors of this volume. A degree of courage was undoubtedly required by some of the authors of the articles in this book. For many of them, it necessitated that they take on a public homosexual identity. This may not be tolerated by some of their families and ethnic communities, who would rather retain their privacy or completely disregard this aspect of the author's life. I have much enjoyed working with Gerard Sullivan and Peter Jackson, the editors of this anthology. Gerard and Peter come from Anglo-Australian backgrounds, but in both their professional and private lives they demonstrate firm convictions to multiculturalism and internationalism.

Tran Binh Dong
Sydney
May 1998

About the Contributors

Tony Ayres is a Melbourne-based writer and filmmaker. He has written extensively for Australian television, including two miniseries, *Naked* (1995) for the Australian Broadcasting Corporation and *The Violent Earth* (1997) for Channel Nine. He has also edited two anthologies of short stories, *String of Pearls* (1996, Sydney: Allen and Unwin) and *Hard* (1997, Sydney: Black Wattle Press). Tony is currently developing a feature film, *Lowlife*.

Hinde Ena Burstin is a founding member of the Jewish Lesbian Group of Victoria, a community worker with NESB women with disabilities, and activist in Yiddish, lesbian, disability and anti-racism communities in Victoria. Her poetry, fiction and essays in Yiddish and in English have been published in the United States, Canada and Australia.

Leon Cantrell is Chair of the Academic Board at Southern Cross University, Lismore, New South Wales, Australia. He holds a PhD from the University of Nebraska and has published widely in the area of Australian literary and cultural studies. His current research interests include Australia/Asia relations and academic governance.

Ling-Yen Chua is currently completing her PhD dissertation examining the intersections of race and sexuality in the Department of Film and Literature, University of Warwick (United Kingdom).

Chuang, Kent Koy-Wah, was born in Hong Kong in 1960 and now resides in Sydney, Australia, where he works as a landscape architect (but he hopes to study full-time in 1998 and become a "struggling artist"). He has also worked on a contractual basis for The Asian Project, a part of the Peer Education program at the AIDS Council of New South Wales (ACON), in which he conducted workshops for gay Asian men and facilitated Silkroad, an Asian social and support group, as well as the Positive Asian group. Kent's other involvements in Sydney's gay community include Asians and Friends, a social and support group; the Community Support Network (CSN), a volunteer group providing support to people living with HIV/AIDS (PLWHA); and Ankali, a volunteer group providing emotional support to PLWHAs.

Abby Duruz is an Anglo-Australian with a passion for identity politics. She has worked as a radio and documentary producer for many years including acting as the Executive Producer of the Muff Divas and Drag Queens project. At the age of 17 she informed her two academic mothers that she would "rather die" than follow in their footsteps. This is her first print publication.

Annie Goldflam is the Director of the Centre for Research for Women, a joint facility of the four public universities in the state of Western Australia. She lives in Perth and has worked in a range of feminist and anti-racist positions and is a keen member of the Coalition of Activist Lesbians in Western Australia.

Amos Hee is a community researcher and writer, who was working as a consultant for the Ethnic Youth Issues Network (EYIN) at the time of writing this paper. He is currently working as a research consultant, along with Damien Ridge, using ethnographic methods with marginalized and disaffected young people at high risk of self-harm, and is engaged in a suicide prevention program in Melbourne. His main research interests are in cross cultural issues, sexuality, ethnicity and youth culture. He is the author of *Sex, Living & Dying: Cross Cultural Meanings & HIV/AIDS* (Melbourne 1997), a manual for community workers. He has also written a number of articles and papers on cross cultural issues in sexuality, design and health.

Rose Kizinska, born in Australia to Polish immigrant parents, is a free-floating, pre-post-panic-punk-siege-Xgrrrl, fully equipped with good eyebrows and "the-world-needs-a-major-overhaul" look in her eyes. During the daylight hours, she works at a youth services office in Melbourne's north-west. At night she plots revenge and scams. She is also a postgraduate at Victoria University of Technology, Melbourne, and is working on her first novel, ©*Dead Cars In Westall.*

Victor Minichiello received his PhD from The Australian National University and is Head and Associate Professor in the Department of Health Studies at the University of New England, Armidale, Australia. His main research interests are in gerontology, sexual health, and sexuality. He is the coeditor of *Venereology: The Interdisciplinary International Journal of Sexual Health* and author of several books including *AIDS in Australia; Gerontology: A Multidisciplinary Approach; Sociology of Aging: International Perspectives*; and *In-Depth Interviewing: Principles, Techniques, Analysis.*

Baden Offord is currently finishing his PhD at Southern Cross University, Australia (Lismore, New South Wales) on "Homosexual Rights as Human Rights in Australia, Indonesia and Singapore." His research interests include queer and human rights theory, Indian philosophy and Australia/Asia relations. He is a member of the International Lesbian and Gay Association, The Theosophical Society (India), Amnesty International and the northern New South Wales gay social group, Tropical Fruits.

Maria Pallotta-Chiarolli lectures in social diversity and sexual health at Deakin University, Burwood, and is a researcher and consultant on the issues of ethnicity, gender, sexuality, and HIV/AIDS, particularly in relation to education and health. She has recently produced the monograph *Cultural Diversity and Men Who Have Sex with Men*, based on a national audit of health services, for the National Centre in HIV Social Research, Macquarie University.

Damien Ridge is a research Fellow in the Faculty of Health and Behavioral Sciences at Deakin University, Melbourne, Australia. He is currently researching and publishing in the areas of culture, health promotion in schools, HIV prevention, marginality and suicide among young people. The analysis for the current article is drawn from his doctoral research (Ridge, 1997), focusing on the meanings, dynamics and contexts which underpin condom use and unprotected anal sex between men.

Rasyid Sanitioso received his PhD from Princeton University and lectures in the School of Behavioural Science at the University of Melbourne, Australia. His research has focused on motivated changes in self-concept and stereotyping. He has more recently been involved in AIDS-related research.

Tran Binh Dong escaped from Vietnam in a boat in 1979 at the age of fifteen. After four months in a Malaysian refugee camp, he was taken to live with a Swiss family in Lausanne through the assistance of the charitable organization *Terre des Hommes*. He migrated to Australia in 1980 and the following year became the first Vietnamese dux (summa cum laude) of Christian Brothers' College in Adelaide. He obtained degrees in Arts, Music Performance, and Science from the University of Adelaide prior to commencing medical training at the Flinders University of South Australia in 1986. He became a Fellow of Trinity College of Music (London) in 1992 and subsequently completed masters degrees in Criminology and Jurisprudence at the University of Sydney. He is currently working as a Trainee Psychiatrist and writing a PhD thesis in French Literature on Andre Gide.

Audrey Yue is Lecturer in Cultural Studies at The University of Melbourne, Melbourne. She was born in Singapore in 1966 and is an immigrant Peranakan Chinese NESBian (cyber)activist and graduate student on the verge of completing her PhD dissertation on postcolonial Hong Kong cinema at La Trobe University in Melbourne. Her writings focus on sexuality, identity and media technologies, and her latest essay, "Colour Me Queer! Some Notes Towards The NESBian" appeared in *Meanjin* (special issue *Australia Queer*). She currently lives in Melbourne, a place where she has temporarily, momentarily, and virtually called "home." Her most recent toy is the all-essential accessory, a matt champagne exoskeletal multi-laser karaoke machine!

Introduction:
Ethnic Minorities
and the Lesbian and Gay Community

Gerard Sullivan

University of Sydney

Peter A. Jackson

Australian National University, Canberra

This book is about the way that people from ethnic minorities in Australia (i.e., those who are not of Anglo-Celtic[1] background) view homosexuality, their experience as homosexual men and women, and their feelings about the lesbian and gay community. It is about people who have double or triple minority statuses–as gay people, as members of ethnic minorities, and for lesbians, as women. It is about minorities within minorities and it looks at how minorities treat one another. Almost all the articles refer to the situation in Australia, but most of the issues raised apply in other multicultural societies, and certainly to western, English-speaking countries including Canada, New Zealand, the United Kingdom and the United States.

In recent years, issues of race, ethnicity, multiculturalism, immigration, and land rights and socio-economic justice for indigenous Australians have been at the focus of a series of contentious and often divisive debates in Australia. This book, looking at the intersections of race, culture, gender and sexuality, is a contribution to an ongoing discussion of key issues facing contemporary Australia. Because of the political immediacy and personal relevance of the issues discussed in the following articles to us, the editors, as Australian-born gay men, our editorial collaboration on this project has at

[Haworth co-indexing entry note]: "Introduction: Ethnic Minorities and the Lesbian and Gay Community." Sullivan, Gerard, and Peter A. Jackson. Co-published simultaneously in *Journal of Homosexuality* (The Haworth Press, Inc.) Vol. 36, No. 3/4, 1999, pp. 1-28; and: *Multicultural Queer: Australian Narratives* (ed: Peter A. Jackson and Gerard Sullivan) The Haworth Press, Inc., 1999, pp. 1-28. Single or multiple copies of this article are available for a fee from The Haworth Document Delivery Service [1-800-342-9678, 9:00 a.m. - 5:00 p.m. (EST). E-mail address: getinfo@haworthpressinc.com].

times required us to think through our respective positions on an array of theoretical, political and other issues. This process has highlighted both the issues on which we agree as well as points on which we hold differing views and perspectives. Some of the issues we have discussed and debated during the editorial process include: the importance of post-structuralist or queer theory for analyzing race-ethnicity-sexuality issues; the place of alternative and experimental forms of discourse in representing and considering these issues; differing conceptualizations of contemporary queer social and cultural life in Australia (e.g., "gay/lesbian community" vs. "multiple queer subcultures"); and how to interpret the recent rise of public discourses of racism in this country. In part, these differences reflect our respective academic training and affiliations. Peter Jackson is a cultural historian concentrating on twentieth century Thailand, while Gerard Sullivan is a sociologist with research interests in lesbian and gay studies, ethnicity and health care. Our differences reflect the diversity of views and outlooks in Australia in the late 1990s and point to the vital need to both imagine and develop forms of collaboration that cross boundaries of race, ethnicity, culture, gender and sexuality.

This introduction examines the context of *Multicultural Queer* within lesbian and gay studies and then looks at some of the issues which face intercultural gay couples. We then provide a brief description of Australian settlement patterns, history of immigration, population and cultural policy for those readers who may not be familiar with Australian geography, history and society. Some figures on "gay immigration" to Australia and on attitudes towards lesbians and gay men in Australia are also presented, and we conclude with some general comments about ethnic identity and an introduction to the articles in this volume, most of which discuss the experience and representation of lesbians and gay men from ethnic minorities.

MULTICULTURAL QUEER IN THE CONTEXT
OF LESBIAN AND GAY STUDIES

This book takes its place among considerable scholarship about homosexuality, and lesbian and gay communities. The pace of this work has been steadily increasing over the past 50 years and the great majority of it has been conducted in the United States. In the immediate post-World War II period, much of the writing on this topic was by psychiatrists, who often discussed homosexuals in very pejorative terms, for example, as mentally ill, if not criminal; unreliable, seditious, hedonistic and sexually obsessed. As such, academia and the professions supported discrimination against homosexuals and acted as a foil against the newly emerging homosexual rights groups in a period when there was concern to shore up traditional family values and lifestyles after the disruptions of the war (Sullivan, 1987).

Gradually, research of a less prejudicial nature was conducted and published, using non-clinical populations as research participants. With the help of early American homosexual rights groups, in 1957, Evelyn Hooker, a psychologist at the University of California at Los Angeles, published a landmark article in which she reported that a group of homosexual men and a group of heterosexual men with similar demographic characteristics were indistinguishable on a battery of psychological tests. Hooker's work was influential in the decision of the American Psychiatric Association in 1973 to remove homosexuality per se from its list of mental disorders (Bayer, 1981; D'Emilio, 1997). Perhaps the next most significant piece of academic writing on the subject which was not negative or homophobic was that of Mary McIntosh (1968) in Britain who noted that while homosexual desire might be present in all societies, only some societies create a homosexual identity, and she was interested in the conditions which encouraged this. Hooker's and McIntosh's work must have taken some courage. Even 25 years later, there was considerable discrimination against social scientists who conducted research about homosexuality, and all the more so if their research conclusions were gay-affirming, or if they were thought to be gay themselves. A study by the American Sociological Association (1981) found that sociologists involved in lesbian and gay studies were less likely to be hired, given tenure or promoted than others.

The AIDS epidemic contributed to gay studies becoming a more legitimate area of research. More information was required about sexual behavior, particularly that of men who have sex with men, and the cooperation of the gay and lesbian community with health departments has been helpful in promoting safe sex practices. With the explosion of HIV/AIDS research came an outpouring of gay and lesbian studies. Most of this was written by white academics who studied and wrote about the communities (or segments of communities) to which they belonged. The result is that we now know a considerable amount about the history and sociology of middle-class, mostly white, gay men and somewhat less about lesbians. Far less is known about working-class homosexual women and men, about those who belong to ethnic minorities, or about those who live in non-western countries. Important, if limited, research has been published about those in these groups.[2] In this respect, lesbian and gay studies is following a pattern set by women's studies, which has progressively investigated race, class and gender, and the intersections of these groups, as well as about the lives of women in non-western countries.

Studies about sexual behavior conducted under the auspices of HIV/AIDS research have reminded researchers that bisexuality is more prevalent than many realized; that many men who are homosexually active do not see themselves as being gay (or have gay identities) and have little connection with the gay community. It now looks as though it may be the case that the gay and lesbian community is largely and disproportionately populated by white,[3] middle-class men and women. For this reason we have used the term "queer" in the title. By it, we suggest the possibility of other forms of homosexual identity and community than that described in most lesbian and gay studies' literature. The authors of the articles in this volume describe somewhat different self-concepts, relationships with family members, and interactions with friends than most white readers experience. It can be argued that different cultural groups share much in common around the issue of homosexuality but there are often cultural differences and some of these are described in this volume.

THE ECONOMICS OF DESIRE

A theme which runs through many of the articles in this volume is that of intercultural sexual relationships. Often ethnicity is coincidental and irrelevant to the partners in these relationships, who love each other for other reasons–it just so happens that they came from different ethnic backgrounds. There are undoubtedly many bicultural couples whose relationship is uninfluenced by the taint of racism, but this is not always the case. The participants in many interracial couples are confronted with issues related to the personal and domestic politics of cultural and economic equality. There is a variety of factors which underlie some people's preference for partners of a different race and/or culture.[4] While some participants are interested in internationalism and in other cases there is a fair exchange of resources, less high minded motives are not uncommon. Some of these can be inferred from the following stories.

> A single, white, gay male colleague who is politically progressive and to the left, quipped, "Well, that's what happens when you turn 50–you either become a rice queen or go in for leather and S&M."[5]

The classified advertisements at the back of many Australian gay publications show that our colleague is not the only person who thinks this way. A not atypical advertisement from *Capital Q*, a Sydney gay newspaper, reads: "I'm looking for a young Asian guy, 18-25 years old, who would like to have an older (50 years old) Aussie guy as a friend." There is a common belief among older, white Australians that Asians have greater respect for their elders than do white Australians, and that while it would be difficult for most older, white gay men who are not wealthy to find a white sexual partner much younger than themselves, "Asian" gay men are available.[6]

Exploitation is a part of some relationships between white men and their partner from a racial minority. Such an experience was likely the reason for the headline, "I don't do laundry" in an advertisement placed in a Sydney gay newspaper by an Australian of Chinese ancestry who had immigrated from Singapore. The only Asian character in Alan Hollinghurst's novel *The Folding Star* is 40-year-old "little" Andy, "a Filipino *boy*" (emphasis added) who is the victim of domestic violence, servitude and paternalism (1995: 332-3). Hollinghurst's book is fiction, but it powerfully reflects the stereotype of Asian gay men as exploited, dependent and powerless.

Another reason for a strong preference by some white gay men for partners from other cultural backgrounds is alienation from their own culture. Some men wish to escape prescriptions of masculinity which they find difficult, or do not wish, to emulate. Homophobia and other restrictions of western models of masculinity sometimes lead to idealization of men in other cultures, from whom it is hoped more compatible roles of what it means to be a man can be learned and a more secure identity established. Though their motives were often complex, elements of this pattern can be discerned in the biographies of E. M. Forster, John Addington Symonds, Paul Bowles and T. E. Lawrence among others (Aldrich, 1996). Alan Patience (1996) and Peter Jackson (1994) describe more contemporary, Australian examples.[7]

These stories may be contrasted with comments by Australian men of Asian ancestry, many of whom report a strong preference for a white partner. A number of these men complain that it is difficult to find white partners of a similar age, educational level, and social class. It is common for them to report only being able to find a partner several or many years older than themselves. An older partner is not always a preference, but a reality. Putting both sides of the story together, it is apparent that the exchange in these relationships is very often not financial in nature, but has more to do with cultural capital and the devaluation of ethnic minorities and the damaging impact upon homosexual men of homophobic forms of masculinity. A number of gay Australians of Asian ancestry say that they would consider it "incestuous" to have sex with another man of Asian ancestry. Why they think this, most are unable or unwilling to say, but some have speculated on the "colonization of desire" due to the prevalence of white males as sex symbols in advertisements and movies, and the extreme under-representation of anyone but white men in gay culture. There may be some truth in this explanation, but as it is not universal that non-white gay men prefer white partners, it appears to be of limited validity.[8] Another explanation contained in the pages of this volume is that some members of some minorities find it difficult to resolve ethnic identity and homosexual behavior, to say nothing of a gay identity, and so leave their cultural heritage to become gay or lesbian. The stories from both sides beg the question of whether or not the desire for a partner of particular ethnic backgrounds (and exclusion of others) involves prejudice, and the use of this preference as a selection criterion for partners is an act of racial discrimination.

AUSTRALIA IN BRIEF

Australia is very unevenly settled and is a highly urbanized society. It is a large country, with an area roughly the same as continental USA, and is divided into six states and two territories. However, much of the land is not arable and half of the area of the continent contains only 0.3 percent of the population. Most of the population lives in cities in the south-east of the country. Only 14 percent of the population lives in rural areas. Sydney and Melbourne are the largest cities, with over three million residents each, and together account for 38 percent of the total population of 18 million. There are three other cities of more than one million residents (Brisbane, Perth and Adelaide) and seven more cities with more than 100,000 residents.

Sydney is often regarded as the most internationally oriented Australian city, and is the largest city in the country. It is also the "gay capital" and hosts the annual Sydney Gay and Lesbian Mardi Gras, a month-long festival of lesbian and gay culture culminating in a huge parade and party, held each summer, usually in February. In recent years, almost half (44 percent) of Australia's new immigrants have chosen the state of New South Wales as their intended place of residence, and most of these settled in Sydney, the state's capital city. Almost one-quarter (23 percent) of the country's new immigrants settle in Victoria (mostly in Melbourne), and 15 percent in Queensland (McLennan, 1996, 1997; Murphy, 1996;---1996a).

At about two percent, indigenous Australians[9] are a small but important component of the population. In the century and a half after the white invasion began in January 1788, strenuous efforts were made to dispossess the country's original inhabitants of their land and culture. In many cases they have been relegated to the fringes of the economy and white society, with their status and experience as ethnic minorities being significantly different from that of minority immigrant groups. For her article in this volume, Abby Duruz interviewed several gay Aboriginal men living in Sydney, but this volume does not deal in detail with the lives of homosexual indigenous Australians. Readers are referred to Gays and Lesbians Aboriginal Alliance (1994) and Hodge (1993) for further information about this group.

AUSTRALIAN MULTICULTURALISM

Since European settlement began in Australia in 1788, race has been a contentious issue. Tragic early chapters in the history of Australia involved the decimation of the Aboriginal population and the destruction of their culture by introduced diseases; racism, including policies that pushed indigenous people onto unproductive land; and even genocide on the part of white settlers. While the intensity of this early racism and ill-treatment abated, racism towards the Aboriginal population has remained widespread. In recent years, however, a national reconciliation process has begun which offers a glimmer of hope for a more harmonious future in which the cultures and rights of indigenous Australians are respected. Although the issue remains contentious in the courts, and in public opinion and political arenas, Aboriginal land rights have been established, and growing numbers of activists have emerged demanding increasing rights for Aborigines. The issues of social and economic justice for Indigenous Australians, based on recognition of land rights and formal statements of apology for past injustices, are widely regarded as some of the most contentious issues in contemporary Australian political and cultural life.

In the past 200 years, Australia has been host to successive waves of immigrant settlers. In the 40 years after the First Fleet arrived in Sydney in 1788, 77,000 people from Britain, the majority of them convicts, were transported to Australia. After the Declaration of Independence in the United States in 1776, British convicts could no longer be sent to the former British American colonies. From the 1820s, free settlers were encouraged to migrate to the Australian colonies and began to arrive from several countries other than Britain. The population increased almost threefold, to 1.1 million in the 1850s, largely due to immigration from around the world as the result the discovery of gold in the colonies of New South Wales and Victoria. By 1861, at 40,000, Chinese residents were numerically third only to British and Germans in the population. However, public opinion against them led to the Chinese Restriction Act being passed in Victoria and other legislative controls by various other colonial governments on the continent. Following the goldrush, unemployment mounted and opposition to immigration schemes increased in the final decades of the nineteenth century (Department of Immigration and Ethnic Affairs [DIEA], 1978).

In 1901, the six British colonies in Australia (New South Wales, Victoria, Queensland, Tasmania, South Australia, Western Australia) formed a federation of states based in part on the U.S. model. A national capital, Canberra, was established in the 1920s as part of the process of federation. By the time the Commonwealth of Australia came into being on the first day of the twentieth century, the population had increased another three-fold to 3.7 million and its composition had changed so that three quarters (77 percent) were born in Australia, with another 18 percent being immigrants born in Britain. One of the first pieces of legislation passed by the new federal parliament was the Immigration Restriction Act, which came to be known as the White Australia Policy. This law contained provisions for a dictation test in a "European" language (abolished in 1958) which was "flexible enough to guarantee failure by unwanted races" (Edwards, 1988:24). A subsequent federal law, the Naturalization Act of 1903, explicitly excluded applicants of Asian, African or Pacific Island ancestry.

Following World War II, Australia was opened up to refugees and other immigrants wanting to leave war-torn Europe. After the Australian mainland had been attacked by Japan during the War, the then prime minister, Ben Chifley, suggested that a population of 30 million was essential to ensure the country's security from threats of "the yellow peril" to the north. Immigrants were also needed to fuel an industrialization drive and to provide labor to develop Australia's many natural resources. A slogan of the immediate post-War period was "populate or perish," and the immigration program had widespread support. By 1961, Australia had a population of over 10 million, of which only 8 percent were not of British or Irish descent, and most of these were of European ancestry. Between 1961 and 1967 the Italian government suspended an agreement to allow migration to Australia following complaints from immigrants about their status, and in 1963 Spain did the same.

By the mid-1950s Europe was making an economic recovery and several countries had labor shortages. Very gradually, Australia began to make minor exceptions to its White Australia Policy. For example, in 1952 it began to admit the previously excluded Japanese wives of Australian servicemen who had been posted to the Allied occupying forces in Japan. Later, highly qualified non-Europeans were considered for temporary visas of indefinite duration (DIEA, 1978).[10] To this point, successive federal governments had followed assimilationist policies toward all ethnic minorities. For example, many Aboriginal children were taken from their parents and placed in residential schools, with white families or in orphanages, and immigrants were strongly encouraged to speak English and adopt "Australian" values and lifestyles.

In 1971, the Labor Party, which had been in opposition for over two decades, formulated an immigration policy which would not discriminate on grounds of "race or colour of skin or nationality," though the Party's policy also stated that it wanted to avoid "difficult social and economic problems which may follow from an influx of people having different standards of living, traditions and cultures" (DIEA, 1978:28). It won office in 1972 but it was not until 1977 and the arrival of large numbers of Indo-Chinese refugees following the end of the Vietnam war that there was a significant increase in the number of Asian immigrants. At this time, restrictions on radio broadcasts in languages other than English were relaxed, a telephone interpreter and ethnic broadcasting service were established (which over the years has come to include gay programming and news coverage), and a pluralistic, multicultural policy was formulated.[11]

The United Kingdom has traditionally been, and is still, the country supplying the largest number of immigrants to Australia, but the proportion from this source is declining. The proportion of Australian residents of Asian ancestry has now risen to approximately 6 percent of the total population of 18 million and is projected to continue increasing (McNamara et al., 1997; Coughlan, 1997; Price, 1994). Between 1986 and 1991, seven Asian countries (Vietnam, China, Philippines, Malaysia, Hong Kong, India and Sri Lanka) were in the top ten sources of immigrants to Australia (ABS, 1993).

When considering the diversity of the Australian population, a distinction needs to be made between immigrants and residents who were born in Australia. New immigrants require special assistance and services. They are added to the national population and gradually change its character, but the existing population, which includes those born in Australia, is much larger and therefore more significant. Presently, almost one-quarter (23 percent) of the population are immigrants and over 40 percent have one or more parents born overseas (Sullivan & Gunasekaran, 1993; Shu et al., 1995; ABS, 1993). One of the best measures of the diversity of the population is language spoken at home. In 1991, 15 percent of the population spoke languages other than English at home. After English, the languages most widely spoken at home were Italian, Greek, Cantonese and Arabic. Most of the people speaking these languages at home would have been immigrants and their Australian-born children.

The two main indicators of ethnicity used in Australia are country of birth and language spoken at home. The data for these are quite reliable, though they are limited in terms of providing an overall picture of racial and cultural diversity within contemporary Australia. For example, an immigrant with Russian parents may have been born in China, while an immigrant from Fiji may speak English at home and be of Indian ancestry. Neither do these data provide any information about the ethnic diversity of the population which was born in Australia and which speaks English at home. Australian officialdom has adopted a policy of not collecting data on the basis of race because it is considered to be a category which should be of little social significance. Ethnic, or cultural, differences are respected but governments do not wish to allocate resources on the basis of race alone or on the appearance of a person.[12] Services for people who need special assistance because of their inability to use English, including HIV/AIDS education programs, are provided on a limited basis, as are programs to help immigrants settle in Australia. Some assistance is also available to groups who wish to maintain their cultural heritage. However, beyond this, people are encouraged to think of themselves as "Australian," and not to discriminate against one another on the basis of race, ethnicity, country of birth, or a variety of other factors (such as age and sex, or in some jurisdictions such as the state of New South Wales, on the basis of homosexuality or transgenderism). One effect of these policies is the unavailability of reliable information about the proportion of people in Australia who are of European, Asian, African or Aboriginal ancestry, i.e., different racial groups.[13] However, for some purposes it would be useful to know more about "visible minorities" (regardless of birthplace and language spoken at home) because many experience discrimination on the basis of their appearance. Examples of types of discrimination are provided in the articles in this volume.

AUSTRALIAN ETHNIC RELATIONS

Since the early 1970s successive Australian governments have been committed to a version of cultural pluralism called multiculturalism. Fundamental aspects of this policy are an immigration program which does not discriminate on the basis of race, ethnicity, nationality or ancestry and that "each ethnic group desiring it, is permitted to create its own commercial life and preserve its own cultural heritage indefinitely while taking part in the general life of the nation" (Grassby, 1973 quoted by Zubrzycki, 1988:130). Under multiculturalism, an attempt is made to strike a balance between social cohesion and cultural identity (or unity and diversity), and to provide equal access to community resources regardless of ethnicity. It was hoped that one effect of this policy shift away from assimilation would be a greater retention of immigrants, about one-quarter of whom emigrated from Australia in spite of earlier intentions to settle here for the long term. Public medical, welfare and media organizations began providing multilingual services.

Though the current Australian Liberal-National Party government under the leadership of Prime Minister John Howard (elected in March 1996) has not officially stepped away from the policy of multiculturalism, it has withdrawn resources from multicultural programs, and community debate on the issue has been ongoing for the past year or more. A catalyst for the debate was the widely publicized opinions of a first-term Member of Parliament, Pauline Hanson,[14] who criticized Asian migration and Aboriginal welfare spending, and supports a stronger military. The Hanson debate has crystallized sentiments about race relations in the Australian community. The racial harmony of which Australian liberals were proud has been shown to be more superficial than they believed. There have been voices in the past critical of Asian immigration, Aboriginal welfare programs and cultural pluralist policies–views similar to those which Hanson represents–but earlier voices were marginalized and failed to obtain significant community support. Pauline Hanson emerged when a conservative government was in power, which was ambivalent about former policies in the area of ethnicity. With the government remaining silent on the issues raised by Hanson and with sustained economic troubles and a bleak outlook, conservatives around the country listened when Hanson dared to publicly espouse her views, urging a return to the "good old days" of full employment, industry protection and Anglo-Celtic monoculture. Many liberals and minorities hoped that the resultant bad press that this produced in Asia would be brief and soon forgotten, and that anti-discrimination laws, a multicultural electorate and trade dependence on Asia would be more influential in shaping public opinion about immigration and multiculturalism. However, for many members of racial minorities, the debate crystallized their experience of racism on a day-to-day basis and has made them question whether they want to continue to live in Australia. We quote now from an article by Indra McCormack, a young woman born to an Indonesian mother and Caucasian father and who was raised in Chatswood, a middle-class suburb in Sydney. For the past four years McCormack has been living in Indonesia but recently she visited Sydney:

> As I was wandering the streets of Chatswood a few weeks ago, an elderly white-haired man approached without warning and . . . slammed his elbow into the small of my back. I was stunned and slightly winded. By the time I turned, he had disappeared around the corner. Maybe he tripped, my mother suggested. Probably a loony, my partner said. But I wondered if my Asian face was the catalyst for the assault. . . . The incident started me thinking about my hometown and how it, and I, had changed. I grew up in Chatswood, living there for almost 20 years. In those days, we were the only Asians around. Not any more. Chatswood has seen an amazing transformation from a red-tile roof residential suburb into a major business and shopping hub and a centre for Sydney's northern Asian community. . . . The old man who hit me must, I suppose, feel like he's landed in a foreign country. In a funny way, so do I.
>
> Growing up, I felt as Australian as the next kid. . . . But looking back now, my sense of Australian identity didn't protect me completely. Discrimination was subtle and mostly, I think, unconscious. My kindergarten teacher divided the class into two groups. By the end of the year, the other group was creating short sentences with magnetic letters. My group, almost entirely children of . . . migrants, was left to concentrate on finger-painting, undisturbed by spelling and dictation. As a young adult . . . I felt liberated by the push for multiculturalism and inspired by debates over Australia's place in the Asia-Pacific. I became interested in my Indonesian origins.
>
> The recent debate about Asian immigration has produced another shift. . . . Take a look at some of my holiday snapshots. My mother and

I attend an auction at Balmain. The toothy estate agent presses brochures on all prospective buyers except us, the only Asians. Stepping into an old corner pub, we attract hostile glares from the 10 am veterans. We are fawned over in a craft shop . . . while other, non-Asian, customers browse in peace. Nothing spectacular or new there. If I hadn't been hit, if I hadn't heard other disturbing stories, I wouldn't have given these incidents a second thought. It's been a long time since the "Asians Go Home" graffiti held any bite for me.

But now . . . I'm hit by two changes. First, the anonymous graffiti seems more threatening and immediate. Second, my . . . sense of belonging to this country "as an Australian" has been shaken. I feel I am viewed as a foreigner. I have become a member of an undifferentiated "Asian community" by virtue not of my ethnicity, cultural background or language, but mainly because I look Asian. Membership of this new club is compulsory if you look like me. Stereotypes apply.

By thumping an Asian-looking woman–a conspicuous representative of unwanted change–the elderly man vented his fears and outrage and, at the same time levelled a blow for the old Australia he still believes in. Biff! That'll show those Asian bastards where to go. It's this gut reaction to change–striking out at difference and newness–that has suffused the mood of some in the community and has made others, like me, feel less welcome in their own country. (McCormack, 1997:17)

THE POLITICS OF IDENTITY

An issue that official statistics fails to provide much light on is that of ethnic identity. In the 1986 national census, a question was asked about which ethnic group respondents belonged to but the answers showed significant differences in self-identification. For example, some people who were born in Malaysia listed their ethnicity as "Malaysian," others as "Chinese," others as "Chinese-Australian," and yet others as "Australian." The self-identification was not necessarily correlated with language spoken at home. Furthermore, people's self-identification is not necessarily the same as the way others see them or treat them. People see themselves as belonging to different groups at different times–their self-perception is fluid and constantly changing according to different contexts. A third element of ethnicity which needs to be noted is that even those who see themselves as "unhyphenated" Australians (i.e., without reference to another nationality or culture such as Irish-Australian) sometimes recognize that their ethnic heritage influences their behavior and the way they see things, experience them and feel about them.

An important difference between the Australian population and that of other multicultural societies is that it is still the case that the great majority of people living in Australia with non-European racial features were born abroad. As years go by this will gradually change, but because of Australia's immigration history, presently second and third generation Australians of Asian, African or Pacific Island ancestry are rare compared to immigrants of these ancestries. Perhaps this explains the widespread use of the term "Australian" to refer to people of Anglo-Celtic or white ancestry, while others are referred to by race, often using the nationality of their ancestors as a code, e.g., "Vietnamese" or "Asian," regardless of their citizenship or country of birth. This practice is not limited to those of Anglo-Celtic background. It is common for members of ethnic minorities to use nationality as a code for race and/or ethnicity. In his research on ethnicity in Australia, Sullivan (1995) found a large difference between the self-concepts of Asian immigrants and those of Asian ancestry who are second or third generation Australians, or who migrated to Australia from Asia at a very young age. While immigrants often do not take offense, and often describe themselves as "Asians," those who have been in Australia from an early age sometimes resent or feel ambivalent about this label, preferring to identify as Australians.

While immigrants often maintain strong connections with their country of origin, those who migrated when they were very young or were born in a country different from that of their parents' birthplaces often do not feel any particular connection with the country or culture of their ancestors. However, because of their appearance, visible minorities are very often excluded and treated differently by others who act towards them on the basis of stereotypes and expect them to possess exotic cultural attributes or biographies, which are often inferiorized. As an example of this, we relate a story of an Australian of Asian ancestry who attended a civic function in Sydney and was asked by the mayor where he was from. He responded that he was from Sydney. "Oh yes," said the mayor, "but where did you live before that?" "In Canberra," said the man. "But where were you from before that?" persisted the mayor. "From Melbourne," said that man. Faced with what was presumably perceived as obstinacy, the mayor turned and walked away without another word. In a different context, this man would have been very pleased to identify as a Vietnamese-Australian, but he would like to retain control over his identity, rather than have it ascribed to him, with all the stereotypes which are too often attached to the labels people use to categorize others, particularly minorities. If a label was to be applied, he expressed a preference to be treated like any other (white) Australian, because that category generally opens doors rather than closes them, and allows one to be seen as mainstream rather than exotic or inferior. This is not to say that he turned his back on his ethnic group–only that it was a private matter, to be shared with whom he chose, rather than presumed because of his appearance.

Richard Fung's article *The Trouble with Asians* (1995) discusses these issues. Fung is of Chinese ancestry and migrated to Canada from his native Trinidad. He tells of how he is often included in conferences as the sole "Asian" in a line-up of minorities. He explains that in these situations he feels the burden of representation from both non-Asians, who would like to hear an authentic account of "the *other* experience," and from Asians, who require that he correctly convey their experience. This he finds difficult, because he is a fourth generation Chinese from Trinidad who speaks only a little Cantonese. Why then, he asks, does he identify himself as Asian? Fung has little choice over the ethnic category others place him in. Most people see him as Chinese and act towards him on the basis of their conception of "what Chinese are like," as they perceive it. Many people persist in doing this, even though he does not meet many of their expectations. Anxious to avoid this imposition, some people suggest that Fung and other minorities are "just like anyone else." This also presents problems, as Fung explains:

> The liberal declaration that Asians (or other people of color) are just like everyone else is as erroneous as the overtly racist precept that . . . [Asians] are fundamentally different–for "everyone" is undoubtedly the white subject by another name.

These concerns are not only raised by the labels others apply, because for Fung, assimilating is to support white supremacy and to deny differences.

Fung says that he knew he was gay before he came to think of himself as Asian. Like many gay people, it took years before he accepted the description of himself as gay. A short period of psychotherapy and belonging to a gay rights group were experiences which helped him overcome the fear and shame he used to feel. But being described as Asian was more complex. In Trinidad, he was considered to be Chinese, pure and simple. When he arrived in Canada, his status changed. He was not recognized as being Trinidadian, even by others from Trinidad, until he spoke with his distinctive accent. People would speak to him in Cantonese, Korean, Vietnamese or a number of other languages which he did not understand. White Canadians found it difficult to reconcile his accent with his appearance. This contradiction between his race and his culture presented challenges for him. As a visible minority, his appearance was used by most people to identity him or place him in a category, though this was not the category he would choose, nor one about which he even knew very much. While he was from a minority in Trinidad and had to prove that he belonged, he found that in Canada he was more easily accepted by people who came from Hong Kong, the Philippines or Korea. But as he spoke none of the languages of those countries, his credentials and affinity were limited. He noted that these groups rarely included people of South Asian ancestry, with whom he perhaps had more in common because of his experience in Trinidad. The thing that made him belong to the East Asian or Southeast Asian community was being an "oriental" in a white society. His identity as an Asian was not so much his choice as it was imposed on him by the way others perceived him. Eventually Fung began to see that he shared a political situation with "Asians" and started to identify himself in these terms. His story shows how his identity is both socially derived and fragile. It all depends on his context. He was an Asian only because of imperialism, colonialism and racism. The category is an externally imposed one which combines people with very different histories and cultures.

GAY AND LESBIAN IMMIGRATION

Since September 1985, Australian immigration policy has allowed partners of lesbian and gay citizens and permanent residents to migrate to Australia provided that they comply with a set of stringent criteria designed to prove the legitimacy of the partnership. This program is also available to unmarried heterosexuals in defacto relationships but has primarily been used by gay or lesbian couples. Between July 1995 and June 1996, 600 applications were received by immigration authorities for permanent resident visas on the grounds of "emotional interdependency" with an Australian citizen. Most of these applications would have been from lesbians and gay men who did not have access to immigration rights under the fiancé(e) or spouse visa programs (Department of Immigration and Multicultural Affairs, 1996; Hart, 1992, 1995; Chetcuti, 1992).[15]

Statistics on the number of lesbian and gay immigrants are not available as not all such immigrants arrive in Australia as members of a couple. Some gay men and women who arrive in Australia on tourist, working holiday or student visas form relationships with Australians while in the country, and some of these qualify for residency under business migration, family reunion and other immigration categories. In his research, Sullivan (1995) has found that it is not uncommon for independent immigrants from Asia who are gay to report that the more liberal environment and greater degree of acceptance in Australia of homosexuals than in their country of origin was an important consideration in their decision to migrate, and one of the most satisfying aspects of settlement here. Sexual orientation can be a motivation for migration both because of a greater degree of freedom to express sexuality in the country of destination and as a way of avoiding family pressure to marry, social restrictions and legal sanctions against homosexual practice in some countries of origin.

AUSTRALIAN ATTITUDES TOWARDS LESBIANS AND GAY MEN

While Australia may be a *relatively* tolerant society in regard to homosexuality, there is much to be done to improve the status of homosexuals in this country. In 1995, as part of the International Social Science Survey, Australian National University researchers conducted a general population survey of 2,338 Australians which included questions about attitudes towards homosexuals. Over half of the respondents reported that "sexual intercourse between two men" or "sexual intercourse between two women" was "absolutely wrong" (56 percent and 50 percent respectively). This result represents a more tolerant attitude than a decade earlier, when almost two-thirds (64 percent) of respondents to a similar survey reported that "sexual relations between two adults of the same sex" is "always wrong." However, in the 1995 survey, when asked to rate various people (such as politicians) and groups on a "feeling thermometer" ranging from zero for "people you feel very strongly against" to 100 for "people you feel very warm or favourable about," 26 percent of respondents gave a rating of zero to "homosexuals (gays)" and a further 27 percent gave a score of 45 or less. Almost one-third (30 percent) recorded neutral feelings (score between 46 and 54) and only 8 percent gave a score of greater than 70. Replicating other research results from Australia and North America (e.g., Van de Ven, 1994; Fraser et al., 1995; O'Hare et al., 1996; Roese et al., 1992), the Australian National University survey found that men are more hostile to homosexuals than women, older people are more hostile than younger people, and that those with more years of formal education are more tolerant of homosexuals.

Respondents aged 20 rated homosexuals 19 points higher on the 100 point "feeling thermometer" rating scale than did those aged 70, and atheists rated homosexuals 14 points higher than respondents with strong Christian beliefs. Churchgoers were even less tolerant. Women were about 10 points more tolerant of homosexuals than were men, university graduates were seven points more tolerant than non-graduates, and urban dwellers were six points more tolerant than rural dwellers. Australian Labor Party supporters were nine points more tolerant than Liberal-National Coalition supporters. Factors which were not associated with degree of tolerance were economic status, public or private sector employment, self-employment or trade union membership (Evans, 1996). Unfortunately, no reliable data have been published about ethnic differences in attitudes toward homosexuality in Australia; however, the results presented indicate that the general context of being a homosexual in Australia is an environment of intolerance, even if civil rights have been established legislatively.

These results indicate general attitudes only. Research on prejudice has shown that bigots often make exceptions for friends and people they like. The opportunity to act on a prejudice is also mitigated by anti-discrimination legislation which protects homosexuals in most states. As indicated, there are segments of society which are more accepting than others and it is possible to minimize the likelihood of experiencing hostility by choosing to live in a neighborhood with a high concentration of lesbians and gay men or in one in which there is little contact between neighbors, and choosing one's friends. While workplace discrimination is not unknown, legislative requirements of employers limit the degree to which this can be practiced.

THE CONTRIBUTORS, ISSUES RAISED AND EXPERIENCES RECOUNTED

Almost all the articles in this volume were written by people who have first-hand experience as a lesbian or gay man and as a member of an ethnic minority in Australia. There are many stories about discrimination in this volume, and members of one minority group not understanding those of another, so that people feel sandwiched in the middle of two groups, each requiring different things of them. Very often, people who belong to multiple minorities feel that they have to choose to belong to one or another of these groups. If they choose to become involved with the gay and lesbian community, it means having less to do with members of their cultural heritage group and taking on Anglo ways. If they choose to spend a lot of time with their families or ethnic communities, this may mean having to be in the closet about their sexual orientation and limiting their participation in the lesbian and gay community. This is not always the case–there are those who manage to integrate the various aspects of their lives, but such integration is often difficult to achieve.

The editors are two Australian-born white men who became interested in the topic partly because of their experience as partners of men of non-Anglo-Celtic background, and of hearing the views and experience of friends in gay and lesbian communities in Australia, North America, Western Europe and Southeast Asia. The immediate impetus for editing this book was a conference that they convened in 1995 on behalf of the Australian Centre for Lesbian and Gay Research at the University of Sydney, on Emerging Lesbian and Gay Identities and Communities. Only three of the authors in this volume presented papers at that conference, but there was considerable interest in preparing a book on the topic on the part of authors and people who were unable to attend the conference.[16] Half of the articles are autobiographical in nature and half are more academic or research oriented, covering the disciplines or sociology, psychology, education, film and literature. The articles use various research methods and some are avant garde or experimental in their writing style. We hope readers will find this volume stimulating and provocative.

The authors of the articles in this volume are seven women and eight men. Several are immigrants but many others were born in Australia. All but one, Ling-Yen Chua, are residents of Australia. Almost all the authors have experience as members of ethnic minorities and as participants in the lesbian and gay community. Five of the articles are about the experience of gay men who are not from Anglo-Celtic backgrounds and four are about the experience of lesbians who are not from Anglo-Celtic backgrounds. Three articles are about the experience of both lesbians and gay men. Half of the articles are about the experience of lesbians and gay men of Asian (predominantly Chinese) ancestry. Although "Asians" comprise only about six percent of the Australian population, it is perhaps not surprising that they are so well represented here, given their prominence as a visible minority and that their cultural backgrounds are probably more divergent from the Anglo-Celtic norm of the Australian majority than the cultural backgrounds of those of other European ancestries. Most of the authors discuss their cultural heritage and ethnic and sexual identities in their articles.

CONTENTS

This book is about the difficulties that non-Anglo queers have found in establishing an acknowledged and honored place for their cultural heritage within Australia's lesbian and gay community. The articles in this volume exhibit the complexity and diversity of the lesbian and gay community and show some of the variety of experience and ideas within it via a combination of traditionally structured academic papers, autobiographical narratives and experimental genres. Listening to voices from outside the mainstream requires us to be open to the fact that not only what these voices say may be challenging, but also how they enounce their challenges may disturb established Anglo-centric notions of discourse.

The first four articles in this volume share a theme in which gay men of Asian ancestry attempt to come to terms with being sexually unattractive to the majority of white men while also being fetishized as ideal sexual partners by a small minority of Caucasian men who are disparagingly called "rice queens." The dominant ideology of commercial culture in Australia defines the muscular, Caucasian, male body as the ideal. All gay men growing up in Australia are socialized into this culture of desire, where having a butch Caucasian partner is to be considered "successful" as a gay man. These articles show in poignant and at times humorous ways how dominant cultural images infuse and mold the sexual desires of gay men. In autobiographical accounts both Kent Chuang and Tony Ayres express a keen awareness of the racial dynamics underlying the expression of their sexuality, but also show that this knowledge does not necessarily change the form of one's desire or break down the structures that have positioned them as subordinate. Chuang uses a characteristically Australian form of ironic humor, in which he criticizes the other (presumably Caucasian readers) yet also belittles himself in order to establish and maintain solidarity and sympathy with the reader. Such self-deprecatory humor is extremely common within Australian popular culture, where an egalitarian ethic dominates much public and private discourse and often demands that speakers adopt strategies that clearly indicate they do not place themselves above the listener in rank or status. However, this Australian egalitarian ethic often masks real social, economic and class divisions, and Chuang subverts this pseudo-egalitarian form of humour by adopting its forms to convey a quite critical message.

Damien Ridge, Amos Hee and Victor Minichiello investigate many of the same issues Chuang and Ayres raise, but show the systematic and Melbourne scene-wide character of racial stereotypes, thereby showing that Chuang's and Ayres' stories are common experiences in the gay scenes in Australia's major cities. Ridge et al. suggest that while Asian gay men in Melbourne have access to the "gay scene," they often do not find any community with other gay men on this scene. Bo Sanitioso takes a social psychological and international approach in writing about members of ethnic minorities who are homosexually-oriented, and shows the conflicts that often arise between ethnic and gay identification and community membership. Trying to reconcile the contradictory demands of the two often proves so difficult that people try to suppress one or the other aspects of themselves.

Ling-Yen Chua continues the focus on the subordinate position of Asian homosexuals within western cultures, but shifts the focus from personal relationships to an analysis of the cultural medium of film. Audrey Yue is also interested in film and other electronic media. Like Chua, she writes from a post-structuralist perspective but Yue analyzes a movie with lesbian characters, and uses an experimental form of presentation which combines a post-modernist critique with personal experience and Internet culture. Yue finds texts from the Internet to be useful models for her own explorations in voicing her exclusion and marginalization, and she has produced a diverse, polyvocal text that rips through the assumptions of white lesbian and gay discourses and the presumptions of white author(ity)ship. Yue both interrogates and resists her minority positions in Australia as "Chinese" and "lesbian."

The next two papers in this book are by Jewish lesbians, from opposite sides of the Australian continent. Annie Goldflam, who grew up in Perth, explains that ever-present thoughts about the Jewish Holocaust and medieval witch burnings color her understanding and imagining of her sexuality. In contrast, Hinde Ena Burstin, who grew up in Melbourne's Yiddish-speaking Jewish community, reflects on the history of anti-Semitism to confront her own racism, leading readers to explore their own positions. As Burstin points out, to be a member of one subordinated ethnic minority does not mean that one does not hold racist views about other minorities. She explains that even among Australians who are very aware of racism and who attempt to excise it from their own thoughts and behavior, it is still often acceptable to knock (or criticize) Japanese and Americans, presumably because they are large, rich and powerful societies, in comparison with smaller, marginalized groups and societies that "deserve" to be respected.

Rose Kizinska explains the frustrations of being tokenized as a "representative ethnic lesbian" by Anglo-lesbians, and relates her experience with the Interlesbian group for non-Anglo lesbians in Melbourne. Through the device of a series of poignantly critical "love letters" to fictional women representing a number of Anglo-dominated lesbian groups in Melbourne in the early 1990s, Kizinska insightfully and incitefully reveals the factions that are often part of the political and social activities of minority groups. Abby Duruz presents material from a series of radio interviews she conducted with lesbians and gay men in Sydney from a variety of ethnic backgrounds, including Jewish, Fijian-Indian and Indigenous Australian men and women. In contrast with the critical and sometimes anxious and threatened tone expressed in some of the other articles, the people Duruz interviewed indicate a sense of achievement and optimism as non-Anglo queers within Sydney's increasingly diverse gay and lesbian scenes.

Maria Pallotta-Chiarolli shifts the focus from racism in lesbian and gay communities to confronting homophobia within institutions and ethnic communities. While Burstin considered this issue in relation to the Jewish community, Pallotta-Chiarolli reflects on her own work to introduce discussion of issues of homophobia in schools. She takes a hard look at multiculturalism and makes the case that this government-sponsored policy should not allow pockets of officially sanctioned homophobia within non-Anglo Australia by permitting anti-homosexual attitudes to remain unchallenged within non-English speaking background communities. Pallotta-Chiarolli draws on notebooks from her work as teacher-educator to argue that challenging homophobia is consistent with respect for non-Anglo cultural traditions.

Most of the articles in this volume are about how lesbians and gay men who are members of ethnic minorities negotiate their sexuality in the context of dual cultural forces–the culture of their parents and their childhood, and the dominant Anglo-Celtic culture of the world outside the home. However, in the final article, Baden Offord and Leon Cantrell examine the complexity and multiplicity of personal identity in contemporary multicultural Australia. In this article, Offord explores his identity as a person coming to appreciate his diverse backgrounds. Multiculturalism affirms diverse cultural traditions, but where do those whose backgrounds have multiple cultural or ethnic traditions fit in? Offord and Cantrell show that multicultural policies which encourage pride in diverse languages and cultural traditions may not cater for an increasingly hybrid population. They point out that choosing between these many traditions is not a realistic option, and recommend negotiating individual complexity and fostering a sense of broad humanitarian unity.

QUEER ANALYSES OF ETHNIC AND SEXUAL DIVERSITY

While the lesbian and gay community may appear to be united to those outside it, most within it are aware of numerous subcultures, the members of which often have markedly different ideas and experience of homosexuality. It is not uncommon for members of some of these subcultures to rarely, if ever, meet as they work, live and socialize in different geographic and social spaces. For example, not all lesbians and gay men participate in the "scene," electing not to go to gay ghettos, bars, saunas, shopping areas or nightclubs, and they often hold different agendas and strategies for political action. Non-Anglo queers are not fully "spoken for" by most ethnic or queer discourses. Those who write about sexuality often ignore ethnicity, while the ethnic media often ignore or criticize those who are unconventional sexually. Epstein (1992:257) describes the issue thus:

> . . . the politics of gay "ethnicity" have tended to foster the hegemonic role in community-building played by white males within the gay movement, and have been articulated to an uncomfortable extent through capitalist enterprise and the commodification of sexual desire.

In the 1970s and 1980s gay men and lesbians in many western countries including Australia adopted what Dennis Altman (1982) and other gay writers have characterized as an "ethnic" identification, with homosexual men and women coming to constitute something like a sexual ethnicity in the course of their collective struggles for civil rights. However, as Epstein points out, while this particular form of cultural politics has produced results in lobbying for gay and lesbian rights in many countries, it has also privileged those groups of homosexual men and women from the most powerful sections of society, namely, those who are white, educated and from the middle and upper classes. The emergence of the notion of "queer" in opposition to "gay," and of post-structuralist "queer theory" in the 1990s has been spurred by the widespread perception that gay/lesbian-based "identity politics" has often excluded homosexual men and women from working-class and ethnic-minority backgrounds as well as transgendered people. The queer critique of gay/lesbian identity politics has been spurred by the need to imagine and construct alternative, more inclusive theories of sexuality and gender and of sex/gender politics.

A greater appreciation of internal diversity–on racial, gender, class and even sexual dimensions–is a prerequisite if homosexual and transgender politics is to move beyond the "ethnic" insularity of gay-based civil rights models of activism which privilege white homosexual people and continue to exclude queer people from cultural and ethnic minorities. Feminists have considered the issue of class and ethnic differences between women for some time, and many of the same issues considered in the course of feminist political theorizing and activism apply to activism in queer communities. As Philippa Rothfield (1991:55) has put it:

> Feminism has been so occupied with naming the enemy without, that it requires some turnabout to look critically within. The issue turns more upon how Western feminist discourse is positioned and less upon its sensitivity towards "the oppressed" and a willingness to empathize.

Those who experience discrimination do not automatically sympathize with others who are discriminated against, and even when they do, they do not necessarily understand what it is like to belong to another minority group. Neither is the experience of being lesbian or gay and from an ethnic minority uniform. We hope that this book will foster a greater appreciation of differences within our community and more acceptance of and support for this diversity.

The papers in this volume do not exhibit any attempt to resolve multiple sexual, gender and cultural differences into any single "true self." Rather they affirm the multiplicity of identity in an increasingly multicultural and hybrid society. The linear character of traditional academic discourse may be singularly incapable of representing the complexity of lived subjectivity and identity in a society such as contemporary Australia. If personal identity is multiple then there may be no single "logical" standpoint from which to view oneself, or from which to reflect on one's experiences. In this situation the allusive qualities of exploratory and experimental genres may be better able to "speak" the complexity, ambiguity, and multiplicity of identity than academic argument.

NOTES

1. Historically in Australia there have been tensions between those of English ancestry and those of Irish ancestry (Fitzgerald & Wotherspoon, 1995). However, in contemporary Australia, these tensions have subsided (perhaps in part because newer immigrant groups have made the population more diverse so that differences between those of English ancestry and those of Irish ancestry are relatively minor), and the two groups combine to form much of the Establishment.

2. Examples include Berube (1994), Chauncey (1994), Connell et al. (1993), Dowsett et al. (1992), Kennedy and Davis (1993) on working-class women and men;

Leong (1996) and Murray (1996) on ethnic minorities; and Murray (1992, 1995, 1997, 1998), Dynes (1992), Jackson (1989, 1995), Sullivan and Leong (1995), Jackson and Sullivan (1998) on homosexuality in non-western countries. Wotherspoon (1996) contains biographies of gay men in Australia, some of whom were from the working class or ethnic minorities.

3. Throughout the introduction we have used a variety of terms to refer to the dominant ethnic group in Australia. Sometimes we have used the term "Anglo-Celtic," which refers to culture but is often used to indicate race as well. We have frequently used the term "white" and occasionally referred to "Caucasians." These last two terms are general categories which mask differences within the group and explicitly refer to race. They are as problematic as any other racial term. For most of this century, Australia has had only a tiny non-white population, and sharp distinctions were made between various (white) ethnic groups. Many older Australians who are not of Western European ancestry (such as those from Italy, Greece and the former Yugoslavia) will remember well the discrimination they faced as members of newly arrived immigrant groups. However, with the arrival of newer ethnic groups from more diverse backgrounds, more established groups are starting to come together much as the English and Irish have done, to form a category which can in shorthand form (and somewhat inaccurately) be referred to as "white" or "Caucasian." The term "Anglo" refers to the language of the dominant group. As such, it refers to a cultural (rather than biological) category, and it allows for distinctions to be made among Caucasians.

4. The examples used in this discussion all involve gay men and are based on ethnographic research conducted by Gerard Sullivan. Many of the issues raised may apply to lesbian couples, but there may also be important differences. To avoid unwarranted generalizations, the section refers specifically to men.

5. "Rice queen" is usually a derogatory term for gay men who prefer Asian partners. Black leather clothes are associated with a gay and lesbian subculture interested in sado-masochistic sexual practices.

6. The same attitude underlies much of the sex tourism to Asia, though in that case financial aspects of the relationship are to the forefront. Relative to many sex workers in Asia, the average, middle-class, middle-age gay man from Australia is wealthy and pays for sex.

7. People from privileged racial, social, cultural or economic groups have not cornered the market in cultural alienation or exploitation, though it is generally easier for them to engage in the latter because of their position of power.

8. Colonization of desire has been written about by Fanon (1967) and Nandi (1983), among others. It might be expected that the politically aware would overcome these colonial ideas, but racial preferences for partners does not appear to be well correlated with sensitivity to ethnic politics. Socialization in areas like sexism and racism are not easily overcome, perhaps especially in private areas like sexual desire where there is generally less scrutiny and pressure to conform than in more public arenas such as a workplace.

9. Indigenous Australians from the mainland and from the southern, island state of Tasmania are often collectively called Aborigines or Aboriginal Australians, while those from the culturally distinct islands between northern Queensland and the neigh-

boring country of Papua New Guinea are called "Torres Strait Islanders." Increasingly, the different nations and tribal groupings of Australian Aborigines are being recognized in official discourse. For example, many Aboriginal people from the southeast of the country are known as Koori, while many of those from the northeast are known as Murri. Many other national and tribal groups exist and preserve distinctive languages, cultural beliefs and practices.

10. Census data show the effect of this policy change. For example, between 1961 and 1971 the number of Australian residents born in India doubled from 14,000 to 29,000 and those born in Malaysia increased from under 6,000 to more than 15,000. Over the same period, the number of those born in Singapore, Thailand and Sri Lanka more than doubled and Filipino residents in Australia increased from 400 to 2,500 (DIEA, 1984a).

11. The effects of these policy shifts were substantial. In the five-year period to 1981, the number of Australian residents born in China, Taiwan and Hong Kong increased 68 percent, from 29,000 to 42,500 and the number of Malaysian-born residents increased by one-third, from under 20,000 to over 30,000 (DIEA, 1984a). This trend has continued and in 1995 there were 866,000 Australian residents who were born in Asia (excluding West Asia or the Middle East), who accounted for 21 percent of Australians born overseas, up from 12 percent in 1985. Those born in Vietnam constituted over 4 percent of the overseas born. Over 2 percent of overseas born Australians were from each of China, Philippines, Malaysia and Hong Kong and Macau. In 1975, 15 percent (N = 8,200) of immigrants were born in Asia but in 1995 this proportion had increased to 38 percent (N = 37,300). In addition, in 1995 there were 45,500 long-term visitors born in Asia, many of them students (Australian Bureau of Statistics [ABS], 1996).

12. Though the terms are sometimes used interchangeably and often overlap, a distinction is often made in sociology and anthropology between the terms "race," "ethnicity" and "culture" in which race refers to a group of people who share common physical characteristics such as the color of their skin, hair type or stature. Ethnicity refers to a group of people who share a common history and culture, including characteristics such as religion, language, diet, music and dance. While race and ethnicity sometimes go together, most social scientists believe that there is no genetic connection between the two. In Australia, information is rarely collected by governments, businesses or other organizations about people's race because of the belief that it is an unimportant social category and one which has been used for inappropriate discrimination. While the term "racism" technically means the belief that races have distinctive cultural characteristics based on hereditary which makes some races superior to others, the term is often used to describe prejudice (beliefs) or discrimination (actions) based on race or ethnicity. Such prejudice may involve a preference for or dislike of particular groups, or assuming that all members of a particular group share a common characteristic, e.g., that all people of Chinese ancestry can speak a Chinese language, or that all Italians are Roman Catholics. Racist discrimination involves the unfair treatment of a person or group based on prejudice about race, ethnicity, national origin or ancestry.

13. Some estimates have been made of the racial composition of the Australian population. Apart from the difficulties in producing these estimates which have al-

ready been mentioned, classification of those of mixed heritage complicates the task and makes it a questionable occupation. Nevertheless, Price (1988) estimated that in 1988, 75 percent of the population is of Anglo-Celtic origin, 7 percent north or west European, 7 percent southern European, 4 percent East European, 2 percent West Asian, 3 percent other Asian, 1 percent indigenous Australian, 0.2 percent Pacific Islander and 0.1 percent African. By 1994, people of Aboriginal and Torres Strait Islander origin numbered 303,000 and constituted 1.7 percent of the population in 1994 (Shu, Goldlust, McKenzie, Struik and Khoo, 1995).

14. Pauline Hanson initially received endorsement from the Queensland state branch of the Liberal Party, as that party's candidate for the outer Brisbane suburban electorate of Oxley in the March 1996 Federal elections. However, she was disendorsed by the party after voicing anti-Aboriginal sentiments but was elected as an independent candidate. She used the occasion of her first parliamentary speech in October 1996 to restate her anti-immigration, anti-multicultural, and anti-Aboriginal views, sparking an intense nation-wide debate and negative reporting of Australian race-relations and racial attitudes in the international press. Hanson garnered enough support to establish a minor political party, One Nation, but there are demonstrations against her wherever she goes, and the ideas she represents are severely criticized by many liberals. While it appears unlikely that One Nation will have much, if any, electoral success, there is a significant proportion of society which has some sympathy for a more moderate form of Hanson's views.

15. The eligibility criteria for qualifying for permanent residency on the grounds of "emotional interdependency" with an Australian citizen or resident have been made more stringent under the current, conservative, federal government. While quotas for almost all categories of immigrants have been reduced substantially since 1996, "gay immigration" applications have suffered one of the greatest proportional cuts.

16. Two other volumes related to the conference themes are currently in production: *Lady Boys, Tom Boys, Rent Boys: Male and Female Homosexualities in Contemporary Thailand* (The Haworth Press, Inc., 1998), and *Gay and Lesbian Asian: Identities and Communities* (The Haworth Press, Inc., 2000).

BIBLIOGRAPHY

Aldrich, Robert (1996) "Homosexuality and colonialism" *Thamyris: Mythmaking from past to present* 3(1): 175-191.

Altman, Dennis (1982). *The homosexualization of America and the Americanization of the homosexual* New York: St Martin's Press.

American Sociological Association (1981) *Report of the Task Group on Homosexuality* Washington D.C.: American Sociological Association.

Australian Bureau of Statistics (1993) *Australia in Profile: 1991 Census* Canberra: Australian Government Publishing Service. Catalog No. 2821.0.

Australian Bureau of Statistics (1996) *Australian Social Trends, 1996* Canberra: Australian Government Publishing Service. Catalog No. 4102.0.

Berube, Allan (1994) "Dignity for all: The role of homosexuality in the Marine Cooks and Stewards Union, 1930s-1950s" Paper presented at the annual meeting of the American Historical Association in San Francisco. 6 January.

Bayer, Ronald (1981) *Homosexuality and American Psychiatry: The Politics of Diagnosis* New York: Basic Books.

Chauncey, George (1994) *Gay New York* New York: Basic Books.

Chetcuti, Joseph (1992) "Relationships of Interdependency: Immigration for same-sex partners" in Aldrich, Robert & Wotherspoon, Garry (Eds.) *Gay perspectives: Essays in Australian gay culture* Sydney: Department of Economic History, University of Sydney pp. 165-175.

Connell, Robert W.; Davis, Mark D. & Dowsett, Gary W. (1993) "A bastard of a life: Homosexual desire and practice among men in working-class milieux" *Australian and New Zealand Journal of Sociology* 29(1): 112-135, March.

Coughlan, James E. (1997) Personal Communication. Department of Sociology, James Cook University, Townsville, Queensland. 15 December.

D'Emilio, John (1997) "Unsung Hero" *Sociologists Lesbian and Gay Caucus Newsletter*, 87, Spring.

Department of Immigration and Multicultural Affairs (1996) *Annual Report 1995-1996* Canberra: Australian Government Publishing Service.

Dowsett, Garry W.; Davis, Mark & Connell, Robert W. (1992) "Gay lifestyles of the not-so-rich and quite unfamous" in Aldrich, Robert & Wotherspoon, Garry (Eds.) *Gay perspectives: Essays in Australian gay culture* Sydney: Department of Economic History, University of Sydney pp. 147-164.

Dynes, Wayne R. & Donaldson, Stephen (Eds.) (1992) *Asian Homosexuality* New York: Garland.

Epstein, Steven (1992) "Gay politics, ethnic identity: The limits of social constructionism" in Edward Stein (Ed.) *Forms of desire: Sexual orientation and the social constructionist controversy* (pp. 239-293), Routledge: New York and London.

Evans, Mariah D.R. (1996) "How much tolerance for homosexuals" *World Wide Attitudes* Canberra: Research School of the Social Sciences, Australian National University.

Fanon, Frantz (1967) *Black Skins, White Masks* New York: Grove Press. Originally published in 1952 as *Peau Noire, Masques Blanc* Paris: Editions de Seuil.

Fitzgerald, Shirley & Wotherspoon, Garry (1995) (Eds.) *Minorities: Cultural Diversity in Sydney* Sydney: State Library of NSW Press.

Fraser, Ian H.; Fish, T.A. & MacKenzie, T.M. (1995) "Reactions to child custody decisions involving homosexual and heterosexual parents" *Canadian Journal of Behavioural Science* 27(1): 52-63.

Fung, Richard (1995) "The trouble with Asians" in Dorenkemp, M. & Henke, R. (Eds.) *Negotiating Lesbian and Gay Subjects* New York: Routledge.

Gays and Lesbians Aboriginal Alliance (Dunn/Holland, Wendy; Fletcher, Maureen; Hodge, Dino; Lee, Gary; Milera, E.J.; Saunders, Rea & Wafer, Jim) (1994) "Peopling the Empty Mirror: The prospects for lesbian and gay Aboriginal history" in Aldrich, Robert (Ed.) *Gay Perspectives II: More essays in Australian gay culture* Sydney: Department of Economic History, University of Sydney pp. 1-62.

Hart, John (1992) "A cocktail of alarm: Same sex couples and migration to Australia, 1985-1990" in Plummer, Ken (Ed.) *Modern homosexualities: Fragments of lesbian and gay experience* London: Routledge.

Hart, John (1995) "Same sex couples and counselling" *Journal of Gay and Lesbian Social Services* 3(3).

Hodge, Dino (1993) *Did you meet any Malagas? A homosexual history of Australia's tropical capital* Darwin: Little Gem Publications.

Hollinghurst, Alan (1995) *The Folding Star* New York: Vintage.

Hooker, Evelyn (1957) "Adjustment of male overt homosexuals" *Journal of Protective Techniques* 21: 18-31.

Jackson, Peter A. (1989) *Male homosexuality in Thailand: An interpretation of contemporary Thai sources* New York: Global Academic Publishers.

Jackson, Peter A. (1994) *The Intrinsic quality of skin* Bangkok: Floating Lotus Publishing.

Jackson, Peter A. (1995). *Dear Uncle Go: Male homosexuality in Thailand.* Bangkok: Bua Luang Books.

Jackson, Peter A. & Sullivan, Gerard (Eds.) (1998) *Lady boys, tom boys, rent boys: Male and female homosexualities in contemporary Thailand* New York: The Haworth Press, Inc.

Kennedy, Elizabeth & Davis, Madeline (1993) *Boots of Leather, Slippers of Gold: The history of a lesbian community* New York: Routledge.

Leong, Russell (Ed.) (1996) *Asian American sexualities: Dimensions of the gay and lesbian experience* New York: Routledge.

McCormack, Indra (1997) "Cri de coeur from an Asian Australian" *Sydney Morning Herald* 15 December p. 17.

McIntosh, Mary (1968) "The homosexual role" *Social Problems* 16(2): 182-192.

McLennan, W. (1996) *Australian Social Trends, 1994* Canberra: Australian Government Publishing Service. Australian Bureau of Statistics Catalog No. 4102.0.

McLennan, W. (1997) *1997 Year Book Australia* Canberra: Australian Government Publishing Service. Australian Bureau of Statistics Catalog No. 1301.0.

McNamara, Deborah J. & Coughlan, James E. (1997) "Asian Settlement in Australia: An Overview" in Coughlan, James E. & McNamara, Deborah J. (Eds.) *Asians in Australia* Melbourne: Macmillan.

Murphy, Jill (1997) *Initial Location Decisions of Immigrants* Canberra: Australian Government Publishing Service for Department of Immigration and Multicultural Affairs.

Murray, Stephen O. (1992) *Oceanic Homosexualities* New York: Garland.

Murray, Stephen O. (1995) *Latin American Male Homosexualities* Albuquerque: University of New Mexico Press.

Murray, Stephen O. (1996) *American Gay* Chicago: University of Chicago Press.

Murray, Stephen O. & Roscoe, Will (1997) *Islamic homosexualities.* New York: New York University Press.

Murray, Stephen O. & Roscoe, Will (1998) *African homosexualities.* New York: St. Martin's Press.

Nandi, Ashis (1983) *The Intimate Enemy: Loss and recovery of self under colonialism* Delhi: Oxford University Press.

O'Hare, Thomas; Williams, Cynthia L. & Ezoviski, Alan (1996) "Fear of AIDS and homophobia: Implications for direct action and advocacy" *Social Work* 41(1): 51-58.

Patience, Allan (1996) "The question of love in a hard culture" *Quadrant* 331, 40(11): 34-41.

Price, Charles A. (1988) "The ethnic character of the Australian population" in Jupp, James (Ed.) *The Australian people: An encyclopedia of the nation, its people and their origins* Sydney: Angus & Robertson pp. 119-128.

Price, Charles A. (1994) "Ethnic Intermixture in Australia" *People and Place* 2(4): 8-11.

Roese, Neal J.; Olson, James M.; Borenstein, Marianne N.; Martin, Angela et al. (1992) "Same-sex touching behavior: The moderating role of homophobic attitudes" *Journal of nonverbal behavior* 16(4): 249-259.

Rothfield, Philipa (1991) "Alternative Epistemologies, Politics and Feminism" in Yeatman, Anna (Ed.) *Postmodern Critical Theorising. Social Analysis* Adelaide: University of Adelaide (30): 54-67.

Shu, Jing; Goldlust, John; McKenzie, Fiona; Struik, Andrew & Khoo, Siew-Ean (1996) *Australia's Population Trends and Prospects, 1995* Canberra: Australian Government Publishing Service.

Sullivan, Gerard (1987) *A Study of Campaigns of Discrimination Against Gay People in the United States, 1950-1978* PhD dissertation in sociology. Ann Arbor: University Microfilms International. Catalog No: 8729425.

Sullivan, Gerard (1995) *The politics of identity and the economics of desire* Paper presented at the Emerging Lesbian and Gay Communities conference, organized by the Australian Lesbian and Gay Research Centre, and held at the University of Sydney on 29-30 September 1995.

Sullivan, Gerard & S. Gunasekaran (1993) "The relative importance of motivations for migration: A pre-departure study of migrants from Singapore to Australia" *Journal of Asian and Pacific Studies* 10:14-32.

Sullivan, Gerard & Leong, Laurence Wai-Teng (Eds.) (1995) *Gays and lesbians in Asia and the Pacific* New York: The Haworth Press, Inc.

Van de Ven, Paul (1994) "Comparisons among homophobic reactions of undergraduates, high school students, and young offenders" *Journal of Sex Research* 31(2): 117-124.

Wotherspoon, Garry (1996) (Ed.) *Being Different: Nine gay men remember* Sydney: Hale & Iremonger.

Zubrzycki, J. (1988) "Multicultural Australia" in Jupp, James (Ed.) *The Australian people: An encyclopedia of the nation, its people and their origins* Sydney: Angus & Robertson pp. 128-131.

_____. (1996) "New Immigration Figures" *Bureau of Immigration, Multicultural and Population Research* 17, August. pp. 59.

_____. (1996a) *Settler Arrivals by State of Intended Residence, 1994-95* Canberra: Australian Government Publication Service for Bureau of Immigration, Multicultural and Population Research. Statistical Report No. 20.

Using Chopsticks to Eat Steak

Kent Chuang

SUMMARY. "Rice queens," "small dicks," and "Asian take-aways," are just a few of the stereotypes that Asian gay men are faced with in Sydney's gay culture. Even though the author grew up in and quickly assimilated to the general Australian society, he felt like an outsider when he came out and moved into the gay community, where race-based sexual perceptions appear to dominate. This article is a personal exploration of how one Asian gay man came to find a place for himself within the predominantly white-oriented gay community. For the benefit of linguistically challenged readers, a glossary of Australian terms is provided at the end of this very serious article. *[Article copies available for a fee from The Haworth Document Delivery Service: 1-800-342-9678. E-mail address: getinfo@haworthpressinc.com]*

I grew up in Sydney, having migrated with my family from Hong Kong in 1968 when I was eight years old. In those days Asian immigrants were still relatively rare in Australia and I can remember people staring at us on the street. I was the only speck of color in an otherwise all white school. It was a matter of adapt or die. Being young, I had no choice, and the lonely transition was full of tears. Yet, a year after my arrival I conversed fluently in English, had learned to walk barefoot in the street, chew the ends of pencils, and eat Vegemite sandwiches like other Aussie boys my age. I considered myself as "one of them." That was until Mum spoke Chinese in public, and so loudly! Apart from that I was happy with my new-found existence, until puberty

Correspondence regarding this paper may be addressed to Kent Chuang at Unit 1209/299 Castlereagh Street, Sydney, NSW, 2000, Australia.

[Haworth co-indexing entry note]: "Using Chopsticks to Eat Steak." Chuang, Kent. Co-published simultaneously in *Journal of Homosexuality* (The Haworth Press, Inc.) Vol. 36, No. 3/4, 1999, pp. 29-41; and: *Multicultural Queer: Australian Narratives* (ed: Peter A. Jackson and Gerard Sullivan) The Haworth Press, Inc., 1999, pp. 29-41. Single or multiple copies of this article are available for a fee from The Haworth Document Delivery Service [1-800-342-9678, 9:00 a.m. - 5:00 p.m. (EST). E-mail address: getinfo@ haworthpressinc.com].

came and spoiled everything. All my Asian "deformities" were gradually outed. In the high school change room, I watched with fear as my classmates sprouted furry triangles while I was still as smooth as a baby's bum. Then their torsos turned into footballers', while mine willowed and drowned into Swan Lake. Worst of all, their gherkins grew into cucumbers, while mine stayed pickled. These were shocking revelations for a little kid who had grown up never having seen a naked man. Even at home we never exposed our private parts. I never saw my father's dick. I felt inadequate and quickly learned the art of dressing very fast and showering without getting wet.

By the time all the boys began dating girls, I was already madly in love with my PE teacher and the school captain–big hairy guys like footballers, swimmers and athletes–people I could never be. I felt insignificant, and to make things worse I came last in maths. No looks and no brains.

Despite feeling totally inadequate and being the only Asian in my year at school, I must have had "something" because almost everybody liked me. I had lots of friends at school, but none of them knew my secret. I was a closet poofter. That's what they called the clumsy fat boys and the girlie ones too. I had no choice but to play it straight, otherwise I too would have been an outcast. Chinese and a poof as well, how could I ever be the same as the others?

At 13 I had my first sexual experience, in a public toilet with a stranger in a business suit who picked me up in the street. I knew exactly what was happening because for months beforehand I had been religiously wanking over pictures of Marlon Brando, the "Wild One," wishing I could rescue him from his tormented soul with my undying love. And finally, on that momentous day when I first tasted the lips of a man, my dream came true when his tongue slithered its way into my mouth. It was sheer ecstasy. After that incident I considered myself a fully-fledged poof. Though I very much wanted to, I was too shy to accept his offer to meet again.

Sure he was a paedophile, but he was also the first man I had ever kissed. At that time he was my first and only contact with the gay world, the Shangri-La where I thought everybody lived in harmony and I could be what I am, where I could be happy. Where could a little 13 year-old poof-in-the-making find love and understanding, not to mention another fuck? At our Chinese Presbyterian Church?

I searched through *The Good News for Modern Man*, our Sunday School version of *The New Testament*, trying to find evidence that being homosexual was OK. But all I found was, "a man shall not lay beside another man." So I concluded that I had only two choices, either live happily in sin and burn in hell ever after or lead a miserable, sexless, life and be rewarded with eternal boredom. Because I wasn't the footballer type I thought I would never get to sin properly with another spunky boy, so there was no point igniting for nothing. The fear of hell became an easy excuse to remain in the closet.

Meanwhile at home, I was sick to death of being reminded that I was the family's sole hope to carry through the prehistoric Chinese virtues of success in career and breeding of male offspring in order to perpetuate the family name. These were my duties as the only son to my parents, my grandparents, and every relative, alive or dead. To them being happy meant that they could boast about their "obedient son's" achievements from the beginning to the end of a twelve-course banquet. I didn't give a damn if they had indigestion. I was obsessed with finding love and a second root, but these chronic cravings which I believed I could never fulfil kept me in isolation, making me more and more bitter towards my family and the world.

A small break came when I was about 15. I accidentally discovered some straight porno magazines at a friend's place. I ripped out the mail order form, paid, posted, and waited anxiously for those throbbing pages in a plain paper packet to arrive. But the hurricane of orgasms quickly subsided into a deep depression. All the men in the photos were gorgeous, blond, macho, hairy studs with big dicks. I took my ruler out and mathematically calculated the sizes of their erections, then measured myself and came to the conclusion that no one could possibly be interested in me.

Everyday I searched desperately for evidence that an Asian could be a sexually desirable object, but neither Calvin Klein advertisements, "Days of Our Lives," nor stories of Rose Hancock on the 6 o'clock news showed me that it was possible. I was certain that I was going to live alone forever without ever tasting love. My life rotted as I continued tripping in sexual misery.

For the next 11 years I was trapped in a vicious cycle of depression and wanking. I saw no way out, until one day at 26 I again discovered something at a friend's place that changed my life. I took it, stuffed it into my trousers, and left. It was the gay classifieds.

> 52 y.o. Caucasian seeks younger Asian for long-term relationship. My interests are gardening, quiet nights at home, movies and classical music. I'm honest, caring and non-scene. (Reply Box 974)

I couldn't believe it! Someone was actually looking for an Asian. In excitement my pen leaked as I spilled out my life story to several mystery men in numbered boxes. A few weeks after the first phone call I ended up settling down with Box No. 3592: "48 y.o., well-hung, masculine Caucasian, seeking long-term relationship."

I thought I had discovered a bright new world, strange and wonderful. Finally I had a man to myself, unlimited sex, intimacy, emotional ecstasy and spiritual fulfillment. At last somebody understood me. I was ready to plant tulips with him for the rest of my life, until Box No. 2451 ("46 y.o., caring, masculine Caucasian") told me, "You married a rice queen."

I stopped dead. Though I wasn't sure what he meant, those words sounded very nasty. Together with my new partner we met other rice queen-Asian couples, and as I found out more about this side of gay life the lovesick boy in me died. I believed that I was trapped in a circle of old men and leeches in their forties, fifties and sometimes older, unfit or fat, unattractive bordering on repulsive. "The only reason they want us is because they can't get a white boy," one Asian friend told me.

I concluded that us ugly Asians couldn't get a white boy so we settled for financial and emotional security with old rice queens. Asians sacrificed youth for security, and rice queens sacrificed color for youth. I heard stories about an infamous Sydney gay bar where rice queens hung out. It used to be nicknamed "Asian Take Away," but after Indo-Chinese refugees started settling in Sydney this was later also named "The Killing Fields." I had flashbacks to the gay classifieds: "Mature man has own place and videos, seeks shy Asian for friendship. Students and beginners welcome. I'm patient and discreet."

My naive romantic dream world crumbled as I wanted desperately to escape from this side-show of freaks in the gay community. I cringed when my older lover held my hand in a gay bar, while all the white boys were with partners and friends of the same age. I didn't want anyone to think that I was worthless, that I'd come to Australia as a refugee on a boat, or that I was being kept by a white man, prostituting my love for an Australian passport.

I wanted one of them, those glamorous Aussies with blue eyes and perfect pecs, the epitome of the gay culture. I felt that until they could accept me, I wouldn't be worthy of being called a homosexual human being. One night, watching my lover undress, I saw the man who I once thought was good-looking and masculine turn into a wimpy, saggy old man. This horribly transformed image destroyed our relationship.

Could I get someone better, younger, more Aussie, so I could be like everybody else? Being Asian on Oxford Street, the heart of Sydney's gay ghetto, was worse than being gay in a straight world. Why did I have to be different? I grew up here, I spoke the lingo, so why did I have to be an outcast even among my own kind? I thought of a solution. Marry a young, fair dinkum Aussie boy.

As I didn't have the guts to express these hurtful and cruel feelings towards my older partner, I acted coldly, brutally, and ended my "life long relationship" of nearly two years to pit myself against the challenges of the Oxford Street scene. By then I was already 28. Fortunately, my Asian genes gave me youthful looks. I could have passed for 21, so there was yet hope for me.

The journey of finding self-worth naturally began at the gym, that factory where White Gods are cloned, and where my shamefully slim Oriental frame could be transformed into a more desirable western body, so that Bonds T-shirts would look tight on my chest. Unlike some of my gay Asian "sisters," who had ended up looking like bulging sacks of rice with a bow-legged cowboy gait, I developed a well-defined "swimmer's body," considered desirable not to mention good reference material for the gay classifieds.

After months of hard work, I was ready to try out my new look at those frightening, mysterious underworlds, those gay venues behind locked doors shunned by many morally correct gays as dirty, unromantic, unethical, places that *they* would never be caught dead in (so they say)–the saunas and the backrooms, the fuckhouses. One of my good friends who "lives" in this underworld of the gay scene gave me instructions on how to suss out the friendly patrons from the stuck up "Muscle Marys" and the young queens with king-sized attitudes. He told me about the regular rice queens and the aggressive sticky rice, the real men (you know, "straight guys" pretending to be straight in a gay sauna) and the queens taking anonymous vacations from their genuine "monogamous" relationships. He told me which nights were "Cabramatta Night," when the Vietnamese gay boys came out in droves, which night was "Chinatown Night" for all the Chinese guys, and at what hours people were most desperate (and therefore more susceptible to settling for an Asian body).

So after weeks of procrastination, and still petrified with stage fright, I tried to be as butch as possible and got myself a crew-cut before entering the sexual gladiatorial arena. I was devastated after the first few "fuck off, Asian" looks. Was it post-rejection over sensitivity or was it really the color of my pecs? Once I had a cubicle door slammed in my face, literally. Obviously the slammer, who I later saw giggling with "her" friends, must have thought it was funny. I didn't get the joke.

"Don't worry, once a bitch called me an ugly chink," reassured my sauna sister. "It's our duty to assimilate our beautiful selves into the Australian culture. Think of the younger generation. We are pioneers for our young up and coming Asian sisters. Just go for it. You'll be a slut in no time."

Post-sauna shock left my ego shattered; it took a while before I mustered up enough courage to look people in the eye again.

Eventually, with persistence and remembering my mission to become "someone" in the gay community, I got a few "good ones," that is, non-rice queen looking, under 30, gym-toned body, the boy-next-door type, and sometimes the even cuter boy-next-door-to-the-boy-next-door types. Most of the time it was hard work, listening to "I Will Survive" over the sauna loud-speaker system did little to wash the shame off my rejection complex no matter how long I stood in the showers. And even the times when I got what

I wanted I wondered whether I'd been chosen out of sheer desperation or chronic promiscuity.

Occasionally on quiet nights in the underworld, I took time to listen to stories from my Asian trolley dolly sisters who worked as QANTAS stewards about their sexual exploits in Europe,

> There we are considered exotic. The Europeans treat us like special people, like a real woman. They buy us dinner and drinks and even drive us back to the hotel. They are proud to be seen with us sensuous creatures, but don't forget the Clarins fake tan–in Europe the darker the better. Even in Melbourne it's easier to get a good root than in Sydney, and the boys in Brisbane, Adelaide and Perth are too isolated to cultivate attitudes. Country guys are so much more friendly. Sydney queens are the worst.

I couldn't have agreed more. Reclining inside my favorite cubicle anxiously keeping an eye on the passing traffic, I wondered what I was doing in this barbaric city?

After a few years of steam therapy I came to the conclusion that a fuck is just a fuck is just a fuck. I wanted more. I wanted real phone numbers I told a friend. "Fat chance," he replied, "All the good ones are only closet rice eaters. They'll root you in the dark but ignore you on the street. Remember our tragic sister and that Aussie prick she calls "my gorgeous gym boyfriend," she's degraded herself into becoming an underground concubine. Her "gorgeous boyfriend" won't go out with her in public or be seen with her when he's with his friends."

I thought it was time, yet again, to give the gay classifieds another try. Perhaps all the "good ones" were hiding in the suburbs under labels like "non-scene, non-saunas," so I religiously advertised myself in every new gay publication in order to lure them out.

When I made it known that the bait was Asian, those over the hill Barbara Cartlands answered again with more lies and reprints of photos taken twenty years ago, so I decided to be daring by not mentioning my nationality. And also to be fair, I thought, not mention any other physical attributes. This time I got replies from a totally different group of Aussie guys in their late twenties to forties. Some were over the scene or did not fit into the scene because of conflicting interests or appearances. Some were just trying something new. And of course there were the usual desperados. When I nervously revealed my "status" on the phone, some brusquely said they'd "ring again." But I was relieved that others were still interested in meeting. There was hope. Ethnically broadminded gays did exist in Sydney!

During all this tedious search for "The One," I wondered whether the average white gay man has similar problems? Just because the hunky ones can get an easy root, and just because blond 25-year-old Jason's ad got over 70 replies (true) to my half-dozen, does that equate to happiness and contentment? Did the average gay man in Sydney really have that much attitude towards Asians, or was I making a mountain out of a mole hill? More importantly, did I myself have prejudiced attitudes? And if I did, how could I expect others to be any different?

I must admit I'm no Mother Teresa full of tenderness and goodwill. During Chinatown Night at a Sydney sauna, in one of those unguarded moments of frustrated selfish fury, I sometimes thought to myself, "So many bloody Asians!" Was it because I felt so helpless seeing us standing out in the crowd appearing to be left untouched (not a pretty sight), or else being cornered by obnoxious vultures (of all nationalities) taking advantage of our seemingly gentle Asian nature. I don't feel special, rare or exotic; more like soggy leftover noodles that nobody wants.

What Anglo queen on the scene was going to associate us with our rich Asian culture of literature and art, and who was to know that some of us had risked our lives to escape totalitarian regimes of both the left and the right to be in this country? Were we not more likely to be associated with fast food, cheap imitation products, "rude" manners, and loud talk? The more they seem to be Asian, the cheaper things look, like Asian financial markets these days. Is this internalized racism? I have lived in Sydney most of my life, so why should *my* territory be invaded by all these Asian new-comers, younger and prettier than me? In my desperate search for approval from Anglo men had I become so selfish, helpless and angry that I would turn against my own kind?

If I was such a hypocrite, how could I expect anyone else to be broadminded? Was this confirmed potato queen–always searching for his opposite: "masculine, hairy with a solid build" according to one of my ads–a victim of brainwashing by endless western pop culture in movies, magazines, and advertisements where the heroes are always perfectly manicured, beautiful and white? I have noticed that Asian gay men who have grown up in Asia before coming to Australia are far more "international" in their sexual tastes.

Realizing my pitiful state of mind, I decided that I should at least make an attempt to be politically correct and to include an occasional meal of rice in my diet. After all, there must be something about us that all those Anglo Aussie rice queens crave for, especially the good ones, the ones who have been converted to rice after travelling or living overseas, as well as the young ones who have been attracted to us from day one. All this talk about "smooth skin and sensuous bodies," I had to find out what I was missing out on and open up more pastures.

My only previous experience with an Asian man had happened a few years before in Hong Kong at the beginning of a short working period there. It was a one night stand, strange, almost bizarre. Naked and looking into another pair of slant eyes, I immediately thought to myself, "This is incest! God, I'm doing it with myself." I was reminded of a guy I know with four blond brothers who can't do it with another blond.

But at the end of that half year period in Honkers, I became so comfortable with being amongst so many gay Chinese men that I found my taste was beginning to change. Who knows, if I had stayed on I might even have been fully converted. But my return to Australia halted this change, and soon after I returned I was gorging myself on steamed potatoes once again.

But reflecting on my Hong Kong episode, how could I explain this change in sexual taste? Was it the opportunity to see Asian men in a different environment without the negative stereotypical images? Did seeing so many color-concordant Asian couples, not visible in the Sydney gay community, sway my taste? Or was I merely attempting to overcome my separateness in a "new" country by again trying to fit in with the local culture?

My sexual perception of Asian men continued its shift some years after my return from Hong Kong during a half-year period working with Silk Road, a social and support group for Asian gay men, and the Asian outreach project of the AIDS Council of New South Wales (ACON). The opportunity to gain personal insights into so many individuals' lives made me see my own race in a completely new light. Whereas previously I had been guilty of dismissing people based on lack of sexual attraction–no gain, no name–the process was being reversed.

I saw a different type of attraction, the person himself. Could lack of understanding of Asian culture and personal insights be one reason why Asians have been left out of the Sydney gay community? After all, the white gays at least have some sort of popular culture in common, be it the Muscle Marys at the gym or leather queens in their dungeons, the daddy bears and their cuddly boys, or the bleached blonds displaying themselves at the beach. All these men had a slot they could fit in and identify with, so why should they bother to get to know such an "incompatible" group, both in looks and in culture? An Asian Muscle Mary or an Asian leather queen will still be looked upon as an Asian first.

Meanwhile, I persisted with my new diet of sampling Australian rice, remembering that I should be opening and not shutting doors, and discovered that things were starting to get more interesting. Certainly, it was a totally different physical, visual and even mental sensation, one that has left me wondering, and sometimes even fantasizing. Can rice be an acquired taste?

It is now more than ten years since I first replied to the gay classifieds, my coming out, and I've reached the ripe old age of 36. My search has taken me from cubicle to cubicle, bar to bar, "all-letters-answered" to "your-photo-gets-mine," and from potato to rice. I now feel I have a better picture of what's around, and what my market value is, so my gay life is now a balancing act between wishful thinking and reality. I know the reality is that being Asian in Sydney means that I have fewer green pastures to choose from. Yellow doesn't make many heads turn in this city, whether Asian or non-Asian.

Let's face it, in this day and age true gay love often begins with a one-night stand. Fuck first, talk later. For most gay men being talkable isn't enough if you aren't fuckable. Take one of my poor little Asian "sisters." Only out for a year, he recently contacted a 29-year-old Caucasian guy on a gay telephone chatline, and after more than twenty minutes of increasingly excited conversation revealed his Asian "status." Instantly, without another word the other guy hung up. Similarly he got zapped several times in Internet gay chatrooms as soon as the word "Asian" appeared on the other guy's screen. The reality is that some Asians are constantly living under the fear of racial rejection. While this can be good for "character building," it can also be degrading.

I sometimes also wonder whether the small-penis syndrome has anything to do with why we are not popular, whereas black men are popular for the reverse stereotype? In today's gay culture it appears that if you can't make someone choke during oral sex you aren't worthy of being gay. From my observations, having been around a bit, here and overseas, I reckon that the average Asian dick is smaller than the Caucasian variety. I'm sure some readers will want to slap my politically incorrect face for saying this, but I'll say it anyway. (This statement always gets angry reactions, especially from Asian men and politically correct Caucasian guys.) Myth or not, it is obviously a sensitive area and one that Asians have to live with. I have been traumatized by this fact for years. Every time I get unzipped by a new man it's like coming out all over again.

So what do we get when we put a small Asian dick onto a slim Asian frame? A woman, of course, implying that we like to take it up the bum. Absolutely passive. I've been brought up to be polite, considerate, listen attentively rather than speak without thought. This kind of behavior does not fit in with the popular Aussie he-man image, extroverted and superficially masculine. Unless you are drop-dead gorgeous and white forget about being quiet and sensitive in a gay pub on the scene. You might just as well crawl in the corner and die. Just look at the posters, movies, magazines (both straight and gay), Asians hardly ever get any attention and when we do we are westernized kung-fu types with hunky gym bodies to make us more palatable. To survive in this kind of environment, I forced myself to go to the gym for cosmetic masochism, and to develop a bigger mouth to disguise my insecurities. If you can't beat them, be bitchy.

Still my bark is fiercer than my bite. My inherently gentle "Chinese" nature can be looked upon as sweet, but when coupled with a low self-esteem it can be disastrous. This lack of assertiveness has led me to endure some painful acts of sodomy and I've gone down on more than one cold Aussie fish for fear of offending or rejection. Lucky this self-sacrificing woman knows better than to risk her life. Sadly, I've known other Asian men who have had unsafe sex because they were afraid to say no.

As for my young Asian sisters who insist on finding a stereotypically good looking young Caucasian boyfriend, "an equal" (but not one who has waded through every rice paddy in Sydney), I admire their courage. I wish them good luck and hope they don't crumble under multiple rejections. It's going to take a lot of guts. Go get 'em! They certainly are not going to come to you. Catch them while they're still innocent, before they succumb to scene clone peer pressure, and adopt the standard "only-white-is-beautiful" attitudes. Of course, there are exceptions to the rule, but the reality is that most Asian men wouldn't get a second look from a young, good looking Caucasian guy. Even if they do look, they still need to be man enough to overcome the stigma of going out with or even picking up an Asian guy in front of their friends. Any Caucasian seen going out with an Asian is in danger of being thought of as desperate unless he is gorgeous, and then everyone is puzzled that he would choose an Asian partner when he could get so many "desirable" white boys. It's simply not cool, yet, for a Caucasian gay man to have an Asian boyfriend.

And as for those Caucasians who think they are in danger of passing the threshold of no longer being young, going out with an Asian will automatically add years to their looks. No one wants to be labelled as an "old rice queen." Anyone who goes out with an Asian is assumed to be a geriatric with yellow fever. This is the grim outlook of some of my Asian friends. While our choices are limited, the up side is that when we do find someone there's a good chance that he will be a self-assured person, down to earth, broad-minded, and less concerned with public images.

For those Asians who prefer other Asians, whether because of the similar culture, ability to communicate or simply because they are fed up with "white trash," it's going to be just as hard. This is due to the limited supply of sticky rice, especially for those looking for a serious relationship with a guy from the same ethnic background who speaks the same dialect.

Thank God I'm an open minded, inquisitive slut! After all, when you've sucked as many cocks as I have (but I'm still a beginner compared to some others I know), and fallen for the wrong man so many times, sexual attraction loses its potency to fool me into falling for the wrong man yet again. More and more, I'm finding the security, the depth of experience, wisdom or sometimes just the plain old common sense of "older men," people who have "been through it all," to be more important than good looks or good body. Who knows, it may be the hero syndrome. Needing to be rescued? A father figure? Once I craved for someone young, and now I doubt that I could put up with someone with the same level of my own mentality of just a few years ago. Is this a sort of age-ism in reverse? The mind is harder to keep excited than the dick, but the orgasm certainly lasts longer.

Alongside this change in attitude, my sexual tastes have also changed. Having been through relationships (well OK, affairs and casual sex) with Caucasians who try to be stereotypically attractive body builders, beautiful young dancing queens, or even the boy-next-door who is no longer the boy-next-door, I've come to the opinion that they are cold towards everyone, sometimes even their own kind. They are up themselves; party-going pill-poppers hooked on finding disposable love. Similarly, Asian men who try hard to fit into these white stereotypes tend to be the same. Of course, this is not true of everyone. Many Caucasian men are friendly towards Asians, but do they take us seriously, genuinely consider us as potential boyfriends? These are only my impressions from watching people on the scene. I wonder if I'm beginning to sound like Mr. Frustrated acting like Fred Nile, a lone moral crusader?

Speaking of moral crusades, what do I now think of the old rice queens? Cross-cultural relationships of this type often involve a younger Asian partner with an age difference of 20 years or even more. Sometimes this age gap is in fact smaller than it looks, because of the ability of Asians to maintain our youthful looks (to a point), whereas the Caucasian partner loses his youthful looks much sooner. Alongside this slightly misleading image (the age gap is not always as great as it appears), there are also often great differences in culture and even level of verbal communication skills.

I once looked upon this type of relationship as a typical case of two groups of "outcasts" in the gay community–the aged and Asians–each settling for second best because they have no choice. But despite these "drawbacks," I have got to know some couples who have found their own recipes for success and happiness. The positive side of these relationships is never promoted in the gay press, so the gay scene continues to look down on the young Asian man and his older rice queen partner.

In other instances, Asian men become an alternative for the Caucasian guy who has been "fucked around" by white boys on the scene. These "fed up" Caucasians become attracted to our loyal, secure, loving, gentle and caring natures. A good choice for the settling down type who also wants these attributes in someone young, or at least young looking. But are we again only a second choice? And if so does it matter?

And are Asians really that loyal? We tend to hear about abuses of power by Asian partners, the Asian house boy, the gold diggers, the passport vampires, because it makes juicy gossip, but sadly these things also do happen at times. The name "Chopsticks and Walking Sticks" which has been given to the

Asian and Friends social group in Sydney is a clever pun, but it reflects a lot of insecurity and frustrations, especially from the young or image-conscious Asians making their way into the big world, wishing to have a young hunky boyfriend.

Even at my stage of mature "enlightenment" I don't deny that sometimes it still feels good to be seen with pretty white boys and hunky guys on the scene, so who am I to point a finger at anyone? After all, we Asians need to get white people more accustomed to this image of seeing young Asian men mixing with young Caucasian guys, rather than geriatrics or in Asian-only groups–so it will appear more "natural," more OK.

And sometimes I still cringe when an "old" acquaintance kisses me in public. Will people think I've slept with him? I admire the young Asian who holds the hand of his older lover walking down Oxford Street.

Looking back at all those years I think to myself, "My God, what a lot of hard work!" Finding a place for myself was a struggle that began from the day I stepped off the QANTAS 727 jet that brought me to this country. A struggle to find acceptance, first in a relatively white straight world and later on in an even whiter gay world. Nevertheless, it's all been for a good cause if only to learn the simple truth that accepting myself is more important than acceptance by others. If only I'd listened to my wise old mother, who told me as boy that there was no need to bleach the yellow out of my skin or wrap myself in a glamorous white fur.

And tomorrow? Tomorrow, I think I'll just continue perfecting the art of using chopsticks to eat steak. As I'm discovering, it can be a lot of fun.

KENT'S AUSSIE GLOSSARY
FOR THE LINGUISTICALLY CHALLENGED

Barbara Cartland–An aged English writer of numerous romantic novels who tries to appear young by dressing up in flamboyant outfits.

Bond's T-shirts–"Chesty Bond"© is a brand of men's singlets and t-shirts often considered to be iconic of butch Australian masculinity.

Cabramatta–A Western suburb of Sydney that is the focus for the city's Vietnamese community.

Cabramatta Night–A night of the week when many Vietnamese men regularly visit Sydney gay saunas.

Chinatown Night–A night of the week when many Chinese men regularly visit Sydney gay saunas (a different night from Cabramatta Night, see above).

Closet Rice Eater–A Caucasian man who secretly enjoys having sex with Asian men, but does not admit this fact to his Caucasian gay peers.

Fair dinkum–Colloquial for "true," "factual" or "genuine."

Fred Nile–A member of the Legislative Assembly or upper house of the New South Wales State Parliament and a minister of the Uniting Church of Australia (formed from the amalgamation of the Methodist and Presbyterian Churches). Fred Nile has long preached against "the evil of homosexuality." He is widely reviled and parodied within the Sydney gay and lesbian communities.

Muscle Marys–Gay men with large, muscular, gym-toned bodies, sometimes also called "gym bunnies."

Oxford Street–A street in Sydney's inner eastern suburbs regarded as the center of the city's gay ghetto.

Potato–A Caucasian gay man.

Potato Queen–An Asian man who is predominantly sexually interested in Caucasian men.

Rice–An Asian gay man.

Rice Queen–A Caucasian man who is predominantly sexually interested in Asian men.

Root–Colloquial term for sexual intercourse.

Rose Hancock–A middle-aged Filipino woman who became widely known upon her marriage to one of Australia's richest men, the late Lang Hancock, who discovered vast deposits of iron ore in the remote northwest of the state of Western Australia.

School Captain–Until recently most Australian high schools followed a British-styled prefect system with one senior boy and girl student being elected boys' and girls' school captains, respectively. In many schools, boy school captains were often the school sporting hero.

Sticky Rice–An Asian man who is predominantly sexually interested in other Asian men.

Trolley Dolly–A gay male flight attendant.

Underground Concubine–This is an expression I made up to describe an Asian friend who is used for sexual enjoyment by his Caucasian boyfriend, who hides this "shameful" act secret from his Caucasian gay peers. My friend is treated like a concubine who has to be kept underground.

Vegemite (©)–A Vitamin B supplement yeast extract eaten as a sandwich spread. Vegemite has an iconic status as a symbol of healthy, homey Australian values, similar to the place of "Mom's apple pie" in popular American culture.

"Asian" Men on the Scene: Challenges to "Gay Communities"

Damien Ridge

La Trobe University, Melbourne

Amos Hee

La Trobe University, Melbourne

Victor Minichiello

University of New England, Armidale, Australia

SUMMARY. This article examines common assumptions behind the notion of "gay community," contrasting these views with the experiences of homosexual men originating from Southeast Asia on the commercial gay scene in Melbourne, Australia. The narratives here reveal fragmented social networks involving various social groups, categories of people and an "In/Out" culture where informants were culturally marginal. Fitting into the scene culture involves processes of assimilation, and loss of connection even with supportive ethnic networks. While all men who look for a place to belong on the scene generally feel pressure to assimilate to a predominantly white middle-class gay culture, Southeast Asian men generally had more cultural distance to cover. Men who are not well assimilated face exclusion, invisibility and

Correspondence regarding this article may be addressed to Damien Ridge, Faculty of Health and Behavioural Sciences, Deakin University, Burwood VIC 3125, Australia.

[Haworth co-indexing entry note]: "'Asian' Men on the Scene: Challenges to 'Gay Communities'." Ridge, Damien, Amos Hee, and Victor Minichiello. Co-published simultaneously in *Journal of Homosexuality* (The Haworth Press, Inc.) Vol. 36, No. 3/4, 1999, pp. 43-68; and: *Multicultural Queer: Australian Narratives* (ed: Peter A. Jackson and Gerard Sullivan) The Haworth Press, Inc., 1999, pp. 43-68. Single or multiple copies of this article are available for a fee from The Haworth Document Delivery Service [1-800-342-9678, 9:00 a.m. - 5:00 p.m. (EST). E-mail address: getinfo@haworthpressinc.com].

43

discrimination. Differences and discrimination within Southeast Asian based networks also contributed towards fragmented relations. This article raises questions about dominant gay cultural forms, assumptions of gay solidarity, and how ethnic minority men make sense of and negotiate their sexual and social experiences. *[Article copies available for a fee from The Haworth Document Delivery Service: 1-800-342-9678. E-mail address: getinfo@haworthpressinc.com]*

INTRODUCTION

"Community" is one of the looser conceptual frameworks used in social research. Besides referring to people in a particular locale or association, and clearly suggesting social connection and support, the concept is somewhat muddy, and the assumptions underpinning it are problematic. In particular, unity and cohesion within social relations are important in conceptual frameworks of "community," including gay communities (Scheff, 1990; Lynch, 1992; Watney, 1995). However, unity requires that members of a community more or less respect one another, view each other as equals and are socially connected (Tinder, 1980). Yet, in modern societies including gay spaces, individuals are stratified along a multitude of social dimensions including ethnicity, gender, class, sexual preference, age and group membership (Weeks, 1991). In addition, the notion of unity implicit in community can mask cultural diversity and the importance of conflict in social networks (Phelan, 1993; Higgins, 1993). For example, people considered by others to be homosexual often prioritize non-sexual identities and social relations instead, such as those based on ethnicity, work, and relationships (Bartos et al., 1993).

While informants as a whole understood the gay world to be diverse, including various gay groups and organizations, gay cafes, bars and nightclubs, warehouse parties and social networks–youth-oriented bars and nightclubs featured most prominently in the informants' narratives and are the focus of this chapter. Such commercial spaces are considered by these men to be a central part of the gay "scene" and community. While these men frequently talked about "community," they also revealed tensions between their ideals of community, and their experiences on the scene. For instance, while there was some sense of belonging, there was also ambivalence and even rejection of gay community. Indeed, it was difficult to gain a sense of gay connectedness from the interviews. The use of the term "community" by these men is therefore not straightforward.

This chapter questions some assumptions behind "gay communities," particularly notions of equality, unity, social connection and cultural commonality. It does this by examining some experiences of men born in Southeast Asian cultures who entered into mainly youth-oriented sections of commercial gay bars and nightclubs in Melbourne, a city of three million people and capital of the state of Victoria.[1] The study explores how informants understand, and are positioned within, scene social networks. Issues associated with assimilation into the gay scene and the implications for sex and social relations are discussed. The analysis shows how focusing on the experiences of ethnic minorities brings into focus critical issues for gay communities, including monoculturalism, diversity, power relations and social justice.

The experiences of ethnic minority men in the gay world tend to destabilize the notion of an inclusive and unified gay identity and community. Cultural insensitivity towards, and racial discrimination against, ethnic minorities in western gay cultures have been well documented in the academic literature, as well as the gay and mainstream media (Duberman, 1991; Milburn, 1994; Maaten, 1994; Altman, 1996; Hee, 1996). However, ethnic experiences of being on the receiving end of cultural insensitivity need to be seen as situated within a wider context. The historical dominance of Anglo culture over other ethnic cultures in straight and queer Australian life is institutionalized to the extent that white privileges often go unrecognized or unspoken, despite more recent multicultural policies (Vasta, 1993; Altman, 1996). For instance, rather than obvious racism, ethnic minorities are often just absent in the gay media (Plummer, 1989).

In terms of cultural insensitivity, universal Western prescriptions of "coming out" and being openly gay are frequently imposed on ethnic minorities despite lacking much relevance to people's cultural circumstances (Wood & Ridge, 1996). Recent overseas and Australian research reveals that when ethnic minority youth "come out" and access the gay world, they can experience rejection and separation from their ethnic networks, emotional difficulties associated with assimilating to the mainly gay white middle-class culture, as well as social exclusion from gay networks (Tremble et al., 1989; McLeod, 1994).

The emergence of queerness in Australia in recent times has challenged assumptions underpinning gay community. Queerness incorporates a postmodern skepticism about the way that gay narratives, including discourses about identity and community, have tended to suit world views arising out of gay liberation movements and politics of the 1970s and 1980s (Higgins, 1993; Angelides, 1994; Reynolds, 1994). Queerness is theoretically based around inclusion and diversity, rather than the exclusion and unity that has characterized gay identity and community. For instance, queer potentially includes bisexuals, transgendered and ethnic minority people. In addition to a postmodern rejection of grand narratives such as liberation and progress, queerness problematizes the notion of the self as a fixed, autonomous and consistent entity. Instead, identities are viewed as fragmented, unstable, discontinuous, and contradictory. Accordingly, notions of a community based on a fixed sexual identity are also de-stabilized. However, as Denis Altman (1996, p. 123) has pointed out, queer theorizing and politics may be limited. With its cultural leaning tending to be "Atlantic-centric in its view of the world," queerness is somewhat entangled in the mainstream culture it seeks to critique.

The current paper is drawn from a doctoral thesis by Damien Ridge which was submitted in 1997. While developing HIV education programs for young homosexually active men at the Victorian AIDS Council in Melbourne from 1989 to 1990, he came to suspect that, regardless of professional discourses about community HIV prevention, little was actually known about younger men and why they engaged in unsafe sex. The result was an analysis that focused on the meanings, emotions, dynamics, and contexts underpinning condom use and unprotected anal sex between men aged mostly in their 20s. A number of Southeast Asian men were encountered in the course of the fieldwork, and it quickly became clear that they were facing particular sexual and social issues related to their ethnicity which went largely unrecognized in wider gay networks. This paper explores themes around ethnicity and sexuality separately from the PhD thesis. While the research and initial analysis and write-up of data from the project were carried out by Damien Ridge, Amos Hee edited the original text and his expertise was important in further developing and refining the analysis in collaboration with Damien Ridge. Victor Minichiello supervized the original thesis and assisted in focusing and editing the final version of the manuscript.

While methodological issues are briefly outlined here, further details are available in other recent publications by the authors (see Minichiello et al., 1995; Ridge et al., 1997).[2] The emphasis in the study was on the meanings, feelings and dynamics involved in sexual and social life within the context of men's life pathways, including their partnerships, informal networks and queer institutions. The study ran from 1993 until 1997. Formal interviews with 24 men were conducted by the main researcher, who is himself Anglo, and over half of all the informants were reinterviewed. A recursive model of interviewing was used so that informants could direct the content of the interviews towards their sexual, social and HIV concerns. Initial research propositions developed using the analytical induction method were scrutinized with further data collected through discussions with informants, other gay men (some of whom are quoted as minor informants in this research), educators, researchers, and health professionals.

Importantly, the analysis in this chapter is limited by a number of considerations. The focus here is on interviews with eight men who were born in various Southeast Asian countries. Five of these men were recruited through advertising, while three were found through networking which developed during the course of the fieldwork. While all eight interviews were used in the analysis, only six of these informants are directly quoted in this chapter.[3] Three of these eight men–Peter, Min and David–were interviewed more than once. However, the interviewer held ongoing discussions with all informants, including those of Southeast Asian background, as part of the fieldwork. Additionally, the concepts discussed in this chapter are grounded in a more general analysis of the experiences of informants on the commercial gay scene. Readers interested in following up themes discussed in this chapter, such as sexualizing social relations and stereotypical social groups, are referred to Ridge et al. (1997). Finally, Damien Ridge held shorter conversations with a range of other men during the study. These men are recorded as "minor informants" in this paper when quoted.

ABOUT THE INFORMANTS

Informants originating from Southeast Asia migrated to Australia at various ages ranging from childhood through to late teenage years. At the time of the first interview, the ages of these informants ranged from 19 to 27. Three men came to Australia as refugees from countries affected by war or social unrest. Two came to Australia along with their families when they were of primary school age, while one, Min, had to make an extremely dangerous escape from his home country in his early teenage years, leaving his family behind. Of the remaining men, Peter went into second year level of an Australian secondary school upon arrival, while David and Martin entered into the final years of secondary schooling. Denis went directly to university as an overseas fee paying student. These eight informants, as with the larger sample, are relatively well-educated and mostly from middle-class backgrounds, reflecting a consistent research finding of "middle-classness" among men sampled from gay social spaces (Prestage, 1995). At the time of the initial interview, one informant had failed his final year of secondary schooling, five men were working towards a tertiary degree, and two had completed a tertiary degree. At the time of the interviews, all men had a good command of the English language, with some being highly articulate.

Denis does not yet have permanent resident status, and has returned to his country of origin while he awaits processing of his application. David has also returned to his country of origin in order to pursue work and explore his cultural heritage. All of the men featured in this chapter are of Chinese ancestry, although country of birth tended to be more central to these men's identities. Most men were highly concerned about confidentiality when revealing their stories. In order to ensure that anonymity was strictly maintained, this chapter avoids directly identifying the actual country of origin of any of the informants. As a consequence, the use of the term "Asian" is problematic in this chapter. "Asian" is used as a constructed identity position, in opposition to the more dominant Anglo-European identities, by these ethnic minority men themselves. However, the term "Asian" is also used in culturally insensitive and racist ways. When used in a racially discriminatory manner, people from very different countries and cultures tend to be lumped together by this term, homogenized and dismissed under the umbrella of otherness. In this text the term "Asian" is used as a shorthand way of signifying that a person has originated from a specific country or culture in Southeast Asia, and as a constructed oppositional identity position that these ethnic minority men may take up themselves.

CHARACTERISTICS OF SOCIAL NETWORKS ON THE SCENE

The most basic units of social organization on the Melbourne gay scene are social groups and individuals (Ridge et al., 1997). However, groups are not clearly defined in relation to other groups, and there are overlaps, connections and movement between groups and individuals. That is, groups and individuals form complex and fragmented social networks. While groups form around acquaintances and friendships, those not included tend to view these particular groups as making up certain categories of people. Such categories often reflect stereotypes which informants use to make sense of social life. Both Anglo informants, and those from Southeast Asia identified a limited number of stereotypical social groups and categories of people with varying attributes, examples of which are included below:

  i. "Party Boys"–connected with the international gay "boy movement" style, dressed in cutting-edge fashion revealing smooth, tanned and well-defined musculature and boyish looks.
  ii. "Clones" and "Leather Queens"–usually older men, these styles were dominant in previous decades.
  iii. "Rice Queens" and "Potato Queens"–rice queens (the stereotype of which is an older man) are Anglo men who pursue so called "Asian" men as sex partners, while "potato queens" are "Asian" men who pursue Anglo men.
  iv. "Young and Gay Crowd"–men who form groups based on a popular course offered by the AIDS Council of Victoria.

Youthful social groups tend to have characteristics–particularly their hierarchical relation to other groups–which have important implications for social organization on the scene.[4] Such social groups are attributed with varying social status by other individuals and groups on the scene. These groups have relatively restrictive and exclusive membership requirements (e.g., based on "in" fashion styles, appearances, ethnicity or social class) which tend to demarcate them from other groups. Each group has its own variation on scene values, knowledge and practices, such as drug taking, dancing styles, and styles of communication (e.g., bitchiness and "camping it up"). Social networks share the scene culture, but are simultaneously separated from other networks, meaning that the culture fractures and intersects in complex ways along multiple dimensions including styles, ethnicities and age. Underlying the importance of group defining attributes is the importance of projecting a "cool" image based on sex and appearance. Alex, a young informant who had only entered into the scene in more recent months, described the required image as "putting on a face" and engaging in restrictive social rituals:

> [L]ike I'm better than you or I'm here to enjoy myself regardless of whether I'm enjoying it or not . . . I have to be happy. I have to dance. I have to wear really tight clothing, have to take off my shirt so everyone can see me without my shirt on. So that the guy standing over there can notice me. (Alex)

Informants in general understood the pressures to fit in with dominant scene styles and social groups to be a homogenizing dynamic. In this commercialized space, only a limited range of styles could be accommodated and promoted as valued. Generally, groups based on relatively limited attributes–Anglo ethnicities, youth, "in" fashion, and masculine styles–tended to have higher status on the scene and were more socially dominant. The accounts of the informants reported here in general pointed to older, lower class, feminine, less stylish, and particular ethnic individuals and groups as having less status on the scene. These people represented "the other" within the commercialized culture which prioritized gay white middle-class styles including masculinity. For example, groups of men from different countries and cultures in Southeast Asia are broadly labelled as "Asians" and are frequently considered–by themselves, Anglo-Australians as well as members of non-Asian immigrant groups–to be situated well down the social hierarchy. Those immigrant men who can assimilate into more valued social groups tend to do so by distancing themselves from the "Asian" identity and thus otherness, and adopting more socially valuable identities such as the hypermasculine "Party Boy."

While unassimilated men from Southeast Asian backgrounds are more likely to face racial discrimination and social exclusion, Asian men on the whole have been able to increase their visibility and establish themselves on the scene through the formation of their own social groups and networks. One Melbourne gay venue which has been known as moderately "Asian friendly" (although some informants felt that this venue turns away unassimilated men through a selective use of a "regulars only" policy or dubious announcements that the venue is full) attracts culturally diverse groups of men from countries such as Malaysia, Vietnam, Singapore, Indonesia, Cambodia, Thailand and Hong Kong. As Martin discovered, some Southeast Asian groups actively incorporate and act as guides for men from similar backgrounds who are new to the scene:

> If you're new, right, they'll introduce you to as many people as they can . . . like it gave me . . . it made me feel good to be an Asian, because I didn't know there were Asians going out, I mean gay Asians. So [it was] something I could identify with . . . so it was very positive, because it's not in the media or anywhere. (Martin)

While there is enormous diversity of cultural heritage among these men reflected in the complexity of their social networks, these differences are invisible to the dominant scene culture from the perspective of these informants, as Min stated:

> They're different, they're not the same, they're different. The Asians feel different among themselves. Depends on where they came from. There's a lot of diversity as a group. (Min)

DISCRIMINATION

> Negative representations were never printed but always around in the subculture. [The stereotype was that] Asians had small dicks, were passive, and wanted older, rich men as partners. (Minor informant, written narrative [WN])

It is valuable to contrast the generally lower status afforded to men from Southeast Asian backgrounds by more dominant groups on the scene with informants' perceptions of gay media representations of "Asians." These men noted that the representation of people from Southeast Asian heritages are lacking in the commercial gay media:

> *Martin*: . . . if you look at like *Outrage*[5] magazine . . . there's nothing about gay Asians. Or even pictures of gay Asians, you know . . . You assume everyone [who] goes out [on the scene] looks like them [Caucasian]. Before I came out it was like . . . you feel a bit reluctant. I thought if I were to go out to the scene that I would be the only Asian there.

> *Ridge*: Do they represent Asian men in the gay media?

Martin: No. Rarely, very rarely. But I think they try very hard to make it better but you know . . . I don't think so. I don't think so. It takes time. I think it will not be happening in a few years.

Those Asian men who are featured as desirable in the gay media are those who have been able to "successfully" assimilate to the dominant Anglo gay culture (e.g., Anglo features, muscular, gay fashions). This preferential representation is common in the wider mass media. For instance, one Filipino informant used the word "mestizo" to describe a "Western-looking" Filipino. The gay media becomes a point of reference where men of Southeast Asian backgrounds, even before they set foot on the scene, learn to situate themselves as marginal within the gay world. By representing assimilated men as valued and desirable, it also suggests a potential path into the mainstream.

Men from Southeast Asian backgrounds in this study were frequently highly sensitive to their subordinate positioning in the dominant gay culture, in ways that Anglos would have had difficulty even noticing. For instance, in addition to being absent in the media, their experiences of being "invisible" to other participants on the scene, such as being ignored by bar staff and catching disapproving glances from Anglo and other European patrons at venues were taken by informants as further evidence of marginality:

> [I]f I was by myself it was very difficult . . . people would often ignore me, on the scene. Not so much being ignored but feeling a bit invisible I think. (Peter)

However, social subordination was not always this subtle. Most ethnic minority men in this study had no difficulty in relating incidences of more overt racial discrimination. For instance, discriminatory remarks from staff, patrons and even Anglo or European friends were reported:

> I'd overhear comments like "This place is crawling with Asians!" Or a particular corner [in a gay venue] where Asian guys hang out being referred to as "Take Away Corner" or "Ho Chi Minh Alley." Or a[n Anglo] drag queen joking that she was late, as her tram had detoured through Richmond and had hit a "slope."[6] (Minor informant [WN])

> [T]he way I feel, gay men should know what it's like to be discriminated against in the first place. And for them to actually discriminate against another minority . . . minority group within a minority group. I think it is really sad. (David)

During the fieldwork, the main researcher recorded remarks from Anglos on the scene including, "this place is swarming with Asians" and "it's like a boat load of Vietnamese just walked in," referring to the number of "Asian" men at a gay pub. The theme underlying such remarks was of discomfort in sharing a largely Anglo cultural space with "the other," that is, with people from cultures which are different from, and little understood within, the dominant Anglo culture. There was also a theme of being overwhelmed by the cultural other.

Importantly, discrimination is also not unknown *within* ethnic groups based on Southeast Asian identities, and occurs on the basis of ethnicity, social status and class. For example, some informants from Malaysia noted that fee paying student friends from their own country studying at Australian universities were from higher social classes. A few of these students reportedly discriminate against Asian men whom they consider to be of lower status (e.g., with statements such as "I came to Australia on a QANTAS jet, not in a boat," that is, not as a refugee) or of "less desirable" ethnic backgrounds (e.g., Indian). Additionally, those men who have successfully assimilated to the dominant gay middle-class culture may consider themselves of higher status than men who have retained elements of their culture, such as men who continue to use languages other than English and engage in non-Western cultural practices. In other words, men who have not adopted the styles of the scene. Some men even avoid contact with visibly Asian groups as a way of fitting in and gaining visibility:

> When there's a lot of Asians, I think I told you before, I feel a bit uncomfortable. I feel uncomfortable because I feel that the other Australians might feel uncomfortable . . . I think like . . . they say, "I don't know why the Asians are coming here," or whatever . . . It's not racism, it's more like if you see a large group of [a] minority in a particular place you just feel a bit threatened . . . that's what I thought they might fear. (Martin)

> I know that I really resented the fact that just being geographically within a space, there would be all these things assumed about me. There were very few Asians on the scene at the time. Some hung around together but were known as "Take Away Rice." Unconsciously, I avoided them as I did not wish to be seen as a faceless other, labelled as Asian again after fighting to be recognized in the dominant culture. (Minor informant [WN])

ASSIMILATION ISSUES

Many informants from Southeast Asian backgrounds assimilate into the largely Anglo, middle-class gay culture in order to gain a sense of visibility and acceptance on the scene. This is because there is limited space on the scene for the co-existence of diverse Southeast Asian cultures when those unassimilated groups are excluded and alienated:

> There are people who hang around . . . like Vietnamese kids who hang around together that don't really know many other people apart from themselves and they have no presence. (Peter)

Denis, an overseas student from a wealthy family in Southeast Asia, had only recently arrived in Australia. He experienced a kind of unremitting discrimination on the scene:

> Well, when I went to a nightclub I didn't feel good because I felt a strong sense of racism. Like I was refused entry and . . . [they said] Asians not allowed. I don't know why. I think probably because it was late in the night and everybody was just getting angry and pissed off and everything. On the occasion that I got to go in, I was being shoved all the time . . . by people on the dance floor. Shoving and when I look at them, they'll stare at me and I quickly turn away. I'd get shoving when I want to get a drink. I was ignored and that kind of stuff. I felt awful. At that time . . . I felt really awful. I felt angry that this kind of thing could happen. I don't think I want to go back there anymore . . . over the four times that I was there . . . it occurs every time I was there. (Denis)

However, Denis did go back to this popular gay nightclub and eventually managed to fit in and assimilate to the scene culture. Importantly, this assimilation included establishing a partnership with a young Anglo man, being accepted into his partner's social network on the scene, adopting gay fashions, and developing a gay "attitude." Since these changes, Denis has reported far fewer instances of discrimination. Additionally, he feels that there are now more men from Southeast Asian backgrounds going to the nightclub he attends, legitimating an Asian presence. Moreover, the narratives suggest that assimilation involves a kind of forgetting and slipping into unconsciousness. At a subsequent meeting, Denis seemed less interested in, and could barely recall, the discrimination he first reported and had been perturbed by.

Other informants originating from a Southeast Asian country escape invisibility and "feminization" through the construction of gay-valued forms of masculinity. Constructing this kind of masculinity involves body building to develop a well-defined musculature, adopting gay fashion and particular demeanors–ways of standing, moving and expression. In the course of the fieldwork, the main researcher observed a number of men who had moved from subordinated Asian groups to become members of dominant social

groups, particularly through body building. Some Southeast Asian informants came to resist pressures to conform to Australian constructions of
valued kinds of masculinity. For instance, David recalled how he cross-
dressed as a child to his parents' amusement and was "camp" at school in his
home country. Once in an Australian high school, under a new regime of
gender, he did not want to be seen as possessing any feminine traits due to the
strong social sanctions against such behavior among his peers. It was not
until David had entered into, and gained experience in, the gay world (particularly the scene and partnerships) that he was able to rediscover what he
considered to be his "femininity." However, rather than mitigating against
social visibility, the "camping it up," theatricality and feminization evident
in David's account afforded him a good deal of social recognition on the
scene. On return to his home town in Southeast Asia where different social
relations operated (including different dynamics of class, ethnicity and gender), Chinese men on the mostly middle-class commercial gay scene often
considered David to have masculine qualities. David now alternated between
camp style (wearing camp shorts which he referred to as his "dress" to
attract heterosexual men at "beats,"[7] who frequently liked feminine men)
and "butch" (to attract gay men on the middle-class commercial gay scene).
That is, David had "negotiated" complex gender performances according to
different social interactions and settings. He also demonstrated how assimilation into the Australian culture can come "undone" once outside of that
milieu.

Assimilation processes often involve a loss of connection to the original
ethnic culture, a loss which may have significant meanings for men, even if
they are not consciously recognized at the time. Disassociation from previous
social networks may seem inevitable to informants of any ethnic background
who understand the scene as a community or place to belong. For instance, in
order to explore his sexuality, Min moved away from his straight Asian
networks toward scene networks which he initially understood to be a community. However, after his overall negative experiences on the scene he
found that he could not return to his former networks, despite deriving important meanings from relations with others who shared his cultural heritage.
The reasons for this are complex but include his assimilation to the Anglo-
centric gay culture at the expense of his own cultural heritage, and the lack of
space for gayness to exist in his particular Southeast Asian network:

> [Y]ou find out the gay community is not a community that you feel you
> belong to or you could become a member of . . . you know. Yeh, and it
> was very sad. I'm caught between the two worlds. But if I have a
> choice, I would choose to be part of the straight Asian community. I'm
> sorry but that's what I feel . . . (Min)

Dislocation from social networks may be problematic, since even "homophobic" networks can be experienced as more culturally supportive than those developed from the commercial scene. While this is particularly the case for ethnic minority informants, it is also an issue for Anglo informants (Ridge et al., 1997). As well as discrimination and pressures to assimilate, Asian men can also find themselves in culturally unfamiliar terrain on the predominantly Anglo gay culture scene. For instance, Min was confronted by the Anglo-centricity of the scene culture and displays of hyper-masculinity:

> Like when I went to a nightclub I [would] feel worse. I think, oh my God . . . Nobody looks at you . . . you know. Who would be interested in you anyway? And you hardly see Asians there. Obviously I don't feel comfortable with very much young, yuppie, pro-active, blond, White Caucasian, you know. Very masculine . . . a bunch of guys without tops and jeans, stuff like that you know. (Min)

SEXUALIZING SOCIAL RELATIONS

There are important differences and similarities between Southeast Asian and Anglo informants in the experiences of sexual relations on the scene. In terms of differences, for example, some informants from Southeast Asian countries were highly concerned about establishing relationships and emotional intimacy as a priority above sex. Unlike most Anglo informants in this study, these particular informants found it difficult to accept having sex outside of an emotionally intimate relationship. In order to avoid a lack of intimacy in sex, some Southeast Asian men attempted, frequently with great difficulty, to establish partnerships with Anglo men *before* sex:

> When I talk to people on the phone . . . Australian, they'll say, "Do you want to go further than that?" "Further than that" means having a relationship. But . . . in Asian culture, when you say "Do want to go further than that?" we mean, having sex after the relationship [has been established]. . . . So, of all the times I meet Caucasians, we end up having sex first . . . (Denis)

Informants in general had similar experiences of the scene in that they noted that social relations at bars and nightclubs tended to be highly sexualized. That is, relations revolved around sexual attributes (e.g., appearance) and activities (e.g., forming friendships with sex-partners). Despite the sexualizing of relations connecting men in some ways, sexualization also acts to insert distance between men, contributing to the fragmentation of social relations and networks. While there are overt elements in sexualizing, it is simultaneously covert; operating in the background, and extending into and influencing all areas of social life. For instance, the way that these informants presented their sexuality to their peers was an important social issue, and could contribute to the hidden sexual currency. One common sexual code in youth-oriented sections of the scene is secrecy. Participants often attempt to appear disinterested in sex despite the contrary being the case. Interestingly, being too sexually available has a stigma of being "sluttish" or "desperate" in some networks.

Sexualization of male-to-male relations becomes more overt at various times, for instance, in "cruising"–when men search for and/or attract potential sexual partners. The sexualizing of relations has important influences on scene social dynamics including militating against building social supports, communication and friendships.

Not only are informants labelled as "Asians" and then socially devalued on the scene, they are also sexually devalued and excluded. Being regularly excluded from sexualized relations as participants, these informants frequently became keen observers of other men's sexual and social relations. For instance, after considerable observation, Peter noted that success in locating scene-valued sexual partners could translate into valued social status among men. As with other informants (such as those who do not fit the low body fat preference on the commercial scene), the sexual devaluing of men from Southeast Asian backgrounds has personal and social consequences. For instance, these men may see their failure as purely personal, rather than as a social issue within the scene itself, adding to feelings of social alienation:

> I'd try and say, pick someone up who I thought was cute or whatever and their response would be so acidic that . . . As if how could you ever imagine that I would want to go with you? And I used to think am I that bad? Am I really that disgusting? (Peter)

Specific social issues involved in the sexual devaluing of Asian men by Anglo men, as opposed to an individualistic explanation, may only become apparent to men after considerable experience. It was only after Min had undergone years of therapy and "social study" that he came to the conclusion that he had "imprisoned" himself through his adoption of racist Western notions of desirable gay men, notions which for Min were encapsulated by an Anglo-American body icon Marky Mark,[8] much admired at one time in the gay culture:

> As an Asian, I have a problem approaching a Caucasian . . . I think that maybe they rejected me. And they may be actual . . . Also I think that they actually are arrogant . . . [and] you don't look like Marky Mark,

you know. I've imprisoned myself through the way I look at myself physically. (Min)

Peter became acutely aware that men would have sex with him in secluded beat situations, but the same men would ignore him on the scene where sex was part of a greater social dynamic, such as when friends and acquaintances might be observing, and there was a greater need to engage with partners on some social level compared to beats. He found that he was rarely able to "pick up" men on the scene:

> It was like when I realized the social dimension . . . like I could be totally ignored by this person . . . on the scene. He wouldn't even look at me twice. Or even if I talked to him, he'd just turn away. But he'd have sex with me at a beat or a sauna . . . they didn't have to interact with me on a personal level. And therefore not bring on the assumptions of what I was . . . what I looked like and translate that into real life. (Peter)

It was only on his return visit to his country of origin in Southeast Asia that Peter considered his failure in the sexual currency system on the scene in Australia not to be a personal failure, but a gay cultural issue. In Southeast Asia, Peter discovered a greater sexual "freedom" compared to Melbourne. Within his home culture, his ethnicity did not exclude him from access to sexual partners. Indeed, Peter found that for the first time, he was desired by men that he also desired. He began to become aware that he might actually be sexually desirable himself. Now back in Melbourne, Peter is attempting to reclaim aspects of his particular culture after an emotionally difficult assimilation to Australian gay culture.

In line with the values of the dominant gay culture, men from Southeast Asian backgrounds frequently value Anglo men as partners above Asian men. Such Caucasian-preferring Asian men are called "potato queens." Caucasian men interested in Asian men (often referred to as "rice queens") are perceived to be far fewer in number relative to the number of Asian men on the Melbourne scene, and are reportedly more likely to be older rather than younger. The limited sexual currency of Asian men on the scene gives these Anglo men a substantial collective power when forming partnerships with men from Southeast Asian countries:

> Recently, one of my Caucasian friends made a remark about gay Asians. He said, if you have OK look–he meant tall and white–you can get any Asian you like. (Min)

Additionally, informants reported that Asian men commonly rejected each other as sexual partners and suspected that there was an element of viewing each other as "competition" for a limited number of Caucasian partners. This situation contributed to division and conflict among these men, undermining threads of solidarity that might exist.

> If you walk in (to the scene) with Asians, they look at you as if to say, "Oh my God, more competition" . . . There's a . . . this general attitude that um . . . Asian men are not desirable. Either because people do not find them sexually attractive or because they are racist towards them. And because of that there's only a select, small pool of men, generally old rice queens, who would only go for Asian boys. And because the group is so select and small, the more Asians that come in, the more threatening it becomes. And because of that then there's this hostility towards Asians amongst Asians, so that's one thing that I find really sad. (David)

> I started wanting to sleep with other Asians . . . and realizing that it was very difficult to because they all wanted white men. I think it doubled the whole feeling I had. It made me feel even worse. (Peter)

There is resistance among these men from Southeast Asia to their low sexual and social status on the scene. Some men resist at an everyday level because they are unfamiliar with, distrust or reject the dominant culture.

> I think culturally they do not feel comfortable, and they do not assimilate . . . some Asians. So they haven't assimilated to the Caucasian culture . . . I mean they are not willing to assimilate, acculturate . . . that's the word. Also the language difficulty . . . the barriers of the language. You can't communicate. (Min)

A few Asian informants resisted at a more organized level by avoiding sexual and/or social contact with Anglo men, and through attempting to develop Asian gay networks. Although there were reports that more Asian men were beginning to consider other Asian men for partnerships, the prospects of developing Southeast Asian homosexual support networks in Melbourne were only just being realized at the time of the study. However, there did seem to be awareness of such networks existing in Sydney:

> [In Sydney] you know people avoid [Anglos] . . . as they start to recognize these institutional power structures . . . they, like me, avoid sex with Caucasian men or, you know . . . seeking out just specifically Caucasian men. They see that as problematic . . . like myself. But that kind of consciousness is not so prevalent here [in Melbourne]. (Peter)

And I haven't seen any network, Asian network . . . a strong support for Asians. They had tried but I think it failed.[9] (Min)

SEXUAL ACTIVITY

This study has tapped into a wide variety of complex personal and social meanings that informants attributed to sex (Ridge, 1996; Ridge et al., 1997). Sex varied in meaning depending on the participants, their feelings, and the specific circumstances. Despite safe sex education for gay men constructing sex in a positive way, sex for informants was not always just about pleasure and positive experiences. Sex could have serious or even negative meanings, particularly for Asian men on the scene. For example, for Anglo and ethnic minority informants engagement in cruising and sex was frequently an "instrumental" way of dealing with emotional issues including insecurities and the "euphoria" of moving from a homosexually negative or exclusionary environment to a gay-positive space. For men of Southeast Asian backgrounds in particular, feelings of cultural isolation and "freedom" could be dealt with instrumentally through sex. In some circumstances, meanings of freedom and empowerment attributed to sex can help to create a context where unsafe unprotected anal intercourse is possible, as was the case for Beng, a man who migrated to Australia from Malaysia, and contracted HIV while exploring his sexuality in a new culture (Hee, 1997). Beng's understanding of his seroconversion was that he moved from a cultural world that emphasized a kind of collective responsibility with clear moral codes, to a Western system which he perceived to be more "free"; where "nothing is right or nothing is wrong." Sex in Australia was experienced by Beng in this new context as being about freedom of "choice" and exploring new bodily and emotional possibilities. Combined with his lack of knowledge about the "rules" of safety in sex, HIV infection through unprotected anal sex was one outcome:

> I come from Malaysia which is like a Muslim country, and it is, you know, very constricted–there are a lot of shoulds and should nots–so when I came here, my first thing that I discovered was my sexuality. I'm gay and life in Australia for the first two or three years was through sex–the opportunity to be able to explore my body, the opportunity to be able to express myself. (Beng)

The personal stakes invested in scene-sexualized relations could be very high. For instance, men of Southeast Asian backgrounds, like other informants, linked their sense of self-worth and social success to finding partners on the scene. However, the additional problems in locating partners for these ethnic minority men could be linked with substantial emotional problems.

> I just couldn't pick up. No one was interested . . . I just couldn't judge
> where I stood. And it really did make me feel bad for the first time I
> think. That's why I say the scene made me learn to hate myself in a way
> . . . this huge wall started to be built. And none of my friends knew that.
> That I was going through all this. (Peter)

While few studies have acknowledged that power relations operate between gay men, power is a routine issue in these men's lives (Ridge, 1996). Men from Southeast Asia who are inexperienced with, and have not assimilated to the white middle-class culture, can be at a distinct power disadvantage in their sexual negotiations with Anglo men. For instance, in a setting where youth is highly valued, and where Asian informants do not tend to reject older men as partners to the same extent as men from other ethnic backgrounds on the scale that other informants reported, older more experienced men may look towards younger Asian men for partnerships. When these Anglo men make sexual approaches, some men from Southeast Asian backgrounds have difficulties refusing these advances, and their apparent passivity or ambivalence can be interpreted as consent for sex. This interaction can be related to various issues including sexual inexperience, a common Southeast Asian cultural respect for older people and an avoidance of confronting authority figures. Such differences in understanding need to be seen as an outcome of an interaction between different cultures where there may be a lack of common ground, rather than merely as an Anglo man consciously pressuring another man to have sex against his will. However, Asian men who are more or less assimilated to western culture can be more critical of such encounters.

> This is one of the cultural aspects . . . they respect older people's right.
> They do not say OK piss off you old bastard, get a life, get away. They
> are so polite. Now I go inside there and I feel like saying "Oh that's a
> disgusting old bastard!" But as Asians are polite and nice they talk to
> them and say "Oh how are you?" you know. (Min)

Men from Southeast Asian backgrounds can be targets of sexual harassment and coercion by older Anglo men, many of whom may not have full awareness of their power advantage. As mentioned above, Anglo men often misinterpret passivity as consent. When a Southeast Asian man means to say no to sex to an older Anglo man, he may do so in a non-confrontational manner, such as by saying "maybe later." In terms of sexual "negotiation," this puts these men at considerable disadvantage if they cannot avoid or directly say no, even to unprotected anal intercourse. It can take experience of cross-cultural misunderstandings before Asian men become more aware of these kinds of power issues. For example, Min related a familiar story whereby his original search for gay Asian friends was utilized as a sexual opportunity by an older Caucasian man:

> And I picked up the *Outrage* magazine . . . and yes I look at the back and it says this community . . . Asian gays and friends. I need Asian there to feel comfortable . . . it didn't work out like I expected it to. The person who rang me is old and Caucasian right. He was false, he said he was a psychologist and I believed that, I was so naive. He you . . . know, he did that to me [tried to have sex] yeah he gave me a blow job. I didn't like it. I said no. Yeh . . . it . . . I did have some control. I said no. But he did that anyway. And ahh . . . I had no idea what gay life was about. I was naive. I didn't have contact with experiences with friends and gay friends. Not with gay . . . I was isolated. You know . . . I was very shy. I didn't know . . . And I didn't understand gay culture of course. It was after 2 years time. . . . I observed, I learnt. I talked to . . . I experienced gay culture from my perspective. And I also became more cynical about myself and the relationships I engaged with. (Min)

Bartos et al. (1993) similarly point to the complexity of power dynamics in Anglo-ethnic minority partnerships, noting that some ethnic minority men had UAI as a means of expressing their vulnerability, as well as related to their lack of power to "negotiate" safe sex with Anglo men. Additionally, they noted that unsafe sex for ethnic minority men could be about acting out a fantasy of surrendering to a more dominant Anglo man, and gaining social support via HIV infection.

CONCLUSION

> I say I would not identify myself as a member of the gay community because I don't comply [with] the rules and I don't comply with their norms and expectations. For me, I am always critical and been cynical about that . . . most of my friends are critical about [the] gay community and that's the way it is! (Min)

Regardless of ethnic background, these informants considered the commercial gay scene to be a central location of the established "gay community." While notions of "gay communities" are a part of popular discourses, there are considerable tensions between the ideals of "community," and these men's actual experiences on the scene. Informants, in general, did not describe their experiences in the scene in terms of finding "unity," "connectedness," "support," "friendliness," "openness" and "acceptance"–aspects of community that they initially anticipated. On the contrary, a major theme emerging from this study was of multiple and fragmented social networks, as predicted in much recent queer theorizing (see Angelides, 1994).

Social groups and networks were relatively exclusive, having varying membership requirements and social status, being maintained and influenced by reasonably rigid social regulation. As many informants from Southeast Asia discovered, not being integrated into a valued group was to risk invisibility, otherness and exclusion. In addition to cultural differences between networks in general, differences within Southeast Asian-based networks contributed towards fragmentation and lack of social cohesion, particularly since there was little space within the dominant culture to express cultural difference. Divisions in Asian networks were compounded by pressures to assimilate to the dominant culture, and sexualized relations which were unfavorable to men of Southeast Asian backgrounds. While all men who integrated into the scene more or less felt pressure to assimilate to the white middle-class gay culture, Southeast Asian men generally had more cultural distance to cover in order to find a place to belong. Men who could not or would not assimilate to the scene culture faced exclusion, invisibility, and racial discrimination. This study seems to have tapped into a high level of anger, sadness and loneliness among informants originating from Southeast Asia. This level of alienation seems connected yet beyond that of other informants within the context of the scene.

Assumptions of unity underpinning gay community conceal the extent to which power operates at an interactional as well as structural level, in scene-based sexual and social relations. In this milieu, many individuals and networks are culturally subordinated and excluded, and not just ethnic minorities. One important dynamic of power operating in this setting is the tendency towards the commodification of social relations. Commodification pressures play an important role in constructing sameness and exclusions on the scene, limiting cultural variations (Whittle, 1994). Under such circumstances, rhetoric about "one community," as is often promoted in gay community HIV campaigning, assumes that there is only one important culture–the western gay culture and those who are able to adapt to it. Such discourses work to silence alternative voices and cultural forms.

However, while limited shared values, knowledges and practices can typically be attributed to these commercialized spaces, such homogeneity tends to obscure considerable individual and cultural diversity that is clearly demonstrated in these men's narratives. These settings comprise diverse individuals and complex social networks which encompass cultural variations and instabilities. These individuals and networks include people with multiple identities and preferences, such as those who prioritized their ethnicity and non-gay social networks over gayness. At this level, there is agency for disrupting and subverting the dominant culture forms, and a number of informants were involved in doing so, such as through avoiding Anglo partners and confronting racial discrimination. Dennis Altman (1997) has recently pointed to the Australian "cultural cringe" or inferiority complex vis-à-vis Europe and North America and consistently pointed to the Australian propensity for following American trends. This inclination is most apparent in the adoption of gay American cultural styles. As gay identities and social spaces are increasingly organized (and homogenized) by commercial transactions (Evans, 1993), discussion and increased awareness of ethnic minority cultural differences may help to open up more local alternatives to current global gay identities and values.

In constructing the universal and increasingly commercialized gay identity and "community," a good deal of restrictive social control is involved. This is particularly evident from these informants' accounts of marked social homogeneity on the scene. There is a tension between ethnic minority experiences of feeling pressure to adapt to the dominant gay culture, and the need to embrace cultural differences in order for officially supported multicultural policies to translate into practice. Unless the proponents of the notion of a unified gay community can become more aware of the values underpinning tendencies toward monoculturalism, then their discourses will continue to be empty rhetoric for these informants.

At the time of writing this conclusion (late 1997), the social and political fall-out from the maiden speech to Australia's Federal parliament by the independent member for the Queensland state electorate of Oxley, Ms. Pauline Hanson, was proving difficult to contain. The Federal electorate of Oxley is located in the western suburbs of Brisbane, the capital of the state of Queensland. In 1995 Pauline Hanson was endorsed by the Liberal Party, the senior political partner of the conservative Liberal-National Party coalition now in power federally in Australia, as its candidate for Oxley for the federal elections held in March 1996. However, the Liberal Party subsequently disendorsed Ms. Hanson because of her outspoken racist views on Aboriginals and Asian migrants. Ms Hanson went on to contest and win the seat of Oxley as an independent candidate not aligned to any political party. She made her controversial maiden speech to Federal Parliament in Canberra in September 1996, when she announced the views and policies she would seek to promote during her period of tenure. In 1997 she formed the One Nation Party as a national political platform for her views.

In her notorious maiden speech to Parliament, Ms. Hanson claimed that welfare, educational and other government policies were giving Aboriginal Australians preferential treatment over white Australians and she also warned that Australia was "in danger of being swamped by Asians" (Leser, 1996). The apparent level of public support for her racially divisive perspectives took many social commentators by surprise, as in the 1980s and first half of the 1990s the mainstream Australian media and state and federal govern-ments had increasingly promoted a view of Australia as a tolerant, ethnically diverse and multicultural society. The chord that Hanson has struck with sections of the Australian public reminds us that the racist "White Australia" immigration policy was only dismantled in relatively recent times in the early 1970s (Sargent, 1994). This official policy effectively barred non-Caucasians from migrating to Australia from the early years of this century until the early 1970s. Since the abolition of the "White Australia" policy a quarter of a century ago, Australia has embraced a racially non-discriminatory immigra-tion policy which has seen significant rates of Asian, Polynesian and other non-Caucasian immigration. However, it seems that residual Cold War era anxieties about an "Asian invasion" of Australia from the north are still an important element of the collective consciousness, including on the gay scene. In the absence of widespread understanding and sympathy for Asian men within the dominant culture of the scene, a projection of fears onto these men seems to be operating instead. Such fear is particularly likely at this time in Australian history, when globalization and years of economic restructuring have ushered in an era of high unemployment, a declining standard of living and a redistribution of wealth from the poor to the already wealthy. More recent immigrants and those who seem to be outside of the mythical "main-stream" are a comforting scapegoat for anxieties about the economic and cultural future.

In the current social climate, it is not clear whether spaces such as commu-nity organizations and queer groups can offer an alternative place to belong for members of ethnic minorities. The accounts of the informants quoted above suggest that dynamics on the scene such as the exclusion of subordi-nated cultural forms are also reproduced in these alternative settings. For instance, men from Southeast Asian backgrounds can be ignored and ex-cluded even by queer groups which claim to be about diversity and differ-ence. Alex, for instance, a bright and warm young man, located a queer discussion group, but found that there was little space to contribute to discus-sion topics based on his own cultural heritage and the perspective this af-forded him. Instead, he felt pressured to adapt to the group's way of interact-ing, such as being loud and talking about "cool" issues which he admitted he had little knowledge of, in order to be heard. In his struggle to establish a socially valued identity since coming to terms with his homosexuality, the irony of how his own sense of self was marginalized on the scene and in this "alternative" discussion group was not lost on Alex. The narratives of a number of informants from Southeast Asian backgrounds have shown how the kinds of regulatory structures on the commercial gay scene also apply to other areas of queer life including gay organizations, events and relation-ships.

Queerness, as the current "light on the horizon" in terms of embracing difference, may only be useful as a precursor to the more substantial cultural shifts that are needed for cultural diversity to be genuinely accepted. The resilience of cultural exclusions and lack of inter-racial understanding across various social settings begs the question–are these kinds of structures and ways of thinking embedded deeply within the consciousness of individuals socialized within western cultures? If Australia is to truly fulfil its potential to become a harmonious multicultural society, as so often proclaimed by Federal and State government policies, rather than follow the path of tense racial divisions found in some other western countries, then there is a need for us to consciously reflect and change at a much deeper level than first anticipated by the architects of multiculturalism in this country. A truly multicultural society needs to make conscious attempts to better understand and engage cultural differences. This is not the same thing as a tolerance which deteriorates when a single Federal politician such as Pauline Hanson suddenly opens up a public space for a society to express its deepest fears and insecurities.

As actual or potential outsiders, the men from Southeast Asia interviewed in this study hold up a mirror to the dominant cultural forms, revealing them from perspectives which are seldom seen or heard. The critiques from the "margins" reveal that perhaps the commercialized gay scene, in reality, cannot be a center of community reflection and change. The work ahead is much harder than merely "attaching" young men to the scene, or bringing together peer "discussion" groups and expecting community development and networking to happen, as past HIV education policy has often assumed. Additionally, counselling and sex education can reinforce western cultural values and ignore other cultural and belief systems (Wood & Ridge, 1996). The results of this study contribute to the current re-thinking about "gay communities" by bringing into the debate crucial issues such as exclusion, power, cultural variations and social justice. Promoting notions of a gay community in HIV/AIDS education and wider political arenas has tended to conceal the cultural dominance of particular social styles, networks, ethnicities, and social class positions within the gay world (Wood & Ridge, 1996). HIV social research has also frequently ignored the experiences of ethnic minority cultures. Over a decade of research has assisted in our understanding of the sexual, social and health issues of white middle-class gay men. However, this collective research effort seems to have unwittingly prioritized Western cultural frameworks and regimes of sexuality above the many different cultural forms now found in Australia. Further social research is required which critically examines dominant gay cultural forms, assumptions of an underlying gay solidarity and uniformity, and how ethnic minority women and men make sense of their sexual and social experiences.

NOTES

1. In line with other studies of gay social networks, participation in the established gay community often amounts to attending gay commercial venues (McLeod and Nott, 1994). While youth-oriented bars and nightclubs are the focus of this chapter, forthcoming publications from this project focus on other institutions in the gay world, including relationships.

2. This chapter is partly based on a paper which appears in the *Journal of Contemporary Ethnography* (Ridge et al., 1997). In writing this earlier paper, it became clear that the experiences of informants originating from Southeast Asia warranted further investigation and this current paper explores these men's experiences in more detail.

3. One interview with a Southeast Asian informant was paraphrased rather than recorded and fully transcribed. While the interview was used in the analysis, only transcribed or written accounts are quoted in this chapter. Another informant, Tommy, had not had much experience on the commercial gay scene.

4. For more detail about these social groups, see Ridge, D., Minichiello, V., and Plummer, D. (1997). Queer connections: Community, 'the scene,' and an epidemic. *Journal of Contemporary Ethnography, 26* (2), 146-181.

5. *Outrage* is a national monthly gay magazine published from Melbourne.

6. Richmond is an inner suburb in Melbourne with a large Southeast Asian population, and "slope" is a derogatory term for a person of Asian background.

7. "Beat" is Australian gay idiom for a cruising place and usually refers to concealed public spaces such as toilets and parks where men seek out other men for sex-related purposes.

8. Marky Mark is an American rap performer/model/celebrity also known for his muscular physique. Although presumably heterosexual, his look has been frequently admired in the gay media such as to model men's underwear.

9. Since this study, SILK (http://www.geocitiees.com/westhollywood/heights/8928), a multicultural group of Asian men, has formed in Melbourne to provide mutual support to men of various nationalities and cultures.

REFERENCES

Altman, D. (1996). The new world of "gay Asia." *Meridian, 14*(2), 121-138.

Altman, D. (1997). *Defying gravity.* St Leonards, Sydney: Allen & Unwin.

Angelides, S. (1994). The queer intervention: Sexuality, identity, and cultural politics. *Melbourne Journal of Politics, 22*, 66-88.

Bartos, M., McLeod, J., & Nott, P. (1993). *Meanings of sex between men.* Canberra: Australian Government Publishing Service.

Duberman, M. (1991). *About time: Exploring the gay past* (revised edition). New York: Meridian.

Evans, D.T. (1993). *Sexual citizenship: The material construction of sexualities.* London: Routledge.

Hee, A. (1996, February 21). An open letter to the gay "community." *Melbourne Star Observer*, p. 13.

Hee, A. (1997) *Sex, living & dying: Cross cultural meanings and HIV/AIDS*. Melbourne: Ethnic Youth Issues Network.

Higgins, P. (1993). *A queer reader*. London: Fourth Estate.

Leser, D. (1996, November 30) Pauline Hanson's bitter harvest. In *The Age* (Melbourne) *Good Weekend Supplement*, 16-23.

Lynch, F.R. (1992). Non-ghetto gays: An ethnography of suburban heterosexuals. In G. Herdt (Ed.), *Gay culture in America* (pp. 165-201). Boston: Beacon Press.

Maaten, F. (1994, October 21). Racist routines: Letter to the editor. In *Brother Sister* (Melbourne, Australia), p. 8.

McLeod, J. (1994). *Curriculum development and peer education project: Third discussion paper*. Melbourne: Victorian AIDS Council/Gay Men's Health Centre.

McLeod, J. & Nott, P. (1994). *A place to belong: Attachment to the gay community and the prevention of HIV infection in young men who have sex with men*. Sydney: Australian Federation of AIDS Organisations.

Milburn, C. (1994, October 25). Gay acts under fire for racism. *The Age* (Melbourne, Australia), p. 9.

Minichiello, V., Aroni, R., Timewell, E., & Alexander, L. (with Ridge, D. & Stynes, R). (1995). *In-depth interviewing: Principles, techniques, analysis* (2nd ed.). Melbourne: Longman Cheshire.

Phelan, S. (1993). (Be)coming out: Lesbian identity and politics. *Signs, 18*, 765-790.

Plummer, K. (1989). Gay and lesbian youth in England, *Journal of Homosexuality, 17*, 195-223.

Prestage, G., Noble, J., Kippax, S., Crawford, J., Baxter, D., & Cooper, D. (1995). *Sydney men and sexual health (SMASH) report A.1: Methods and sample in a study of homosexually active men in Sydney, Australia*. Sydney: HIV, AIDS & Society Publications.

Reynolds, R. (1994). Postmodernism and gay/queer identities. In R. Aldrich (Ed.), *Gay perspectives II: More essays in Australian gay culture* (pp. 245-274). Sydney: University of Sydney Printing Service.

Ridge, D. (1996). Negotiated safety: Not negotiable or safe? *Venereology, 9*(2), 98-100.

Ridge, D. (1997). *Why men still have unsafe sex: Meanings, dynamics and contexts among younger gay men*. PhD Thesis, Faculty of Health Sciences, School of Public Health, La Trobe University, Melbourne.

Ridge, D., Minichiello, V., & Plummer, D. (1997). Queer connections: Community, "the scene," and an epidemic. *Journal of Contemporary Ethnography, 26* (2), 146-181.

Sargent, M. (1994). *The new sociology for Australians* (3rd edition). Melbourne: Longman Cheshire.

Scheff, T.J. (1990). *Microsociology: Discourse, emotion, and social structure*. Chicago: The University of Chicago Press.

Tinder, G. (1980). *Community: Reflections on a tragic ideal*. Baton Rouge and London: Louisiana State University Press.

Tremble, B., Schneider, M., & Appathurai, C. (1989). Growing up gay or lesbian in a multicultural context. *Journal of Homosexuality, 17*(3-4), 253-267.

Vasta, E. (1993). Multiculturalism and ethnic identity: The relationship between racism and resistance. *Australian and New Zealand Journal of Sociology, 29*(2), 209-225.

Watney, S. (1995). AIDS and the politics of queer diaspora. In M. Dorenkamp & R. Henke (Eds.), *Negotiating lesbian and gay Subjects* (pp. 53-70). New York: Routledge.

Weeks, J. (1991). *Against Nature: Essays in History, Sexuality, and Identity.* London: Rivers Oram Press.

Whittle S. (1994). Consuming differences: The collaboration of the gay body with the cultural state. In Stephen Whittle (Ed.), *The Margins of the City: Gay Men's Urban Lives* (pp. 27-40). Arena: Hants.

Wood, R., & Ridge, D. (1996). All in the family. *National AIDS Bulletin (Sydney), 10*(6), 18-21.

A Social Psychological Perspective on HIV/AIDS and Gay or Homosexually Active Asian Men

Rasyid Sanitioso

University of Melbourne

SUMMARY. This paper employs findings in social psychological research to analyze HIV/AIDS-related issues among gay and homosexual Asian men living in western countries, specifically in Australia. This includes analyses of: (1) the impact of collectivistic cultural ideologies on self-conception and self-esteem; (2) self-identity related to the status of Asians as numerical and status minorities; (3) the existence of stereotypes of Asians in the gay communities and their consequences on individual Asians; and (4) issues related to self-esteem of gay Asian men as determined by their identification with the Asian and/or the gay communities and acculturation to the dominant Australian Anglo-Celtic culture. *[Article copies available for a fee from The Haworth Document Delivery Service: 1-800-342-9678. E-mail address: getinfo@haworthpressinc.com]*

INTRODUCTION

This paper presents a social psychological analysis on HIV/AIDS-related issues among gay and homosexually active Asian (GHA) men. The focus

---

Correspondence regarding this article may be addressed to Rasyid Sanitioso, PhD, School of Behavioural Science, University of Melbourne, Parkville, Victoria, 3052, Australia.

[Haworth co-indexing entry note]: "A Social Psychological Perspective on HIV/AIDS and Gay or Homosexually Active Asian Men." Sanitioso, Rasyid. Co-published simultaneously in *Journal of Homosexuality* (The Haworth Press, Inc.) Vol. 36, No. 3/4, 1999, pp. 69-85; and: *Multicultural Queer: Australian Narratives* (ed: Peter A. Jackson and Gerard Sullivan) The Haworth Press, Inc., 1999, pp. 69-85. Single or multiple copies of this article are available for a fee from The Haworth Document Delivery Service [1-800-342-9678, 9:00 a.m. - 5:00 p.m. (EST). E-mail address: getinfo@haworthpressinc.com].

will be those Asians who live in western countries such as Australia and the US and therefore are considered an ethnic minority in a dominant majority Anglo-Australian or White-American culture. Theories and findings in social psychology will be used to identify issues that may be relevant to GHA men because of their ethnic and sexual minority status, including issues related to cultural ideologies, self-conception, and stereotyping–all of which may influence GHAs' response to HIV/AIDS.

Though an extremely diverse group, for the purpose of this paper the term "Asians" will be used to refer to those men who trace their origins to countries such as Malaysia, Singapore, Indonesia, Thailand, the Philippines, Vietnam, Hong Kong, and China. (This categorization issue will be addressed again in a later section of the paper.) This grouping is to facilitate discussion and research into the experience of Asians in Australia, which is still in its early stages. Within this heterogeneous group, there need to be acknowledged distinctions related to degrees of acculturation to the dominant Anglo-Australian or White American culture (Rosenthal & Feldman, 1992). One measure of acculturation has been the length of stay in the host country (from birth to recently arrived) and the adoption or rejection of cultural values and habits of the host country (e.g., language spoken at home, food) by the individual and his family (Feldman & Rosenthal, 1990). The grouping of Asians into a single category, even if an inclusive one, may be justified since cross-cultural research shows that, despite differences in specific experiences associated with countries of origin, factors which relate to cultural ideologies tend to be similar among Southeast and East Asian countries and collectively differ markedly from countries commonly referred to as "western" nations such as Australia, the USA, and western European countries (Smith & Bond, 1993). Since this paper focuses on differences at the level of cultural ideologies, the inclusive and heterogeneous grouping of Asians into a single category will be used–with an awareness of significant differences within the category itself.

COLLECTIVE CULTURAL ORIENTATION, MINORITY STATUS, AND SELF-CONCEPT

Most Asian countries and cultures are characterized by collectivistic cultural orientation. In contrast, western nations are characterized by a more individualistic orientation (Smith & Bond, 1993). This orientation refers to the importance of others in the society to the individuals' sense of self, well-being and existence. Individuals in collectivistic cultures define their self in an interdependent manner, for instance, in terms of their relationship with others in the social group (e.g., "I am the daughter of X," "the mother of Y") and give priorities to collective over personal goals (e.g., sacrificing personal wishes for the good of the family). Individuals from individualistic cultures, on the other hand, emphasize independence in the form of a unique, bounded self which is not dependent on others, true expressions of this uniqueness and independence, and an emphasis on personal over collective goals. For the self to be meaningful, an individual from collectivistic cultures cannot forsake primary support groups such as family and relations. To fit in within one's roles and duties as a member of social groups such as family contributes to a person's worth. When asked to describe themselves, individuals from collectivistic cultures are more likely to mention social roles which reflect the importance of social context in their self-definition, compared to individuals from individualistic cultures who are more likely to mention trait words (e.g., "extroverted," "independent," "intelligent") reflecting independence from others and consistency of the self and behavior regardless of whom the individuals are interacting with (Markus & Kitayama, 1991).

The difference in self-construal between people from collectivistic and individualistic cultures means that different factors influence its evaluation (i.e., self-esteem). One of the clearest pieces of empirical evidence pointing to cultural differences in self-esteem is the findings in attributional biases for success and failure. Attribution is the explanation one gives for behavior or outcomes. This is the answer to the "Why" questions people may ask in order to explain their social world. Whether consciously or not, people engage in attribution analyses most of the time, though perhaps more likely when something occurs which contradicts everyday expectations. When a friend fails to greet us, for example, we want to figure out why. Attribution also applies to one's behavior. When one succeeds, one may explain his/her success as being due to one's intelligence (disposition) or to the situation (e.g., the task was easy) or various combinations of the two. Empirical findings suggest that Anglo-Australian and White-American subjects are more likely to attribute success to the self (i.e., disposition) compared to subjects from collectivistic cultures (e.g., Korea, Japan, and China; see Kashima & Triandis, 1986). Among collectivistic subjects success is often attributed to luck, help from the group, or other factors that would minimize differentiation of the successful person from his or her group. Thus, whereas being better than one's peers contributes to the self-esteem of a person with an individualistic orientation (Sanitioso, Kunda, & Fong, 1990), fitting in and being a good member of a group may be an important factor to the self-esteem of a person from a collectivistic culture (see Luthanen & Crocker, 1992).

The importance of the group in the self-esteem of someone from a collectivistic culture is further enhanced by minority status. Asians in Australia and in the US are both numerical (Asians make up only about 4 percent of the total Australian population [Australian Bureau of Immigration, Multicultural and Population Research, 1991], and 3 percent of the total US population [US Bureau of Census, 1990]) and status minorities (Asians occupy a lower social status than the dominant majority group). Being a minority could enhance the salience of the group (i.e., Asian-ness) to the person (the Asian himself or herself) and to others (e.g., other Americans or Australians). A study conducted by Phinney and Chavira (1992) illustrated the importance of groups to minority members by examining the influence of ethnic identification in the level of self-esteem shown by individual members.

There are theoretically clear expectations that minority members will have a lower self-esteem. Social psychological theories such as social comparison (Festinger, 1954; Gergen, 1987) and reflected appraisal (Mead, 1934; Gergen, 1987) can lead to this expectation. Social comparison specifies that a person learns about himself or herself (about one's abilities, worth, traits) by comparing him/herself to others. To understand whether one is intelligent or not, for example, one compares to others on this dimension. Since minorities often occupy a lower status in the societal strata, it can be expected that minority members may compare poorly against the dominant majority group and therefore show a lowered self-esteem level. Reflected appraisal also concerns how we get to know ourselves. The theory specifies that we know who we are (or how we are evaluated) from the feedback and reactions we receive from others. Since stereotypes of Asians (perceptions of Asians held by the dominant majority) tend to be negative, it will not be theoretically surprising to find that Asians have lower self-esteem compared to members of the majority groups (i.e., Caucasian-Americans or Anglo-Australians). Phinney's findings, however, showed that minority individuals have as high self-esteem as individuals from the majority group. And more importantly, identification with their ethnic group is correlated with minority individuals' level of self-esteem. That is, the higher the ethnic identification, the higher the level of self-esteem of an individual. This correlation was not found among individuals belonging to the majority or dominant group. Ethnic identification refers to the importance of ethnicity to the individual, the personal involvement of the individual in the ethnic community (i.e., whether one thinks of oneself as a worthy member of the group) and personal evaluation of the group (i.e., whether one thinks of one's group as worthy) (see Luthanen & Crocker, 1992).

The findings that strongly identifying with groups which have minority and often lower status in society actually increases self-esteem can be explained by referring to referents and standards used by high identifiers in their reflected appraisal and social comparison. Increased identification means that the group is more important in defining one's self. This could mean that the feedback about oneself from other members of one's group (e.g., from other Asians and from family) represents the single, most important source of self-esteem. If the group indeed has a positive self-stereotype (roughly speaking, this is how a group thinks of itself), then higher group identification ensures a positive evaluation of oneself by *important* others who are made up of other members of one's own group. Indeed, self-stereotypes (e.g., how Asians think of themselves as a group) tend to be more positive than stereotypes held by others (e.g., how Anglo-Australians or White-Americans think of Asians in general). High identifiers also compare themselves to others in their own group rather than to others in, for instance, the dominant majority group. Additionally, the importance of the minority group to a person's self-conception may render him or her more aware of potential discrimination from others. This may protect a person's self-esteem if failures and inability to control outcomes are attributed externally (i.e., to discriminatory systems) than internally (i.e., to shortcomings about oneself).

Self-esteem has been related to likelihood to engage in safe sex (Rotheram-Borus, Rosario, Reid, Koopman, 1995). More importantly from a social psychological view point, self-esteem is related to perceived self-efficacy which may influence the acquisition of skills necessary to negotiate safe sex with a partner or in translating knowledge (e.g., about HIV/AIDS) and intention into behavior (e.g., safe sex; see Bandura, 1977, 1982). In the case of ethnic minorities, high self-esteem is correlated with increased identification with one's ethnic groups (note that an actual causal relation has not been empirically documented). GHAs, however, have double minority status based on their ethnicity and sexuality. As a member of both Asian and gay groups, a gay Asian man may experience a conflict of identity because the two identities often contain discrepant and contradictory values. Many Asian cultures emphasize the importance of family and propagation of the family name. Most Asian cultures view homosexuality as a form of social deviance that brings shame and dishonor to the family and the community (see Aoki, Ngin, Mo, & Ja, 1989). HIV/AIDS, often perceived as being associated with homosexuality, leads to the same consequences for family and community. It is therefore not surprising that some GHAs may have to face the issues of being HIV positive and coming out at the same time.

Reconciling two identities which may be incompatible is a difficult process often characterized by approach-avoidance conflicts. Indeed, many GHA men felt that they had to choose one identity over the other (Choi, Salazar, Lew, & Coates, 1995). Choosing one identity over another means that one deliberately denies certain important aspects of the self and this may hinder the formation of a positive self-concept (Espin, 1987). Rejection of ethnic identity can potentially lead to lowered self-esteem as Phinney and Chavira's (1992) research has shown.

This could also mean denial of any identification with the gay community which often leads to feelings of isolation, and reduced access to information concerning HIV/AIDS and other support groups. If indeed the person rejects his gay identity, this could lead to HIV/AIDS issues not being the primary concern of the person. Indeed, other issues such as protecting the secrecy of one's sexuality may become more important and this can have negative HIV/AIDS-related consequences. Exposure to information about safe sex and HIV/AIDS will obviously be affected because the person may deliberately avoid approaching places or sources where such information may be available (e.g., gay newspapers, gay community centers, and gay clubs). Receptivity to HIV/AIDS information may also be affected since this may be considered irrelevant to the individual's concerns. And social isolation also impedes any development of gay identity. In this case, we may question the findings of Phinney and Chavira (1992) relating high self-esteem with ethnic identification. Indeed, it may be theoretically difficult to sustain the proposition that a minority person will have high self-esteem in a context where high ethnic identification is coupled with total rejection or denial of another important aspect of one's self (Chan, 1989).

US studies show that isolation is common among GHA men, especially among new migrants (Carrier, Nguyen, & Su, 1992). This isolation could result from not acknowledging their gay identity, homophobia in the Asian (or larger) communities, language and cultural barriers, and minimal knowledge of the gay community. This points to specific needs to address HIV/AIDS issues among Asian communities. First, information has to be disseminated in a manner that bypasses language difficulties (e.g., visual), and, second, that information must reach those who are homosexually active but not gay identified through channels that are not obviously gay identified and need not be actively sought (e.g., gay community radio).

Even if a GHA man adopts a gay identity and immerses himself in the gay community, this does not always lead to a conflict-free existence. The adoption of gay identity often means the rejection of ethnic identity and possibly primary groups such as family (Choi et al., 1995). The loss of an important support is one of the highest sources of stress and depression. The gay communities in the US and in Australia are also for the most part White or Anglo communities. Whereas homophobia may be a major problem for GHA men living in their own ethnic communities, racism may be a major problem faced by GHA men living in a predominantly white gay community. US data suggest that racism in the form of denying entry into gay clubs and bars does occur (Chan, 1989). This, however, only refers to overt or blatant racism that can be easily detected and recorded. As studies on racism in general have shown (see Dovidio, Gaertner, Anastasio, & Sanitioso, 1992), more covert or subtle forms of racism may in fact be more common, harder to detect, and have consequences that are at least as negative if not more severe, as overt racism.

Stereotypes about GHA men exist within the Australian and US gay communities (Choi et al., 1995). GHAs tend to be perceived as submissive, feminine, and sexually available or "easy." They are also perceived as being "clean." One consequence of a group occupying a low status in the society for which a stereotype exists is homogeneity. That is, members of the group are depersonalized and are thought to be interchangeable with one another. In everyday parlance, this is akin to statements such as "They all look alike. They are all alike." The host of factors such as stereotype and perceived homogeneity of GHA men, and the adoption of gay identity by GHA accompanied by the rejection of ethnic identity together may influence the dynamics of relationships GHA men may have with non-GHA men or partners.

One consequence that may follow the adoption of gay identity is the adoption of White values. This includes a strong preference for White compared to other GHA partners. White partners may embody the notion or desire for gay identity due to lack of positive portrayal (or any portrayal) of gay Asian men in the gay press or media. GHA men may, in a relationship that crosses ethnic and cultural boundaries, face issues related to Asian stereotyping. Stereotypes may exert an influence within a relationship even if the non-Asian partner of an Asian man may be aware of their inaccuracies. That is, stereotypes may exert an automatic influence on behavior and be exemplified in attitudes and behaviors that may not be deliberate (Devine, 1989). For example, a Caucasian man who approaches a GHA man may feel more confident that he will be able to achieve his goals (whatever they may be) because the predominant stereotype of Asian men includes the notion that they are "easy." The Caucasian partner may be assertive because he believes that Asians are submissive, and he may also behave in a more dominant manner sexually because he believes that Asians are "effeminate." As research has shown (Darley & Fazio, 1980), behavior tends to be reciprocated. This implies that GHAs in turn may respond in a manner consistent with their stereotyping, not because the stereotype is valid or accurate but rather because of people's tendency to respond in a reciprocal manner. A US study examining why Black interviewees showed greater physical distance to a White interviewer than to a Black interviewer unequivocally ruled out explanations based on the Black interviewees' own characteristics, and shifted the cause of the greater physical distance shown by Blacks to the White interviewer's behavior (Word, Zanna, & Cooper, 1974). White interviewers maintained less eye-contact and offered fewer verbal reinforcements when interviewing Black compared to White interviewees. Thus, it is reasonable to assume that GHA men may also behave in a stereotypical manner not because of their characteristics, but in response to the behavior shown by others who hold the stereotype.

When a GHA man "enters" the gay community, there is no clear role of how he should behave due to the lack of gay Asian role models. Most gay media portray a White or Anglo person, who may fit certain conceptions of the community's ideal gay person, but perhaps not most gays. This uncertainty may render GHA men even more susceptible to stereotyping by others. Others influence our behavior and our behavior in turn may influence the way we think about ourselves. Similarly, being treated as a certain type of person leading to reciprocal behavior may influence the way GHAs see themselves in the gay community. The process of stereotyping (by others) leading to actual incorporation of the stereotype into the self-concept of the stereotyped group may be speculated as happening as follows. First, other gay men treat GHA men according to existing stereotypes which leads to reciprocal behavior from the GHA men. Then, GHA men may observe their own behavior and, in the absence of a clear prior self-conception in the context of gay interaction, may interpret this behavior as reflective of their self. That is, the self-concept of GHA men may be influenced or changed, and become consistent with the stereotype held by others in the larger gay community (Darley & Fazio, 1980). This does not mean that a person will always acquire stereotype-consistent self-conception. In cases where people are certain of who they are (Swann, 1983), the influence of stereotypes may be diminished. This again points to the need for greater exposure of GHA men in all their diversity who could provide role models for others within the gay community.

What consequences does the stereotyping of GHAs have in terms of safe sex and HIV/AIDS? Being perceived as submissive certainly confers a lower status in the decision-making or negotiation about safe sex. Rather than attempting to come to a mutual decision, a GHA man may not be involved in the decision-making process and be expected to conform to the decision (whether safe or unsafe) made by the most likely White/Anglo partner (Tsui, 1986). The emphasis in Asian cultures on respecting others who have more knowledge and more experience, such as older people, may also contribute to the relinquishing of control regarding safe sex solely to the partner who, if White/Anglo, may be perceived to have a higher status. In other words, GHAs may respect without question decisions made by partners who are perceived to be of higher status. The stereotype of Asians also includes the characteristic of being "clean"–both in terms of personal hygiene and health. This could lead partners to believe that it is safe to engage in unsafe sexual activities with GHA men. If indeed this is the case, coupled with the expectation that GHA partners need not be involved in decision-making regarding safe sex, the exposure of GHA men to potentially risky situations will be significantly greater than is the case among non-GHAs in the gay communities.

How can stereotyping and racism be combated within gay communities?

Common sense would probably dictate that the gay community be tolerant of ethnic and cultural differences, having itself experienced prejudice and discrimination. But as a minority, the so-called gay community may also display characteristics shown by most minority groups. These include expectations of members to conform to a particular group identity (i.e., the ideal gay man), which leads to depersonalization of individual members. This can be observed in the images of gay men produced by gay-oriented organizations and media, which tend to be of White or Anglo gay men. These role models aid in the formation of "possible selves" for other gay men.

Possible selves are future selves which represent what an individual can be, wishes to become, or is afraid of becoming (Markus & Nurius, 1986). They are personalized and vivid images of oneself in the future. They serve as a goal to be approached (or avoided) and contain means by which one can reach that goal. Possible selves are reality bound (i.e., we cannot, for instance, have "being the Queen of England" as a possible self), but since they are future-oriented the constraints of reality are of a lesser degree compared to the current self (i.e., I can be a happy person in the future even if I am unhappy now). Imagined possible selves do, however, affect how we feel presently about ourselves. Lack of culturally provided possible selves may leave an individual unmotivated (there is no goal to strive for) or unhappy. Role models help an individual to create what is possible for him/her in the future. Geraldine Ferraro (who was once a Democratic Party vice presidential candidate in the US), for instance, may help create possible selves as US presidents for young women in that country. She certainly conveyed the message that it is possible for a woman to succeed in the political arena. Less lofty perhaps than a US presidency but certainly no less important, role models of happy and well-adjusted GHAs in the gay press and media would help in the creation of positive possible selves among GHA men. These possible selves may bridge the discrepancy between current self and the ideal self by providing hopes, motivation, and perhaps the means by which the ideal self can finally be attained (or discrepancy between the current and ideal selves may be minimized).

Feared, or negative, possible selves are also powerful motivating factors as long as they are accompanied by means which can be used to avoid the feared self. HIV/AIDS may simply not have been embodied in the feared possible self of GHA men for it to have any effects on their sexual behavior. Indeed, Choi et al. (1995) found that GHA men have a high level of knowledge of HIV/AIDS, though many still practise unsafe sex. HIV positive Asian men have not been widely reported in the gay or non-gay media in Australia. Exposure to images and representations of HIV positive GHA men may increase the relevance of HIV/AIDS issues among GHAs, motivate them to seek information on how to minimize risks and exposure, and incorporate this into their current self-concept and behavior. Both positive and negative possible selves are necessary in order for GHA men to develop a healthy self-identity and HIV/AIDS-conscious behavior patterns. The presence of positive possible selves alone, though better than none, may not be as strong a motivating force as the presence of both negative and positive possible selves. It should be noted that what is referred to here as negative possible selves are not simply fear tactics, but rather an embodiment of a future self that one wishes to avoid (e.g., becoming HIV positive or becoming ill) and also contains means by which this unwished-for self can be avoided.

DELINEATING HIV-RELATED ISSUES SPECIFIC TO ASIAN MEN

The above analysis presents social psychological factors that may be relevant to GHAs who, because of their cultural origins and minority status, differ from the dominant majority Anglo-Australian or White-American groups in their needs and concerns to deal with homosexuality and HIV/AIDS. Several general conclusions may be inferred from the analysis and new or other questions can also be posed.

In the US, Asians and Pacific Islanders comprise a group which still has the lowest HIV rates. However, the rate of infection within this population is higher compared to White-Americans (Centers for Disease Control, 1995). In most cases, HIV transmission was through sexual contacts rather than other means (e.g., needle sharing). Asian-Americans in general have highly accurate knowledge about HIV/AIDS transmission but still engage in risky sexual activities (Choi et al., 1995). This suggests that Asians may not perceive themselves to be at risk, despite engaging in unsafe sexual practices. This also suggests that accurate knowledge about how HIV is transmitted is not sufficient to influence sexual practices. Thus, an examination into how knowledge translates into behavior among this particular population needs to be investigated.

From the factors identified earlier in the paper, we may speculate how they may be involved in the lack of translation of HIV/AIDS knowledge into safe sexual practices. First, HIV/AIDS may simply not be the primary concern of GHAs when it comes to homosexual contacts. Threats of bringing shame to the family and a loss of face may be more salient guides in GHA men's sexual behavior than HIV/AIDS concerns. Second, despite the knowledge, GHAs may not be involved in the decision-making or negotiation of sexual activities with their sexual partner, especially in cases where the partner is perceived to be of higher status such as White/Anglo, older, and more experienced. In this case, personal knowledge simply is not relevant and will not be translated into actual behavior. Third, the lack of positive role models of gay Asians and HIV positive Asians may render HIV/AIDS and issues of identity irrelevant or perceived as untenable for GHAs. Fourth, the issues related to racism and stereotyping of GHAs (or Asians in general) in the gay communities need to be addressed.

Several suggestions on the development of prevention programs specifically targeted towards GHAs have been proposed by researchers which appear consistent with the concerns identified here. HIV/AIDS services need to be perceived as confidential by GHAs (Choi et al., 1995). Dissemination of information which bypasses language barriers (e.g., through visually based information channels) and social barriers (in the sense that the individuals need not actively seek information from gay-related sources) are also needed in order to reach GHAs who are isolated from the mainstream gay cultures. Since, as is also true for others, the issue of being HIV positive is in some instances the driving force of coming out among GHAs, HIV/AIDS-related services need to effectively address issues related to social support groups for GHAs who may anticipate the loss of their primary social groups (i.e., family and the community) and feelings of isolation. That is, HIV/AIDS services must address identity issues (related to both homosexuality and ethnicity) as well. For example, the (HIV) Positive Asians Group operated by the Victorian AIDS Council in Melbourne addresses this issue of isolation, which may be quite profound for individuals coming from collectivistic cultures. To be able to share experiences with others who may have gone through similar experiences and conflicts may aid individuals to understand their own experiences. Increasing the visibility of gay cultural diversity and specifically gay Asians and HIV positive Asians can assist homosexually active Asians in overcoming isolation, changing the perception of what is possible for themselves, and increasing awareness of HIV/AIDS and its relevance to them. Finally, an increased awareness of (potential) racism in the gay communities can help minimize (at least deliberate) racist attitudes and discriminatory behaviour which may hinder non-White or non-Anglo individuals in identifying themselves as being part of the gay communities. I turn now to other issues that have not been addressed in this paper.

CULTURE-BOUND CONCEPTIONS OF HOMOSEXUALITY AND HOMOSEXUAL BEHAVIOR

How relevant is gay identity to homosexually active Asian men? Gay identity such as we know it in the West is a novel phenomenon that may not have a direct counterpart in Asian countries and cultures. Homosexuality may have been an integral part of many traditional Asian societies. But perhaps due to the clear gender differentiation of these societies (that males and females have specific and separable roles in the society), homosexuality may often involve men who take on the role of women (e.g., *fa'afaafine* in

Samoan society) or ritualized to fulfil specified functions. A homosexual couple in traditional Asian societies may involve a man who takes on the role of women (e.g., in behavior and duties) with another who takes on the traditional male role (e.g., dominant). Thus, gay identity may be a new concept that has to be learned for GHA men who are not acculturated to western societies. Even in the West, homosexual activities do not mean that the person will be willing to view himself as gay. This possible lack of recognition of gay identity (rather than say of cross-gendered identity) again points to the importance of gay role models in Asian communities in Australia, especially for unacculturated new migrants who are likely to feel a sense of displacement and isolation (related to coming to a new country) and to face language and cultural barriers.

Are there cross-cultural differences in the preferred or normative sexual activities among homosexually active Asian men who come from diverse backgrounds? Studies have shown that Vietnamese immigrants in California tend to engage in fellatio and mutual masturbation, but not anal intercourse (Carrier, Nguyen, & Su, 1992). We can also anticipate regional differences in preferred sexual activities which may reflect different attitudes toward, and conceptualization of, sexuality (Lottes & Kuriloff, 1992). The preferred behavior may reflect gender roles in the cultural groups of origin (e.g., as long as you are the insertive partner, you are not perceived as being "gay"), but this may change as people learn more about homosexuality and the gay community. Indeed, the adoption of gay identity may, in some cases, expose the individuals to potentially more risky situations (i.e., more frequent and varied partners, more varied sexual activities). However, immersion in the gay communities also means exposures to information related to HIV/AIDS, especially pertaining to safe sex. Data on preferred activities can be used to formulate effective intervention programs which target specifically the normative behavior of the different Asian groups.

Doubtless there are other factors not identified here which may be important to GHA men's experience. This calls for systematic gathering of data concerning GHAs, which can begin by acknowledging the need to focus on GHAs and their concerns as a group in Australia and the US. As in any other minority group, self-empowerment may be one of the means by which GHAs respond to issues that may affect them in unique and specific ways such as HIV/AIDS and homosexuality (Choi et al., 1995). In the US and more recently in Australia, in the absence of the availability of information directly relevant to and targeted toward Asians as a distinct group of homosexual men, Asians themselves have organized to provide support and education for GHAs to deal with issues of identities, coming out and HIV/AIDS. This can be seen as a response to the absence of information directly relevant to and targeted towards Asians as a distinct group of homosexual men. In the US groups such as Gay Asian Pacific Alliance (GAPA) in San Francisco illustrate the self-empowerment of GHA men (Choi et al., 1995). In Australia, organizations such as the Victorian AIDS Council and AIDS Council of New South Wales recognized in the mid-1980s the needs to specifically target GHAs and have supported the formation of Positive Asians in Melbourne and Silk Road in Sydney (which has since disbanded). HIV/AIDS has helped bring to the fore issues related to homosexuality in the Asian communities. Disclosure of one's HIV positive status and/or illness often means revealing one's sexuality to family and friends. Thus, HIV/AIDS raises homosexuality-related issues not only for the individual, but also for others (i.e., friends and family).

Australia has not yet begun recording AIDS data on Asians as a distinct category at the Federal level (categorization varies across the states), whereas the US has done so since 1988. Even though the total percentage of AIDS cases among Asian-Americans (including Pacific Islanders) is small compared to other groups, the rate of increase of AIDS among Asian and Pacific Islander Americans is higher than the rate for White-Americans (Centers for Disease Control, 1995). The most common means of transmission also differs in that most cases (almost three-quarters) can be attributed to homosexual contacts. This pattern of data again points out the importance of information about HIV/AIDS to be coupled with information about homosexuality and gay identity.

Increased self-esteem/self-efficacy, control, knowledge, and communication skills may be important to GHAs in negotiating safe sex with their partners. This may indeed go against the cultural norms of collectivistic Asian cultures whose members often perceive their behavior as controlled by situational factors (e.g., the partner's status and behavior) rather than internal factors (e.g., one's knowledge of safe sex and one's wishes), either to save the face of the higher status partner or to keep harmony within the partnership/situation (Smith and Bond, 1993). However, changing aspects of culture has been accomplished before with arguable success. An instance within Australia is the perception of drink driving. Changing the habit of drink driving need not necessarily include changing alcohol drinking behavior overall. Indeed, the Transport Accident Commission (TAC) of Victoria has been successful in isolating the culture associated with drinking and driving. In the early 1990s, using messages presented in television, on billboards, in newspapers and on radio, the TAC changed the perception of drink driving as normal or even "cool" to one that is undesirable and irresponsible. It also firmly conveyed the message that control or responsibility rests with the individual himself or herself, with hard-hitting colloquial messages such as, "If you drink, then drive, you're a bloody idiot!" This example illustrates that even particular cultural norms can be changed, though the means to achieve such changes still need to be explored further.

CONCLUSION

To conclude, different factors have been proposed which may be important and unique to gay and homosexually active Asian men living in Australia and the US. Past studies on HIV/AIDS prevention programs indicate that these programs need to be tailored specifically for the target population. Asians as a group are extremely diverse. Yet, there are also commonalities which differentiate Asians and the Asian experience from those who make up the dominant/majority groups in Australia and the US. This refers to their cultural ideology which is based on collectivity, emphasizing the importance of groups over individuals. This points to preventative programs which need to address the collective aspect of Asians' psychological well-being and behavior. Asians as a group also occupy a minority status both numerically within the population and in the hierarchy of social status. In Australia, many are also immigrant newcomers. These are probably the common features that need to be addressed in programs directed towards GHAs. Any HIV/AIDS services need to broach the issues of isolation, feelings of loss of control and social support, language and cultural barriers (in integrating to both the dominant majority and the gay cultures), and identity conflicts unique to individuals who are a minority in their sexuality as well as ethnicity. Yet, research also shows uniqueness related to country of, or cultural, origins. An instance which is addressed here is the type of sexual activities preferred or normative to different Asian groups. Thus, in the context of common collectivistic ideologies, variability with respect to target behaviors needs to be explicitly approached in HIV/AIDS preventative attempts.

This paper is not meant to be a comprehensive look at HIV/AIDS issues relevant to GHA men. Rather, it is an attempt to illustrate points of convergence in issues that have been identified in HIV/AIDS research, on the one hand, and social psychological research related to minority/racial and cross-cultural issues, on the other. Choi et al. (1995) have identified many of the HIV/AIDS-related factors presented in this paper. Relevant social psychological theories and findings have then been used to identify the socio-psychological determinants of these factors (e.g., delineating determinants of levels of self-esteem of individuals who belong to minority groups), and to suggest means by which these factors may be dealt with effectively. Social psychological theories have also been used to cohere factors that have been independently identified in HIV/AIDS research (e.g., the relationship between stereotypes of Asians and the self-concept of individual Asians). Social psychological research concerned with minority status, cross-cultural phenomena and the effects of stereotyping appear to be directly relevant to the subject and have therefore been applied to the context of HIV/AIDS and GHA men. The validity of these applications remains to be explored in future studies.

Many ideas included in this paper are drawn from American studies, which reflects the amount of social psychological research devoted to minority groups in the US compared to Australia. The use of American research does not imply that the US and Australia are comparable at all levels (Rosenthal & Feldman, 1992). However, the experience of dislocation associated with immigration, or the impact of minority status of Asians in the two countries, may show some similarities (see Lord & Saenz, 1985; Feldman, Mont-Reynaud, & Rosenthal, 1992). An important difference between the two countries includes the relative recentness of large scale immigration of Asians into Australia (post 1975), and the different composition of the groups (based on country of origin) making up the Asian communities in the two countries (de Lepervanche, 1984). Asians are not the only minority group in multicultural countries such as Australia and the US. Some experiences addressed here as being related to the status of Asians as a minority (e.g., racism) may also be applicable to other minority groups (e.g., African-Americans, Greeks and Italians in Australia, and people of Hispanic origins in both the US and Australia; see Dovidio et al., 1992; Trembel, Schneider, & Appathurai, 1989). Studies need to delineate factors related to minority status which may be common to all minority groups, cultural ideologies which may be unique to each immigrant/minority group, as well as degrees of acculturation (or assimilation) to the host country (Triandis, Kashima, Shimada, & Villareal, 1986), to fully understand the impacts of, and how best to deal with issues related to, HIV/AIDS in a multicultural and multi-ethnic society.

AUTHOR NOTE

The author would like to thank anonymous reviewers and editors, and Doctors Peter Jackson and Gerard Sullivan for their useful comments and suggestions on draft versions of this paper.

REFERENCES

Aoki, B., Ngin, C.P., Mo, B., & Ja, D.Y. (1989). AIDS prevention models in Asian-American communities. In V.M. Mays, G.W. Albee, and S.F. Schneider (Eds.), *Primary prevention of AIDS: Psychological approaches* (pp. 290-308). Newbury Park, CA: Sage Publications.

Australian Bureau of Immigration, Multicultural and Population Research (1991). *Australian Immigration Statistical Focus: Estimated Resident Population.*

Bandura, A. (1977). Self-efficacy: Toward a unifying theory of behavioral change. *Psychological Review, 84*, pp. 191-215.

Bandura, A. (1982). Self-efficacy mechanism in human agency. *American Psychologist, 37*, pp. 122-147.

Carrier, J., Nguyen, B., & Su, S. (1992). Vietnamese American sexual behaviors and HIV infection. *Journal of Sex Research, 29*, pp. 547-560.

Centers for Disease Control and Prevention (1995). *HIV/AIDS Surveillance Report No. 6.* Atlanta: CDC.

Chan, C.S. (1989). Issues of identity development among Asian-American lesbians and gay men. *Journal of Counselling and Development, 68*, pp. 16-20.

Choi, K-H., Salazar, N., Lew, S., & Coates, T.J. (1995). AIDS risk, dual identity, and community response among gay Asian and Pacific Islander men in San Francisco. In G.M. Herek and B. Greene (Eds.), *AIDS, identity, and community: The HIV epidemic and lesbians and gay men.* Thousand Oaks, CA: Sage Publications.

Darley, J.M. & Fazio, R.H. (1980). Expectancy confirmation processes arising in the social interaction sequence. *American Psychologist, 35*, pp. 867-871.

Devine, P.G. (1989). Stereotypes and prejudice: Their automatic and controlled components. *Journal of Personality and Social Psychology, 56*, pp. 5-18.

Dovidio, J.F., Gaertner, S.L., Anastasio, P.A., & Sanitioso, R. (1992). Cognitive and motivational bases of bias: Implication of aversive racism for attitudes towards Hispanics. In S. Knouse, P. Rosenfeld, and A. Culbertson (Eds.), *Hispanics in the work place* (pp. 75-106). Newbury Park, CA: Sage.

Espin, O.M. (1987). Issues of identity in the psychology of Latina lesbians. In Boston Lesbian Psychologies Collectives (Ed.) *Lesbian psychologies* (pp. 35-51). Urbana, IL: University of Illinois Press.

Feldman, S.S., Mont-Reynaud, R., Rosenthal, D.A. (1992). When East moves West: That acculturation of values of Chinese adolescents in the US and Australia. *Journal of Research on Adolescence, 2*, pp. 147-173.

Feldman, S.S., & Rosenthal, D.A. (1990). The acculturation of autonomy expectations in Chinese high schoolers residing in two Western nations. *International Journal of Psychology, 25*, pp. 259-281.

Festinger, L. (1954). A theory of social comparison processes. *Human Relations, 7*, pp. 117-140.

Gergen, K.J. (1987). Toward self as relationship. In K. Yardley & T. Honess (Eds.), *Self and identity: Psychosocial perspectives* (pp. 53-64). Chichester: Wiley.

Kashima, Y., & Triandis, H.C. (1986). The self-serving bias in attributions as a coping strategy: A cross-cultural study. *Journal of Cross Cultural Psychology, 17*, pp. 83-97.

de Lepervanche, M. (1984). Immigrants and ethnic groups. In S. Encel, M. Berry, L. Bryson, M. de Lapervanche, T. Rowse, and A. Moran (Eds.), *Australian society* (4th ed.). Melbourne: Longman Cheshire PTY. Limited.

Lord, C.G., & Saenz, D.S. (1985). Memory deficits and memory surfeits: Differential cognitive consequences of tokenism for tokens and observers. *Journal of Personality and Social Psychology, 49*, pp. 918-926.

Lottes, I.L., & Kuriloff, P.J. (1992). The effects of gender, race, religion, and political orientation on the sex role attitudes of college freshman. *Adolescence, 27,* pp. 675-688.

Luthanen, R. & Crocker, J. (1992). A collective self-esteem scale: Self-evaluation of one's social identity. *Personality and Social Psychology Bulletin, 18,* pp. 302-318.

Markus, H., & Kitayama, S. (1991). Culture and the self: Implications for cognition, emotion, and motivation. *Psychological Review, 98,* pp. 224-253.

Markus, H. & Nurius, P. (1986). Possible selves. *American Psychologist, 41,* pp. 954-969.

Mead, G.H. (1934). *Mind, self, and society.* Chicago, IL: University of Chicago Press.

Phinney, J.S. & Chavira, V. (1992). Ethnic identity and self-esteem: An exploratory longitudinal study. *Journal of Adolescence, 15,* pp. 271-281.

Rosenthal, D.A., & Feldman, S.S. (1992). The nature and stability of ethnic identity in Chinese youth: Effects of length of residence in two cultural contexts. *Journal of Cross-Cultural Psychology, 23,* pp. 214-227.

Rotheram-Borus, M.J., Rosario, M., Reid, H., & Koopman, C. (1995). Predicting patterns of sexual acts among gay/bisexual male adolescents. *American Journal of Psychiatry, 152,* pp. 588-595.

Sanitioso, R., Kunda, Z., & Fong, G.T. (1990). Motivated recruitment of autobiographical memories. *Journal of Personality and Social Psychology, 59,* pp. 229-241.

Smith, P.B. & Bond, M.H. (1993). *Social psychology across cultures–Analysis and perspectives.* New York: Harvester/Wheatsheaf.

Swann, W.B. (1983). Self-verification: Bringing social reality into harmony with the self. In J. Suls & A.G. Greenwald (Eds.), *Social psychological perspectives on the self* (Vol. 2) (pp. 33-66). Hillsdale, NJ: Erlbaum.

Tremble, B., Schneider, M., & Appathurai, C. (1989). Growing up gay or lesbian in a multicultural context. *Journal of Homosexuality, 17,* pp. 253-267.

Triandis, H.C., Kashima, Y., Shimada, E., & Villareal, M. (1986). Acculturation indices as a means of confirming cultural differences. *International Journal of Psychology, 21,* pp. 43-70.

Tsui, P. (1986). Power and intimacy: Caucasian/Asian gay relationship as an indicator of self-oppression among gay Asian males. *Asian-American Psychological Association Journal,* pp. 59-61.

US Bureau of the Census. (1990). *Statistical abstract of the US.* Washington D.C.: US Government Printing Office.

Word, C.H., Zanna, M.P., & Cooper, J. (1974). The nonverbal mediation of self-fulfilling prophecies in interracial interaction. *Journal of Experimental Social Psychology, 10,* pp. 109-120.

China Doll–
The Experience of Being
a Gay Chinese Australian

Tony Ayres

SUMMARY. This article is a stylized blend of personal history and po-
lemical essay which investigates the relationship between race and
sexuality. What starts out as a history of the narrator's experience of being a "banana"–yellow (Chinese) on the outside and white (Caucasian)
on the inside–becomes a complex exploration of the various ways in
which male homosexual desire is constructed and how race is both included and excluded from western constructions of homosexuality.
*[Article copies available for a fee from The Haworth Document Delivery Service:
1-800-342-9678. E-mail address: getinfo@haworthpressinc.com]*

INTRODUCTION

What brings you here, Johnny Chinaman,
Why do you come to New South Wales?
Why do you sail when breezes fan
The north side of your sails?

"Our native country scarce can hold
The increase of the year;

Correspondence regarding this article may be addressed to Tony Ayres, 365
Barkly Street, Elwood, Victoria, 3184, Australia.

[Haworth co-indexing entry note]: "China Doll–The Experience of Being a Gay Chinese Australian."
Ayres, Tony. Co-published simultaneously in *Journal of Homosexuality* (The Haworth Press, Inc.) Vol. 36,
No. 3/4, 1999, pp. 87-97; and: *Multicultural Queer: Australian Narratives* (ed: Peter A. Jackson and
Gerard Sullivan) The Haworth Press, Inc., 1999, pp. 87-97. Single or multiple copies of this article are
available for a fee from The Haworth Document Delivery Service [1-800-342-9678, 9:00 a.m. - 5:00 p.m.
(EST). E-mail address: getinfo@ haworthpressinc.com].

So, we, allured by love of gold,
Will try our fortunes here."

What do you bring, John Chinaman,
As offering of your heart,
To us who feed, protect your clan,
And let you rich depart?

"We bring you small pox from our land–
Nay, no not raise you ire,
We opium bring–a noble band,
and to your wealth aspire."

–Anonymous, "The Chinaman"
published in *Sydney Punch*, 1881

A few months after my family migrated to Australia from Hong Kong in 1964, my mother divorced my Australian stepfather. Not being qualified for anything else, she went to work in Chinese restaurants, mainly as a waitress or dishwasher. The people we knew were greedy, obese restaurateurs and their nosy, simpering wives. Their houses were decorated with walnut veneer panelling and red plastic lanterns made in Hong Kong. These were people who pretended to be our friends, so they could pay my mother $2 an hour and keep her tips. I was too young to know that the *nouveau riche* are a cross-cultural phenomenon, so I blamed this exploitation on their being Chinese. Most of my childhood I associated "Chineseness" with money-grubbing, back-stabbing, and kitsch "copper art" house decorations.

As a teenager growing up in Perth, Western Australia, in the 1970s I cut myself off from the Chinese restaurant world by sticking my head into comic books and only emerging from my bedroom to watch "I Love Lucy" on television. I started to see Chinese people through Caucasian eyes–a small, oily race with noisy table manners. I had an obvious blindspot (i.e., the mirror), but then I kept telling myself I wasn't Chinese. I shunned the other Asian kids at school. I grew tall on Australian food. I forgot how to speak Mandarin, my first language. I became a "banana." Yellow on the outside, white on the inside.

At university, I had shoulder length hair and wore army pants like everyone else. I studied English literature and philosophy, became involved with student politics, started up men's groups. I had no Chinese friends, nor did I seek them out. I did not even know where the Department of Asian Studies was on campus. My friends used to say, "I never think of you as Chinese, Tony," and I would feel pleased with myself, as if this was an accomplishment.

When I discovered my sexuality in my late teens my carefully constructed disguise fell to pieces. I went to my first gay bar when I was 18 years old. In gay bars you can't dazzle people with insights into D. H. Lawrence or T. S. Eliot. You can't talk politics or art or assert the million and one cultural signifiers which testify to your Western-ness. Apart from anything else, the music is too loud. Gay bars are places where you are what you look like, even if that is at odds with how you feel about yourself. In gay bars, I was/am Chinese. That is how I was/am judged. As it turned out, being Chinese in a gay bar was one of the worst things you could be. At least that was my experience when I came out in the early 1980s.

It was in a gay bar that I learnt, contrary to my university demagogy, that being gay did not give a person privileged insight or an ideological commonality with other lives and oppressions. "Gay" describes our sexual practices, not our attitudes, and certainly not our prejudices.

Over the years, I have experienced three typical responses on the gay scene. First, there is overt belligerence: the drunk queens who shout in my face, "Go back to your own country"; the tag line at the end of gay personal classifieds–"No Fats, Femmes or Asians"; the guys who hissed at me in the back room, "I'm not into Asians." Still, these incidents are rare and easily dealt with. It is racism, fair and square. I shrug my shoulders, put up a barrier of condescension. It is they who have the problem, not me.

The second response is the exact opposite of this racist antagonism. It is an attraction to me *because* of my Asianness, my otherness. Again, this has nothing to do with who I think I am, my individual qualities as a person, or even as an object of desire. It is the fact that I conveniently fit into someone else's fantasy. Frankly, I would not mind this except that the guys who want me for these reasons tend to be well on the way to their first superannuation cheque. In other words, they are often (though thankfully not always) the older, less "desirable" men: out of shape, not particularly fussed by personal appearances. And they expect me to be so flattered by the attention of a white man that I will automatically bend over and grab my ankles. Out of pure contrariness, I refuse to comply . . . unless, of course, it's really late and I'm really drunk.

For the most part, though, my experience in the gay scene has been characterized by neither outrageous abuse nor outrageous attention. Instead, it has involved a wearing, subtle, almost imperceptible feeling of exclusion. For example, I am introduced to a group of men at a party and realize within moments that no-one is interested in talking to me. Or I am at a gay bar with Caucasian friends, watching enviously as they make contact with a room-full of possibilities, while the only guy who fancies me is having trouble keeping his toupee on straight. Or I am at a beat and someone is coming towards me because they are attracted to my shape or size, but turn away as soon as they see my face. It is the demoralising feeling that I am, in the eyes of the majority of the gay male population, as undesirable as a woman.

What is so difficult about this form of exclusion is its elusiveness. I think, "Maybe it's just me, maybe I'm being paranoid." After all, everyone has to deal with rejection. What makes mine worse than anyone else's? Maybe I have to face up to the fact that I am not the most attractive man in the world. For years, I have wrestled with doubts. Do other people have the same problems? It has only been recently, when I have met other gay Asian men who suffer from a similar lack of self-esteem, that I have realized that there is something more to it than my own foibles and vulnerabilities. Yes, of course everyone has to deal with self-doubt and the possibility of rejection. But not everyone has to deal with it at the fundamental level of skin color. To deny inequalities in race is as silly as denying inequalities in class or gender, or denying that the earth moves around the sun. There is a profound dynamic which has, at some level, affected all gay Asian men in the West.

DISCRIMINATION AGAINST ASIAN MEN IN THE GAY SCENE

This article is my attempt to understand how a particular brand of "racism" characterized by sexual discrimination occurs within the gay male community. I would like to start by making a few assumptions. The first is that sexuality is the underlying dynamic which draws gay men together into a "scene." Obviously, this is simplistic. Other factors such as friendship and a mutual adoration of Kylie Minogue and Madonna also bring us together. But at the end of the day, the gravity that cleaves us towards each other, the restless inspiration that keeps us out until all hours trawling the bars, backrooms and beats, has a scrotum at its base.

This explains why I feel so ill at ease in the gay bar. It is an environment where being physically desirable is closely related to being socially desirable. We have all experienced just how charming, witty and clever a sexy body can be (especially if he does not open his mouth). But it is often the case that not being considered physically desirable also means that you are not deemed worth talking to.

My second assumption is that the objects of our desire are not fixed or given but are interactions between personal history and the artifacts of culture. By personal history, I mean the little accidents and events which make up our sexual lives. By artifacts of culture, I mean all the pictures, magazines, porno videos, books, movies, television programs, and so on which are the cultural representations of homosexuality by which we have learnt what "homosexuality" is.

Personal history often shapes our adult sexuality: that first adolescent fumbling, the crush on your best friend at school, the slap and tickle on Uncle

Pete's knee. Since, for the most part, gay Caucasian men in Australia have their earliest experiences with other Caucasians, it does not surprise me that this is the template by which desire is stamped, at least initially.

But sexual history does not form the immutable shape of our desire. Sexuality, as far as I understand it, is fluid. In my case, when I first became conscious of being gay, there was not a particular kind of male body I was attracted to. To be honest, anything with a dick would have done. However, as I became a participant in the gay world, I found myself increasingly influenced by the imagery which determined what was desirable. An "Ideal Body" began to take form in my head. In the mid-1980s my Ideal Body was modelled on the "clone": moustached, butch, and hairy. Later, the "gym body" became increasingly attractive: muscled, tanned, and buffed. The images of the Ideal Body which saturate mainstream and gay media and cultures gradually insinuated themselves into my fantasies.

There is no single Ideal Body. Advertisements are variously filled with blondes, brunettes, latinos, chunky men, lean men. But the closer you look at what is considered "sexy," "hunky," "desirable," the more you realize that there is a limited range of parts which make up Ideal Bodies. The recurring themes are youth, masculinity and race.

It is in this area that the question of politics arises. The act of making the Ideal Body concrete by giving it physical expression–whether through photographs, films or live shows–is a political act. It defines in a social sense what is deemed to be desirable. And it is from this arena that the Asian man has been excluded. Gay magazines rarely use Asian men in their pictorial spreads. Gay-targeted advertising rarely, if ever, uses Asian models. State and territory AIDS Councils in Australia rarely use images of Asian men in safe sex campaigns, except in campaigns targeted specifically at gay Asian men. Gay pornography–American, European or Australian–almost never includes Asian actors, except for porn targeted at the "rice queen" subculture. Each of these sins of omission contributes to the invisibility of the Asian man's body on the scene.

If our sexual fantasies, at least in part, are populated by endlessly renewable Ideal Bodies, how can we Asian men see ourselves as desirable? This is true not only for Asian men, but for all excluded categories: old men, fat men, short men, Aboriginal men.

The sexually marginalized Asian man who has grown up in the West or is western in his thinking is often invisible in his own fantasies. Our sexual daydreams are populated by handsome Caucasian men with lean, hard Caucasian bodies. This creates the phenomenon of the Asian man who does not find other Asian men attractive. For most of my adult life, this has certainly been true of me.

When I am out cruising, I do not look other Asian men in the eye. And they do not look at me. It is a mutual acknowledgment and a mutual elision of desirability: "I'm not interested in you, you're not interested in me." Often in these cruising situations in bars or saunas, there's a sense of competition between us. We are competing for the attention of the limited number of Caucasian men who desire Asian men. Intellectually I know that this inability to feel attracted to other Asian men is a form of internalized racism. I know that at some basic psychic level I am unable to come to terms with my own body. But I have never known what to do about this. My dick has a mind of its own, and it does not subscribe to politically correct views.

I have no idea what percentage of the gay Asian population in Australia feels this way. My suspicion, despite the increasing numbers of Asian men advertising for Asian lovers in the personal columns of gay magazines in this country, is that it is still the vast majority.

Another consequence of being unseen within the mainstream of gay culture is that we are also invisible in other people's fantasies. This is the phenomenon of the Caucasian man who does not find Asian men (as a category) attractive. Again, it is impossible to attribute percentages to this group. As an experiment, I once posted two advertisements in successive weeks on a gay personal column on the internet. The first advertisement read: "Attractive 35-year-old, 5' 11", black hair, brown eyes, lean, gymnasium-toned body, looking for hot sexual encounters." The second read: "Attractive 35-year-old Chinese man, 5' 11", black hair, brown eyes, lean, gymnasium-toned body, looking for hot sexual encounters." The first advertisement attracted twenty-two responses; the second attracted three responses. Of course, this is not a scientifically proven result, but it does seem to confirm my suspicion that the number of men who are not into Asian men is depressingly large.

But you cannot point a finger and say, "This man is a racist because he doesn't want to sleep with me." I don't think people consciously choose their desires. But, the very fact of this separation of desire into racial categories indicates a kind of institutionalized racism.

This is not surprising in a country like Australia with a long history of institutionalized racism. From the early 1900s when the first legislative act of the newly formed Federal Parliament of Australia was an immigration policy which actively excluded all racial/ethnic groups other than Caucasians, the Chinese in Australia have been marginalized and demonized. Large numbers of Chinese, most from the southern province of Guanghzou, had come to Australia in the middle decades of the nineteenth century to work on the Australian gold fields. After the "gold rush" many stayed on and worked as small traders, market gardeners, and laborers. But because of the "White Australia policy," the Chinese population in Australia dwindled to a small, invisible minority who mainly congregated around Chinatowns in the major cities.

After the Korean War, the general perception of the Chinese was equally negative. They were the "Yellow Peril," on the verge of storming the vast underpopulated Australian continent from the north. Australia was a European outpost precariously perched in the underbelly of the world. Asians in Australia, no matter how long they had lived in the country, were viewed with suspicion, to the extent of being investigated by the Australian Security Intelligence Organisation during the anti-communist era of the government of Prime Minister Sir Robert Menzies in the 1950s. "Made in Taiwan" and "Made in China" were symbols of an inferior product.

Inevitably, these deep-seated socially engineered prejudices against Asians have had their corollary on a psycho-sexual level. Even though the current mood of our society suggests a liberal, multicultural tolerance when it comes to racial difference, there is a part of our conditioning which is automatic and which stems from preconditioned fears. It is this unconscious prejudice which manifests itself in the gay scene in sexual negotiation and interaction.

An attempt to promote a desirable Asian Body was made in December 1991 by the Sydney-based gay lifestyle magazine *Campaign*. For the first time in its 20-year history *Campaign's* editor placed an Asian model on the cover. In January 1992 the following letter was printed in the magazine's letters to the editor section:

> I have to compliment you on that beautiful guy on the November cover, Linden Davidson. But when I looked inside I was disappointed to see that Asian queen, Chee Kun Woo.[1] He would probably look good in the *Hong Kong Weekly*. How come there are thousands of gay men coming out from Asian countries? Who lets them in when there are thousands of American, German, Irish, Hungarian and Italian queens who could immigrate getting knocked back? . . .

> It is OK to go to bed (for one night) with a colored person but to have an everlasting love affair is out of the question. So you are really kidding yourself when you feature an Asian on the cover and try to be multicultural. It is only the stupid Australian (gay poofters) who want the so called "multicultural pot." We hate each other. There are only a few white men interested in the small Asian dick. You can show me a small dick and show me a big black one and it is more important to go off with the big black one than the small Asian one.

> David Phillips.

Obviously this letter comes from the extreme end of the political spectrum, but it manifests the same fear of the Asian hordes–the "Yellow Peril"– invading from the north which I suspect informs a more general sexual prejudice. What is also disturbing about this letter is that the author, David Phillips, is actually an Eastern European migrant who has anglicized his name. One of the peculiarities of race relations in Australian, as distinct from race relations in the United States and Europe, is a lack of identification between minority racial groups, e.g., between Aboriginal and Asian groups.

There have been attempts in Australia in recent years to represent an Ideal Asian Body, the most significant site being *OG (Oriental Guy)* magazine, which specializes in representing young Asian men for a predominantly Caucasian audience. My response to this magazine is mixed. Part of me feels that there is something positive in any representation of an Asian man as desirable. Another part of me wonders if a "specialist" magazine such as *OG* plays a part in keeping the Asian body marginal. By separating the Asian body out as something "exotic," is *OG* reinforcing its "otherness"? Certainly, in an ideal world, there would be no need for *OG* to exist as Asian men would be proportionally represented within the mainstream gay media.

I am not familiar with all of *OG*'s output over the past few years and the following comments are based upon issues that I purchased in 1993. What struck me about the representation of Asian men in these issues was how "feminine" they were. By this, I mean that certain qualities of representation line up with the way in which women are typically represented. Feminist arguments of the past two decades have drawn attention to the differences between the depiction of the female body and the male body. Essentially, the "masculine" body is aggressive, in control, and powerful while the "feminine" body is passive, relinquishing control, and powerless. Most images of gay Asian men that I've seen, including many although not all of those in *OG*, are "feminine" in nature compared to representations of the Caucasian body in the mainstream gay media, which are aggressively masculine.

In gay media photos of Caucasian men the focus of attention is often the man's erect penis, the most aggressive symbol of masculinity. In contrast, the focus in photos of Asian men is the curve of the body, a typically feminine emphasis. This representation shows the Asian male as passive and subservient. Mirroring this feminine image is the stereotypical Asian/Caucasian relationship. In this the western man is older, the Asian man is younger. The western man is wealthy, the Asian man is poor. The western man is sexually active, the Asian man is sexually passive.

Until relatively recently, the majority of relations between gay Caucasians and Asians seemed to confirm this stereotype. Older gay Caucasian men would frequent the sexual meccas of Bangkok and Manila to buy sexual favors from younger, financially destitute boys. Not all of them are the "sexual predators" and "pederasts" that the scare-mongers among the straight press would have us believe them to be. Many have come out late in life. Coming onto the youth-oriented gay scene in their forties or fifties, they find that there is little place for them. It is often easier for them to have relationships with younger Asian men. They feel that they have something to offer these younger men.

Caucasian men primarily attracted to Asians are called "rice queens." Because of the lowly status of the Asian within the gay community, the term "rice queen" is a term of disparagement. The implication is that "rice queens" are not desirable enough to cut the mustard in the mainstream scene so they have to resort to having sex with Asians. Within the race-power dynamics of the gay scene, these Caucasian men become second class by default.

CHANGING TIMES

If this were the whole story, it would be incredibly depressing. Fortunately, it is not. In reality there are many variations on the stereotype I have described. Some people take up with each other irrespective of and not because of their race. With the rapid economic development of countries such as Korea, Vietnam, Malaysia and Thailand, many gay Asian tourists and migrants are now highly educated, well-travelled, cosmopolitan in outlook and the economic equals (or superiors) of their Caucasian Australian partners.

Even the seemingly most inequitable and stereotypical Caucasian-Asian relationships also have some degree of negotiation and consent. They cannot simply be reduced to interplays of power. The "rice queen" might have more socio-economic power, but the Asian man often has youth and looks on his side, both of which are powerful bargaining tools on the gay scene. And as well as a level of financial security, the "rice queen" offers the Asian man the power of being desired, which is often denied him within the mainstream gay culture. Superficial and high-minded judgements about the inequalities between rice queens and their young Asian partners are based upon the western gay fantasy of the "equal relationship." But in reality no relationship is equal. Men are not equal to women; men from different classes within the same society are not equal to each other; and neither are men from different cultures and societies equal. There are exchanges of power in all relationships.

We live in a historical period when all of the assertions that I have made above are in a state of flux. In many economic and cultural ways, Australia is becoming a part of Asia and the gay scene in this country is following that trend. In the late 1990s there are far more Asian men on the gay scenes in cities such as Sydney and Melbourne than ever before, and there seems to be a greater intermingling of races than was the case even a few years ago, especially amongst younger gay men. In Australian gay venues it is now increasingly common to see young Asian men with young Caucasian men, something which was almost unheard of as little as five years ago, or Asian men with other Asian men (called "sticky rice"), equally unheard of in the recent past. Young gay Asian men are forging new spaces in which to explore their identity and sexuality.

Since the racist letter in *Campaign* six years ago an increasing number of gay Asian men and women have become engaged in the politics of race, such as organising Asian Pride workshops and making their presence felt in Sydney's annual Gay and Lesbian Mardi Gras festival and parade. In fact, the Asian lesbian float won the award for the best entrant in the 1995 Mardi Gras parade with the photo of this float prominently displayed on the front page of the gay press the following week. For the first time, racial politics has, to some degree, forced itself onto the gay agenda. Even the mainstream gay press is starting to show images of the Asian body, albeit cursorily.

Inevitably, sheer demographics will break down some of the racism which I have described and experienced. As the Asian section of Australia's population grows as a result of the racially non-discriminatory immigration policies that have been in force since the early 1970s, and as more wealthy gay Asian tourists holiday in this country (often to escape homophobia in their home societies), then more gay Asian men appear on the scene. It will then become harder for the Caucasian majority to ignore us and continue to render us invisible. And slowly, inexorably, the Asian body will begin to appear as ordinary, normal and desirable as any other.

Last year I went back to China for the first time as an adult to do some research on a television miniseries I was working on for the Australian Broadcasting Corporation about the Chinese in Australia. The great irony of that journey was that, having decided to at last embrace my country of origin after years of denial, no-one in China thought of me as Chinese. Everyone assumed I was Japanese, possibly because of the Nikon camera I had around my neck.

But one important thing happened. I had sex with a Chinese man for the first time in my life. It was in a gay sauna in Hong Kong called "Game Boy." All I ever found out about him was that his name was Robert. He was tall and solid–a physical type I like. Touching him was a foreign sensation. I am used to the touch of Caucasian skin–hairier. Chinese skin is smooth, yet there is also a hardness to it, a polished ivory muscularity. I found myself giving way to it, being swept away by a desire which I had never experienced before. It was desire which had nothing to do with politics. He did not want me because I was Chinese. I did not reject him because he was Chinese. We just wanted each other. It was simple. For a brief moment I felt that for the first time in my life I understood what desire was about. And in that understanding, there was the most exquisite feeling of liberation.

NOTE

1. The author of the letter had obviously confused the November 1991 issue of *Campaign*, which had Linden Davidson on the cover, with the December issue with Chi-Kan Woo on the cover.

The Cinematic Representation of Asian Homosexuality in *The Wedding Banquet*

Ling-Yen Chua

University of Warwick, UK

SUMMARY. Over the last decade, there has been an increasing number of western films which represent both homosexuals and Asian people. However, the homosexuals depicted in these films are often white, and the Asians are almost always heterosexual. In an attempt to account for the scarcity of western films containing Asian homosexuals, this paper aims to examine some of the common cinematic tropes and theoretical discourses used to depict and define both Asians and homosexuals. As one of the few feature-length films containing an Asian homosexual central character, Ang Lee's *The Wedding Banquet* will also be discussed. *[Article copies available for a fee from The Haworth Document Delivery Service: 1-800-342-9678. E-mail address: getinfo@haworthpressinc.com]*

INTRODUCTION

Over the last decade, there has been an increasing number of western films which represent both homosexuals and Asian people. However, to date there

---

Correspondence regarding this article may be addressed to Ms. Ling-Yen Chua, Department of Film and TV, University of Warwick. Coventry CV4 7AL, United Kingdom.

[Haworth co-indexing entry note]: "The Cinematic Representation of Asian Homosexuality in *The Wedding Banquet*." Chua, Ling-Yen. Co-published simultaneously in *Journal of Homosexuality* (The Haworth Press, Inc.) Vol. 36, No. 3/4, 1999, pp. 99-112; and: *Multicultural Queer: Australian Narratives* (ed: Peter A. Jackson and Gerard Sullivan) The Haworth Press, Inc., 1999, pp. 99-112. Single or multiple copies of this article are available for a fee from The Haworth Document Delivery Service [1-800-342-9678, 9:00 a.m. - 5:00 p.m. (EST). E-mail address: getinfo@haworthpressinc.com].

are still few films which represent Asian homosexuals. The recent New Zealand film *Desperate Remedies* (Stewart Main & Peter Wells, New Zealand, 1993) and Australian film *Priscilla, Adventures of Priscilla Queen of the Desert* (Stephan Elliot, Australia, 1994) which both contain white homosexual characters and (presumably) heterosexual Asian characters are just two Australasian examples of such a trend. The most obvious reason for the scarcity of representations of Asian homosexuals in western cinema is that there are simply fewer Asian homosexuals in the West. However, in this paper, I wish to explore two alternative reasons for this omission.

Firstly, I posit that homosexual characters are frequently depicted as white because contemporary western definitions of homosexuality have been largely constructed by and for white subjects. In *The History of Sexuality Volume 1* Foucualt (1978, p. 43) writes that with the development of psychological theories of the invert, the homosexual became a sexually aberrant "species" with an "indiscreet anatomy" and "a mysterious physiology." Chauncey (1995), Young (1990), McClintock (1995) and Hart (1994) have suggested that although racist assumptions have historically constructed non-white people as being (homo)sexually deviant, western psychoanalytic definitions of homosexuality became foreclosed to include only white middle- and upper-class subjects when white homosexuality threatened the procreation of the (white) race.

As psychoanalytic definitions of homosexuality were pivotal to the establishment of contemporary understandings and definitions of the homosexual, and since psychoanalytic theories of (homo)sexuality were based almost solely on white middle-class (homo)sexuality, it is thus not surprising that contemporary cinematic discourses of homosexuality often exclude non-white and working-class subjects. This led to the contemporary separation of the category of the homosexual from the non-white person. Asian-Canadian filmmaker Richard Fung has also suggested that there are few cinematic representations of Asian and other non-white homosexuals since homosexuality is popularly constructed as a white phenomenon:

> Even as recently as the early 1980s, I remember having to prove my queer credentials before being admitted with other Asian men into a Toronto gay club. I do not believe it was a question of color barrier. Rather, my friends and I felt that the doorman was genuinely unsure about our sexual orientation. We also felt that had we been white and dressed similarly, our entrance would have been automatic. (Fung 1991, p. 148)

By arguing that homosexuality is commonly seen as a white phenomenon, Fung is not suggesting that Asians are thought to participate only in heterosexual activities. This leads me to my second reason why there are so few representations of Asian homosexuals. Besides, Fung, Pratibha Parmar (1993) and Rudi Bleys (1996) point out that an old stereotype that all Asians are perceived as sexually deviant already exists. Because of this racial stereotype, Asians are perceived as "naturally" capable of practising all forms of "unnatural" sexual acts, including homosexual ones. Hence, the Asian's homosexual practices are more likely to be interpreted as an illustration of his/her deviant raciality. Bleys (1996, p. 31) elaborates that since "the Far East [was] seen by many a traveller as a hotbed of sexual lasciviousness," homosexual practices are seen as part of their range of sexual activities. Asians are consequently not identified as "real homosexuals." The weight of racialist discourse has thus proved considerable as the very distinction between "congenital" versus "situational" homosexuality allowed for the simultaneous upholding of an etiological model of "endemic" homosexuality when applied to non-western societies, and a "minority" model when applied to the West (Bleys 1996, p. 192).

Films such as *The Last Emperor* (Bernardo Bertolucci, Italy/Hong Kong/United Kingdom, 1987), *M. Butterfly* (David Cronenberg, USA, 1993) and *The Buddha of Suburbia* (Roger Mitchell, United Kingdom, 1993) depict Asian men and women who engage in homosexual acts without being identified as strictly "homosexual." Instead, their homosexual practices are depicted either as being a "natural" result of their being more open (than Western subjects) to sexual exploration, or a result of their Asian sexual "decadence." Thus, I suggest that the simultaneous coexistence of the two racial and sexual stereotypes–Asians as being more sexually lascivious than Westerners, and homosexuals as being white–provide plausible reasons for why there are so few identifiably Asian homosexual characters in western films. Parmar, a British South Asian lesbian filmmaker, writes that the scarce number of films containing black/Asian[1] lesbian and gay characters can be attributed to the exclusive definitions of homosexuality and "Asianness" within the various communities:

> One of my concerns as a filmmaker is to challenge the normalizing and universalizing tendencies within the predominantly white lesbian and gay communities–to assert the diversity of cultural and racial identities within the umbrella category of gay and lesbian. There is a need to define "community," and just as there isn't a homogeneous black community, similarly there isn't a monolithic lesbian and gay community. (Parmar 1993, p. 9)

Parmar further argues that the transgressive Asian lesbian and gay subjects who exist at the intersection of the separate discourses of "the homosexual" and "the Asian" call into question rigid racial and sexual categorizations. It is important to note that Parmar is not suggesting that the monolithic discourses of homosexuality and racial identity be replaced by a model which emphasizes the Asian homosexual's "multiple identities."

I suggest that her position is more similar to that of Richard Fung who writes that his identity, as a Trinidadian born Canadian Asian homosexual, is *not* "any more 'multiple' than that of a straight white man, who is also raced, classed, gendered, and sexually oriented" (Fung 1995, p. 128). Lawrence Grossberg (1996, pp. 89-90) also cautions that an emphasis on a minoritized subject's "multiple identities" is not as politically progressive or useful as once might have been thought. This is because an emphasis on the Asian homosexual's "multiple realities" paradoxically reinstates his/her position as the more socially devalued half of the binaries white/colored, male/female, hetero/homo, abled/disabled, and so on. Instead, Julien and Mercer suggest that the necessary beginning of any project about non-white homosexuals must be the attempt to identify the relations of power that determine which forms of issues and representations are prioritized in the first place:

> The initial stage in any deconstructive project must be to examine and undermine the force of the binary relation that produces the marginal as a consequence of the authority invested in the centre. (Julien & Mercer 1996, p. 451)

Consequently, any discussion about the scarcity of films containing Asian lesbian and gay characters will first have to examine how the processes of contemporary discourses work against the representation of subjects who transgress the separate categories of racial and homosexual difference. This leads me again to the subject of this paper, which is to look beyond the seemingly obvious reason that the proportionately fewer number of Asian homosexuals in the West adequately accounts for their scarce cinematic presence in order to interrogate the conditions for their representation.

Some of the few feature length fiction films and shorter documentaries featuring an Asian homosexual subject include *Chinese Characters* (Richard Fung, Canada, 1988), *Khush* (Pratibha Parmar, United Kingdom, 1991), *The Wedding Banquet* (Ang Lee, Taiwan/USA, 1993) and *Fresh Kill* (Shu Lea Cheang, USA, 1993). However, for reasons of length and manageability, I will here consider only the widely known and commercially successful *The Wedding Banquet* by director Ang Lee. I am particularly interested in exploring if, and how, this film negotiates the two stereotypes of Asians as being sexually deviant and homosexuals as being white, since they both affect the representation of the central Asian homosexual character.

THE WEDDING BANQUET

Although *The Wedding Banquet* contains a predominantly Asian cast, it was filmed entirely in New York with a production and post-production crew that was largely white. The film also received a financially and critically successful mainstream release in the West. For these reasons, although the director of the film Ang Lee[2] is Taiwanese, *The Wedding Banquet* is arguably a "western" film.

I am aware that because *The Wedding Banquet* contains many Chinese characters and is also a Taiwanese production, an argument could be made that it is not a "western" film. However, I posit that the argument that it is not "western enough" on the basis of national or ethnic origin is highly problematic. Stuart Hall (1996b, 1996c) and Mercer (1994) have debated at length about the problems of national identity and racial authenticity. Mercer (1994, p. 243) observes:

> When the trope of "authenticity" is used to define the question of aesthetic and political value, it often reduces an argument about who does, and who does not, "belong" in the black communities.

Mercer writes that trying to determine who is more racially "authentic" often leads to the exclusion of certain black people (such as mixed race people and non-white homosexuals) from black communities. I suggest that his argument can be extended to apply to issues about what is deemed "western" or not. If one wishes to argue about what is "western," then questions such as whether the films have to be produced in the West or directed by a white person have to be properly addressed. I suggest that this line of questioning is unproductive and fraught with highly problematic essentialist notions of identity, ethnicity and nationality. Films already commonly accepted as being "western"–such as *Fresh Kill, Chinese Characters, Khush* and *Looking for Langston* (Isaac Julien, United Kingdom, 1989)–would also be called into question for not being western enough since none of these films' directors are white or were born in the West. Thus, when we start trying to determine how long a filmmaker has to live in the West before his or her films are accepted as "western," the territory of what is deemed "western" risks inscribing the hierarchies of racial or cultural "authenticity" which critics like Mercer (1994), hooks (1994), Hall (1996a, 1996b, 1996c), and Julien (1996) warn us against.

I also resist alternative arguments that *The Wedding Banquet* is not western enough because it contains a large cast of Chinese characters on the grounds that films such as *The Color Purple* (Steven Spielberg, USA, 1985), *Young Soul Rebels* (Isaac Julien, United Kingdom, 1991) and *Panthers* (Mario Van Peebles, USA, 1995) are all accepted as "western" even though they also contain large casts of African characters, some of whom were born in the West and others in Africa. It is, after all, not so long since people of African descent were seen as un-British, un-American, or un-Western because of their racial difference. The work of activists such as Paul Gilroy (1987, 1993), Hall (1996a, 1996b, 1996c) and hooks (1994) has assisted in the gradual acceptance of black people as being part of a culturally diverse West. Thus, it would seem to be highly problematic to accept a film containing characters of predominantly African-derived race as western while rejecting *The Wedding Banquet,* ostensibly because it contains Chinese characters even though it is set entirely in New York and deals explicitly with the experience of living in West and was widely released for a western audience.

I am not suggesting that the issues of ethnic or cultural difference or filmic and narrative style should be ignored. These factors must be taken account of in any film analysis. However, as Fung (1991, p. 160) argues, the racial or national identity of a director is not a guarantee that the film will be more "politically correct" or depict issues of race or nationality in a more "authentic" manner. Hence, for all the above reasons, I resist the essentialist argument that *The Wedding Banquet* is not "western enough" because the director is not white or because it contains a large cast of Chinese characters. Having explained my reasons for including *The Wedding Banquet* in the category of "western film," I will now look at the film itself.

The film narrative is uncomplicated and largely revolves around the "coming out" of Wang Wei Tung, a homosexual Taiwanese-born Asian-American. From the very first scene of the film we are made aware of his parents' desires for him to get married and to have a son. Wei Tung's fear of disappointing his parents prompts his white partner, Simon, to arrange a "fake" heterosexual marriage between Wei Tung and a Chinese woman, Wei Wei. Delighted that their son is finally getting married, his parents, Mr. and Mrs. Wang, leave their home in Taiwan to come to New York for his wedding. Unfortunately, their arrival triggers Wei Tung's disastrous "coming out" to his parents when his bogus marriage is exposed. Although the film is a comedy with a lighthearted happy ending, it tackles and deals with many of the issues raised by critics and activists such as Fung, Mercer and Parmar. I will start with a general discussion of the film's representation of Wei Tung as an Asian homosexual.

First of all, the film portrays Wei Tung very sympathetically. Wei Tung is depicted as the "hero" of the film, and the events are largely shot and narrated from his point of view. This point-of-view cinematic structure ensures that few blatantly negative racial or sexual stereotypes of Asians or homosexuals emerge in the characterization of Wei Tung. More interestingly, the film does not universalize Wei Tung's Asian homosexuality as a common phenomenon. I will now show how the film interrogates popular stereotypes of homosexuality as being "a white thing."

HOMOSEXUALITY AS "A WHITE THING"

I pointed out above that homosexuality has generally been defined according to and for white subjects in western discourse. However, it is not only white western subjects who assume that only white people are homosexuals. There is also a popular discourse circulating within Asian communities that homosexuality is "a white man's disease." Parmar (1993) and Fung (1991) have both pointed out that Asian communities often disavow that lesbian and gay people exist within their midst or that Asian people can be "born that way."

While white communities distance white homosexuals as being similar to perverse "foreigners," Asian communities often construct a converse form of stereotyping by regarding Asian homosexuals as being people who have become contaminated through excessive "westernization" or social contact with white people.

Paradoxically, whether in order to challenge the assumption that homosexuals do not exist "naturally" within one's racial community or in order to counter the fear that one may become a homosexual through "social contamination," lesbian and gay activists have commonly adopted an essentialist argument that "one is born gay" as part of the struggle to gain political and social rights. I suggest that *The Wedding Banquet* attempts to negotiate all these social and political discourses about homosexuality circulating both in the West and within Asian communities when the film's narrative repeatedly emphasizes that Wei Tung is a homosexual because he was "born that way."

There is a crucial scene in the film where Wei Tung's mother suggests that he is now a homosexual because he has been led astray by Simon, a white man. Wei Tung argues emphatically that he was not "socially contaminated," but that he was "born this way." Later in the film, there is another scene where his mother again suggests that Wei Tung's homosexuality could be a "passing phase." Here, Wei Tung's arranged bride-to-be, Wei Wei, contradicts her future mother-in-law by emphasizing that Wei Tung is indisputably a homosexual, not a bisexual or a heterosexual. Hence, the film persistently illustrates that homosexuality is not exclusive to white people, and that one cannot become a homosexual through being led astray by white men. I thus posit that *The Wedding Banquet*'s characterization of Wei Tung's homosexuality problematizes the myth that homosexuality is an exclusively "white thing."

However, besides this progressive representation of Wei Tung, all the other homosexual characters in the film are white. By the same token, all the white characters in the film are also homosexual or at least pro-gay and involved in some form of gay activist work. There are no other Asian or non-white homosexuals. All of Wei Tung's Asian friends, as seen at the wedding, appear to be heterosexuals. Therefore, despite the groundbreaking and sympathetic representation of Wei Tung as an Asian homosexual, *The Wedding Banquet* still seems to suggest that being gay is predominantly a white thing. By depicting all Wei Tung's gay friends as white and his Asian friends as heterosexual, the film colludes with the popular stereotype that to be gay is to become "more white," or to be submerged into white culture. This stereotype has been noted in various English language anthologies about being Asian homosexuals such as *Witness Aloud* (Chi Tsang, 1993) and *A Lotus of Another Colour* (Rakesh Ratti, 1993).

One possible explanation for the unquestioned heterosexuality of the Asian characters is the film's emphasis on the strong family ties within Asian/Chinese communities. There is a scene in the Chinese restaurant where Wei Tung and Wei Wei's wedding reception banquet is held in which the restaurant's old Chinese proprietor, old Chen, points to Simon (the only white character present at the banquet) and tells the Wang family that they cannot "lose face" in the United States of America. By pointing to Simon, he draws a line between being white and Asian, suggesting that in the West the bonds of being Chinese extend beyond the nuclear family and even the extended family structures to include all Chinese people as part of one large expatriate family.

THE FAMILY

Old Chen indicates that Wei Tung's father's desire for his son to get married for the sole purpose of his, in turn, having a son is related not only to his desire to continue the patriarchal Wang family line, but is also related to the maintenance of the Chinese race in the West. Since heterosexuality is considered necessary for the purposes of reproduction, the film's unquestioned acceptance of the Chinese patriarchal desire to preserve this large Chinese family means that, other than Wei Tung, the Asians in the film are all implied to be heterosexuals.

Although the film engages in an admirably sympathetic portrayal of Wei Tung's homosexuality, even he eventually fulfills his duty of being a good Chinese man by getting married and having a son when he has sex with Wei Wei when drunk. Through a long comic description of Simon's dysfunctional family, the film emphasizes that the western white American family unit has collapsed. This scene suggests that unlike Simon and his family, the preservation and continuation of the family line is important to Wei Tung and other Asians.

The build-up early in the film provided by Wei Tung listening to his mother's tapes from Taiwan informing him of his father's desire for a grandson, scenes foregrounding an anonymous boy at the marriage ceremony, and Wei Wei's decision to keep the baby that Wei Tung has fathered (which leads to the resolution of the film), all serve to emphasize the importance of heterosexuality to the continuation of the Asian family line.

The emphasis on the familial attachments of Asian characters is a commonly used stereotype in western films. *Bhaji on the Beach* (Gurinda Chadha, United Kingdom, 1993), *Sammy and Rosie Get Laid* (Stephen Frears, UK, 1987), *The Lover* (Jean-Jacques Annaud, United Kingdom/France, 1992) and *Indochine* (Regis Wargnier, France, 1992) are examples of other films which employ the Asian family stereotype. It is important to note that stereotypes themselves are not necessarily negative. Richard Dyer (1993, pp. 11-12) points out that it is how stereotypes are used which is more important, "The position behind all these considerations is that it is not stereotypes, as an aspect of human thought and representation, that are wrong, but who controls and defines them, what interests they serve."

Some activists/filmmakers such as Julien (1992) and Parmar (1993) have further suggested that constantly rebelling against utilizing stereotypes to show "positive images" can also be stifling. Although "positive images" are constructed in opposition to demeaning stereotypes, their reverse relationship signifies that they are still dependent on and subject to the limits of representation laid out by the stereotypes. Consequently, the emphasis on the importance of the Chinese family in *The Wedding Banquet* cannot simply be dismissed as reinscribing the stereotype that Chinese people are very family oriented. What is more important is to examine the personal and economic negotiation of power in the film's representation of the Chinese family in relation to the social circumstance of Wei Tung and the white society in which he exists. Therefore, while it can be argued that Wei Tung's father is depicted as a dictatorial authoritarian, it is ultimately Simon's white family that is set up as being more negatively dysfunctional. It has been suggested by Mercer (1994) that the family is more important to non-white homosexuals living in the West than to white homosexuals because the family unit acts as a support in their fight against racism in western society. Parmar's film *Khush* further illustrates this point. Fung (1991, p. 149) also writes positively about the importance of the family to the Asian homosexual:

> Creating a space for Asian gay and lesbian representation has meant, among other things, deepening an understanding of what is at stake for Asians in coming out publicly. As is the case for many other people of color and especially immigrants, our families and our ethnic communities are a rare source of affirmation in a racist society. In coming out, we risk (or feel that we risk) losing this support . . .

Consequently, although *The Wedding Banquet* is not preoccupied with issues of racism, the film's representation of Wei Tung's experience of coming out to his family (although ending perhaps rather over-idealistically happily) in fact reflects a reality that many Asian homosexuals have to face. I thus posit that the film's emphasis on the importance of the family is not negative. In fact, to a certain extent it is admirably "realistic." This leads me to consider the significance of the bride Wei Wei's Chinese racial identity and the boyfriend Simon's white racial identity.

INTERRACIAL HOMOSEXUAL ROMANCE

The importance of racial identity in choosing one's partner is first introduced by "Little Mao." Little Mao is a Chinese woman Wei Tung is paired up with by the Taiwanese dating agency his mother enrolled him in. There is a crucial scene in *The Wedding Banquet* where little Mao reveals she was also enrolled in the same dating agency by her parents because she faces similar difficulties as Wei Tung. Little Mao explains, "Like you, I am also going out with a white man."

She suggests that heterosexual interracial relationships are as taboo as homosexual relationships because both types of relationships do not result in the production of an acceptable (Chinese) family heir to continue the family line. As Wei Tung's case reveals, preservation of the correct family line is important to the Chinese. However, little Mao's case further suggests that it is not only crucial that a son is produced, but that this son be a racially correct "pure Chinese." This explains why, despite having a white boyfriend, Wei Tung chooses to marry a Chinese woman for the sake of pleasing his parents. It is thus vital that his arranged bride Wei Wei is Chinese. By marrying the right race, Wei Tung will have racially correct children.

On the other hand, I suggest that it is also crucial to the film's narrative that Simon be white. In the few other films containing lesbian and gay people of color, such as *My Beautiful Laundrette* (Stephen Frears, UK, 1985), *She Must Be Seeing Things* (Sheila McLaughlin, USA, 1987), *Young Soul Rebels*, *Salmonberries* (Percy Adlon, Germany/USA, 1991), *The Crying Game* (Neil Jordan, UK, 1992), *Grief* (Richard Glatzer, USA, 1993), *Go Fish* (Rose Troche, USA, 1994), *Boys on the Side* (Ross Herbert, USA, 1995), *Bar Girls* (Marita Giovanni, USA, 1995) and *When the Night is Falling* (Patricia Rozema, Canada, 1994), the non-white homosexuals are all depicted as being sexually involved with white homosexuals, like Wei Tung and Simon in *The Wedding Banquet*.

It is as if Asian and other non-white homosexual characters still cannot be seen outside of the western subculture of homosexuality. Almost always depicted as being interracially involved with white homosexuals, the non-white protagonist's homosexuality seems almost unable to exist outside of popular western discourse of homosexuality as being "a white thing." So although interracial heterosexuality is frowned upon in *The Wedding Banquet*, an interracial homosexual relationship with a white man is arguably essential to the "authentication" of Wei Tung's homosexuality. Despite the radical characterization of Wei Tung as an Asian homosexual, the film still firmly locates his homosexual identity as existing only within a white cultural discourse.

Superficially, the cinematic representation of the non-white homosexual as being involved in interracial homosexual relationships appears racially progressive in its disregard of the taboo against miscegenation. However, Young (1995, pp. 25-26) argues that the fear of miscegenation applies specifically to heterosexual interracial sex, and not to homosexual interracial sex. Same-sex sex, though clearly locked into an identical same-but-different dialectic of racialized sexuality, poses no threat because it produces no children; its advantage is that it remains silent, covert and unmarked. On the face of it, therefore, hybridity must always be a resolutely heterosexual category.

So interracial homosexuality is not similarly transgressive like heterosexual interracial relationships. Jackie Stacey (1992, 1995) posits that lesbian films have often borrowed the conventional heterosexual romantic tropes of casting characters who are romantically involved with one another with contrasting (sometimes racial) lightness and darkness to create the romantic tension of difference which is perhaps not so obviously present because of a lack of heterosexual gender difference. She additionally explains that another trope borrowed from heterosexual romance films is the creation of obstacles to heighten the romantic tension. However, Stacey (1995) writes that in order to produce an affirmative lesbian film, these obstacles cannot be unsurmountable since popular portrayals of lesbian relationships are already unfulfilling. Although Stacey writes specifically about lesbian romance films, her theories are also applicable to male homosexual romance films since she refers in particular to the lack of gender difference in lesbian films, a phenomenon which is also evident in films about homosexual men.

Given the popularity of *The Wedding Banquet* and the relative commercial or critical successes of the few other recent interracial homosexual romance films, it appears that interracial homosexual liaisons are not socially threatening, but are in fact used effectively as a device to create romantic tension and obstacles. Hence, when *Priscilla, Adventures of Priscilla Queen of the Desert* is "re-done" by Hollywood as *To Wong Foo, Thanks for Everything, Julie Newmar* (Beeban Kidron, USA, 1995) it is not surprising that one of the white homosexual characters in *Priscilla . . .* is replaced by a non-white homosexual character (played by Wesley Snipes).

Although none of the above-named films are about Asian homosexuals, I suggest that *The Wedding Banquet* is part of a larger group of films containing non-white homosexuals involved in interracial homosexual relationships. Hall (1996c) suggests that this unexpectedly popular representation signals that racial and sexual stereotypes can be shifted.

Mercer (1994, p. 71) concurs that the popularity of films containing Asian and other non-white homosexuals can also be read positively as a reflection of the changing expectations of the audience. This shift indicates that the audience is not one homogenous mass but rather is made up of diverse groups of people whose tastes vary according to what they are "taught" to like or dislike. Stoller (1995, p. 151) argues that desire can be educated. Likewise, I suggest that one's tastes in filmic representations can also be educated according to what is released for mainstream consumption. It is thus with a political agenda in mind that Asian lesbian and gay filmmakers like Parmar and Fung have voiced the need for more films containing Asian lesbian and gay characters which do not unproblematically utilize negative racial and sexual stereotypes.

As I have indicated earlier, this is not a simplistic call for "positive images" since they can be limited to reacting against negative stereotypes rather than depicting the diversity of experiences of the particular minority. However, since there are so few representations of Asian homosexuals, regardless of the filmmakers' intentions, the few existing texts often risk being forced to take on the responsibility of attempting to speak for all Asian lesbians and gay people, as Fung (1995, p. 129) observes:

> Speaking as gay, as Asian, or as a gay-Asian man is a tricky proposition. For one thing, speaking as any one thing implies not being listened to on any other terms . . . In making a videotape or speaking on a panel I cannot escape the burden of representation . . . This burden, which accumulates over the history of representation, cannot be transcended any more than the socially defined categories of race or gender can— they affect our lives whether we recognize them or not.

Julien and Mercer (1996, p. 453) also write that because access and opportunities are often rationed to marginalized groups so that only one token minoritized "representative" gets to "speak" at a time, whether by choice or otherwise that delegate becomes burdened with the responsibility of representing the entire community of which they are but one member. This privileging of only one point-of-view often leads to the creation of an alternative hegemonic norm in films where only certain "experiences" are deemed "correct" or "authentic."

Additionally, since most politically motivated projects are to some extent dependent on a notion of a unitary identity and a model of "correct" representation, films which feature previously marginalized characters often run the risk of creating an alternative "norm" by which all such subjects are measured. Therefore, when viewing films with Asian homosexual characters, such as *The Wedding Banquet*, one must also bear in mind that they are only *one* particular form of representation. To avoid perpetuating the politics of tokenism and imposing the "burden of representation" on the filmmakers, such films should not be judged solely for whether the Asian homosexual character is "authentic" according to a racially or sexually homogeneous yardstick.

This is a reason why I do not conclude here with a definitive statement about whether *The Wedding Banquet* is a "positive" or "negative" film. What I instead hope to have done in this paper is to contextualize the film within a larger group of films about non-white homosexuals and discuss some of the pressing issues surrounding the problems involved in the representation of Asian homosexuals in western cinema.

NOTES

1. Like Kobena Mercer (1994), Isaac Julien (1996), and Stuart Hall (1996a), Pratibha Parmar uses the term "black" within the British context to refer to all non-white people, including Asians. The term "black," when used in this paper, similarly refers to all "people of color," including Asians.

2. Since directing *The Wedding Banquet*, Ang Lee has gone on to direct other critically and financially successful films which can be considered "western films." The Oscar-award winning *Sense and Sensibility* (USA, 1995) is one such film.

REFERENCES

Bleys, Rudi C. (1996). *The geography of perversion*. London: Cassell.

Chauncey, George. (1995). *Gay New York*. London: Flamingo.

Dyer, Richard. (1993). White. In Richard Dyer (Ed.). *The matter of images* (pp. 141-163). New York: Routledge.

Foucault, Michel. (1978). *The History of Sexuality, Volume 1*. (Trans. Robert Hurley). London: Penguin.

Fung, Richard. (1991). Looking for my penis. In Bad Object Choices (Ed.). *How do I look?* (pp. 145-168). Seattle: Bay Press.

Fung, Richard. (1995). The trouble with Asians. In Corey Creekmur & Alexander Doty (Eds.). *Negotiating lesbian and gay subjects* (pp. 123-130). London: Cassell.

Gilroy, Paul. (1987). *There ain't no black in the Union Jack: The cultural politics of race and nation*. London: Hutchinson.

Gilroy, Paul. (1993). *Small acts*. London: Serpent's Tail.

Grossberg, Lawrence. (1996). Identity and cultural studies–Is that all there is? In Stuart Hall and Paul du Gay (Eds.) *Questions of Cultural Identity* (pp. 87-107). London: Sage Publications, 1996.

Hall, Stuart. (1996a). What is this "black" in black popular culture? In David Morley and Kuan-Hsing Chen (Eds.) *Stuart Hall: Critical dialogues in cultural studies.* (pp. 465-475) London: Routledge.

Hall, Stuart. (1996b). Introduction: Who needs identity? In Stuart Hall & Paul du Gay (Eds.). *Questions of cultural identity* (pp. 1-17). London: Sage Publications.

Hall, Stuart. (1996c). New Ethnicities. *ICA documents 7: Black film, British cinema.* In Kobena Mercer (Ed.). London: ICA, 1989. Reprinted in David Morley & Kuan-Hsing Chen (Eds.). *Stuart Hall: Critical dialogues in cultural studies* (pp. 441-449). London: Routledge.

Hart, Lynda. (1994). *Fatal women.* London: Routledge.

hooks, bell. (1994). *Outlaw culture.* New York: Routledge.

Julien, Isaac. (1992). Black is . . . Black ain't: Notes on de-essentializing Black identities. In Gina Dent (Ed.). *Black popular culture, a project by Michelle Wallace* (pp. 255-263). Seattle: Bay Press.

Julien, Isaac and Kobena Mercer. (1996). De margin and de centre. In David Morley and Kuan-Hsing Chen (Eds.), *Stuart Hall: Critical dialogues in cultural studies* (pp. 450-464). London: Routledge.

McClintock, Anne. (1995). *Imperial leather: Race, gender and sexuality in the colonial contest.* London: Routledge.

Mercer, Kobena. (1994). *Welcome to the jungle.* London: Routledge.

Parmar, Pratibha. (1993). That moment of emergence. In Martha Gever, Pratibha Parmar & John Greyson (Eds.). *Queer looks* (pp. 3-11). New York: Routledge.

Ratti, Rakesh (Ed.) (1993). *A lotus of another color: An unfolding of the South Asian gay and lesbian experience.* Boston: Alyson Publications.

Stacey, Jackie. (1992). Desperately seeking difference. *Screen: The sexual subject: A screen reader in sexuality* (pp. 224-260). London: Routledge.

Stacey, Jackie. (1995). "If you don't play, you can't win": *Desert Hearts* and the lesbian romance film. In Tamsin Wilton (Ed.) *Immortal, invisible* (pp. 91-114). London: Routledge.

Stoller, Ann. (1995). *Race and the education of desire.* London: Duke University Press.

Tsang, Chi. (Ed.) (1993). *Witness aloud: Lesbian, gay & bisexual Asian/Pacific American writing, The APA Journal* (New York: Asian American Writers Workshop), *2*(1).

Young, Robert. (1990). *White mythologies.* London: Routledge.

Young, Robert. (1995). *Colonial desire.* London: Routledge.

<interface: reflections of an ethnic toygirl>

Audrey Yue

La Trobe University, Melbourne

SUMMARY. This essay interrogates the colonial modernity of Anglo-Australian lesbian hegemony through an experimental text which plays with the aesthetics of cyberspace. Mobilizing the hypertext mark up language (HTML) form of the Internet, it spatializes the creative, the erotic, and the political that landscape the vicissitudes of everyday life for a lesbian of Southeast Asian background living in Australia. "interface" performs as a tryst that drives the queer body politic through the postcolonial in-formations of color, race, gender and identity. This text bears indelible marks from multiple sites and sources: the charges of electronic conversations and etchings on the World Wide Web; the raw pulp of inner-urban graffiti scrawls; passionate voicemails; racist policies in queer venues; fury banner posts; luscious lesbian cinema screenings; sexy fantasy malls; and fleshy style shopping. *[Article copies available for a fee from The Haworth Document Delivery Service: 1-800-342-9678. E-mail address: getinfo@haworthpressinc.com]*

The meaning of a digital message is not usually explicated by reciting tokens of numbers. We experience (the reality of) what lies hidden in a digital medium through an *interface* which transforms numbers into events (or vice versa) by implementing a systematic and automated connection between them. (Binkley, 1993, p. 111, emphasis mine)

Correspondence regarding this article may be addressed to Audrey Yue, Department of English with Cultural Studies, The University of Melbourne, Parkville, Victoria, 3052, Australia.

[Haworth co-indexing entry note]: "<interface: reflections of an ethnic toygirl>" Yue, Audrey. Co-published simultaneously in *Journal of Homosexuality* (The Haworth Press, Inc.) Vol. 36, No. 3/4, 1999, pp. 113-134; and: *Multicultural Queer: Australian Narratives* (ed: Peter A. Jackson and Gerard Sullivan) The Haworth Press, Inc., 1999, pp. 113-134. Single or multiple copies of this article are available for a fee from The Haworth Document Delivery Service [1-800-342-9678, 9:00 a.m. - 5:00 p.m. (EST). E-mail address: getinfo@haworthpressinc.com].

"Interface"[1] colors the queer body politic. Visualized through a hyper-texted[2] translation of contexts, subtexts, politexts and literatexts, it bitmaps a memory trace of (inter)connections, connections which interweave alongside and in-between the borderlines of NESBian[3] politics, gay and lesbian coalitions, (immigrant) queergirl desires and (Chinese) cyberdyke dreams. Criss-crossing a labyrinth sexing raced bodies and queer hopes, it is a local cartography interfacing in fragments that meander the homelands of (transnational) nostalgia and (cross-cultural) imagination; map the contours of type, touch and tears; and embody the remnants from the recollection zone of becoming future-perfect-past.

This paper mobilizes a hybrid of form and content in an array of discourses which range from grass-roots activisms, community conferences, clubbing and cruising cultures, and electronic mail communication. For lesbians from minority backgrounds in dominant cultures, the narrative of sexuality is also the narrative of race. Because it is race (and not racism) that has met with its invisibility in the queer public arena, this paper aims to intervene and complicate the paradigms of contemporary gay and lesbian culture(s) through recoding how the workings of race (in)form the workings of sexuality. Invoking a migratory consciousness as a strategy of reading and writing, this paper is, in the words of De Lauretis (1988, pp. 164-165),

> [A] formally experimental, critical and lyrical, autobiographical and theoretically conscious . . . practice . . . that crosses genre boundaries . . . and instates new correlations between signs and meanings, inciting other discursive mediations between the symbolic and the real, language and flesh.

Scrolling along very much like the tentative pixels of an interactive computer screen, this text performs as a circuit, inviting readers to interline the webs of their configurations into this fabric, which can only be the beginning of an on-going platform for further points of critically queer departures. Articulating the oral, the vernacular and the subaltern, "interface" injects as a kind of postmodern self-writing which presents an emerging visuality and functions as a postcolonial entry into the metropolitan Australian queer culture.

@   @   @

```
<html>
<title>MainliNe</title>
<body>
<h1>This link defies queer comfort zones.</h1>
```

eXrotica
a viral circuit infecting ethnosexual paradigms
presents
moments of passing
decodes in parsing
Shudder from the visceral templates of a slippery piss!
| Lick | Rub | Quiver | Tremble | Smack |

Bluefish

Today. Everyday. I am counting Time, counting repetitions. Everyday at Five. One X, Two Xs, Three Xs. Branded with recycled codes, my token recites the mechanics of my Olympic press. In. Out. In. Out. The abated breath of labor. Twenty Xs times Six times Three. Trickling sweat. Rhythmic rush. Methodic. Periodic. Soaked Bonds t-shirt. Stuffed Nikes. My hands are pricked by yesterday's thorns. Trimming rose bushes is not my forte. Today, my PVC pads are slicked and I have no calluses on my palms. Zero. My body is a Number. An *interface.*

I'm outside the living machine; pierced by the dangerous edges of little Swiss knives with nothing to jab, nothing to thrust. Just the skeletal frame of a living dead doll hangin' by a 3.5 inch thread. I see many face(less) ducts squirting yellow green pus in frantic moments of frenzied squeezing. The scene is reminiscent of one toilet spew in a garbage-strewn windswept alley-way, like a Tarantino pastiche. Remnants of half-digested salami pizza slices splattered across mouldy sepia bowls reeling in acid waste, ammonia burns and shit stains. I am stroking a surface, pressing my digits against the solidified crust lining her steamy wet cunt.

> Synthetic-plus cyberdyke wants non-blonde (fakes OK), non-herbal types for sexual interfacing. Required: Oozing, pumping clit-tit machines for non-stop surfs, virtual and/or otherwise. [Reply Box 2001]

@connect Living_Doll
You have mail.
Letter from Subject X entitled "Honey seeks Doll"

DollFace,
I've been looking for you, for a finger that responds logged in. My screen is a self reflexive entity, a standalone reproducing parthenogenetically.
So what will Doll be seeking this time?
Hmm. You tell me. I imagine I've been a great disappointment to you.

Extr@corporeally yours, Xslashslashslash.[4]

@ @ @ @ @ @

> Leaving for Another Country
> Sex With Women
> Secrets

Australian Department of Immigration, Local Government and Ethnic Affairs
Applicant's Nationality: *Singaporean*
Visa Category *Granted: Interdependency*
~~Border Crossing~~
Class: 154
Resident: P
Visa No. S523464

Boarding Pass
Singapore Airlines Flight # SQ7
Passenger Name: Yue, A.
Destination: Melbourne
Departure: 14.25 hours.
Economy Baggage Qty: 30kgs

"Interdependency" is a visa category under Australian immigration policy which permits existing permanent residents in same-sex *de facto* relationships to seek permanent residency for overseas partners.[5]

@ @ @ @ @ @

To: Subject X
From: Living_Doll
Subject: imagi ~ nation

Dear Migrant X,

You asked me if you have disappointed me. The notion of a fuckspace is a living perplexity. If I tell you I want you as much as I really do, then you will know that you have not failed in your manifestation as my clit-tit machine. So I will not. Because I still want a fuck.

Your sign in my life has become a trope that lies precariously on the borderline. I think about you sometimes and I remember the flash of your form down Brunswick Street[6] last winter in the hope of not-wanting-to-forget. And it scares me because you are very real. I think about wanting to touch you, and it is a yearning that lies beyond the chronotip of my keyboard.

I have projected an excremental nostalgia. Is this the body of extr@ that you say can be mine?

Names are unnamed the moment they are named. Yours. Mine. Theirs. I will take you in your map when we next meet. Is this still gameplay, or are we now locating desires via extr@MOOmail? I am confused because we have exceeded the tokens of our contract but this is the reality of our intertextual liaison. I know you must think of me as I do you and perhaps sometimes, in a temporal moment or two, that you do want me as much as I want you.

The ownership of illicit desire is something that needs to be worked out, and it's probably something that you already have. I don't know. The relationship between imagined desires and imagined bodies is complex. My subjectivity to your manifestation is different to the usual jack offs.

What about your subjectivity in relation to me? What does it sign? And I have missed you if you really must know. ~ Doll.xx

@ @ @ @ @ @

Interlesbian Presents:[7]

The Sappho Was a WogGrrrl Conference

Our aims are to create a forum to name and challenge our differences as well as shared experiences, and to create a voice for ourselves, in our many shapes and forms, in the larger community. Given the disparate nature of the group, the strategies we employ can only be described as being in constant negotiation. We don't claim to have an understanding of race and ethnicity, as we are ourselves grappling with the dynamics involved both within our group and in the wider community. That is why we see this as an opportunity to initiate a dialogue with groups such as yours which might lead to a better understanding of these issues in the gay and lesbian community. (Interlesbian Collective, 1995)

Dear Diary   6th June
X called . . . refused table at a queer cafe on Brunswick Street again. Fucked. I am jacked.

@ @ @ @ @ @

RETURN

I have been a regular patron of the 3 Faces queer nightclub for well over a year. On Friday 3 February I decided to take two of my friends (one Indian, the other Malaysian) there.

We were greeted at the door by security staff who told us that we couldn't *ENTER*. . . I am tired of the treatment I get when I'm with my Asian friends. I came here from South Africa where racism was part of the law of the land. Back there I knew that I could rely on all members of the gay community to accept and support each other regardless of background or colour . . . The only thing missing at some Australian venues here are the signs saying "*Vir Blankes.*" (Grimsell, 1995. Emphasis mine.)

Dear X,

Gay Venues Code of Practice
The draft "Code of Practice" was initiated by members of the Multicultural Gay Group[8] in Melbourne in the summer of 1994. It proposed that gay venues adopt an anti-discriminatory policy in the selection of staff members, content of entertainment and treatment of customers. The draft was never endorsed by the community.

Would like your support on this issue.
Many thanks,
Audrey Y.

@ @ @ @ @

jack@inter~face desperately seeking hybrid eyeballs, lurid oculars and Carnation Brand taste.

Slipzone

A geodesic zone of evanescent orificial peepholes. The Slipzone is your temporal euplastic paradox.
Outzone, inzone, nozone, becoming zone.
You are nowhere, everywhere.
Hear.
Here is Elsewhere.
You see *Zip*, a ventriloquist doll.
Living_Doll (awake) is here.

@ @ @ @ @ @

Asian lesbian, new to Melbourne, into films, music and theatre seeks new friends. Age and nationality open. [Reply Box 5230]

@ @ @ @ @ @

Dear Diary   25th September
Fleshmeet. 3 pm.

Look. Living_Doll returns your gaze. Suspended in an elliptical paradox, you are intoxicated by the excesses of its festering bites. Stripped bare, the naked gaze speculates the naked flesh. Synthetic. Sublime. Drenched in the pungent sweetness of toxic vapor, you suddenly feel dizzy. Her swollen callus trembles as your fingers slither across the scabrous membrane. Tender. Raw. The naked gaze desires the naked flesh.

<tasty> costs millions of $ </tasty>[9]

On 7th August 1994, 43 Victorian State police officers stripped-searched 463 male and female patrons of the Melbourne queer night-club "Tasty." About 150 of the patrons have since filed suits against individual police officers charging assault and abuse of civil rights. Following a State parliamentary ombudsman's report which pro-claimed the raid discriminatory and unjustified, Victorian State Police admitted that they had breached their own regulations. In the first case to reach trial, a woman has been awarded $10,000 in compensation.

Color Matters[10]

I am dreaming of livedolls, whitedolls and playdolls. Constructing desires, speculating fantasies. Touch typing on my keyboard, imagining sex beyond the screen and making forms without codes. In the virtual world of cyberspace, there are no visual signs except the plain words that are fabricated on the screen. Words that encode and denote, words that decode colorcodes, racecodes, gendercodes, sexcodes and fuckcodes. My only possession was words that recode.

I began this slippery journey consisting of frequent electronic mail conversations with a local queer activist who I had only met once. I have no maps, except the fading memories of a fast-disappearing face. She is an Anglo grrl.[11] A white femme body. These are the real traces of a real life.

This is a space where I cannot see colors. White is colorless, invisible, transparent. White is blank (Dyer, 1988). White is the blank, black screen that my words are typed on, everyday, twice a day. I began to map an imaginary whiteness, an imagination constructed by the familiar confines of my location. My island location was once a British colony. A colony ruled by a white race that deserted the place when the Japanese Occupation began in 1942. At the same time that I cringed at my mother's Nippon-phobia, I also learnt from her how to meticulously reproduce the Grand Rituals of Empire. I watched myself repudiate the traditions of my own Chineseness. I mastered the English language and memorized the literature of the Great Canon. This is the History of my place.

I constructed a desire for whiteness based on a yearning to be white. Yellow Skin. White Mask. But at the same time that I am yellow and not white, my desirability was already coded by the stereotyping of my skin, this History of my map. The Great Asia. The Great Receptacle. The Great Femininity. My postcolonial body is a deterritorialized body, constantly marked by western colonial fantasies of living dolls with long black hair, almond eyes and fair, smooth skin, prescribed by the ethnocentric Oriental signs of native beauty, passive femininity and docile subservience (Yue, 1996). Doubly displaced. Doubly colonized. I cannot desire.

But I am not. But this is not me. And this is not how I want you to desire me. And I know this is not how you see me. But how do you look? What do you see when you look? *"'I am like you. I am different'."* (Yue, 1993, p. 19.)

White is not the only color I see. But I see colors. I am thinking colors. I am remembering colors. Fresh pink nipples. Unblemished pale flesh. I remember the fear. I remember the first time I touched and tasted whitemeat. It was bland, a sort of dryness that left a biting aftertaste on my tongue. I remember the same fear when I kissed those fresh pink lips that I stole kisses from at the park behind the school, those same fresh pink lips that embody the darkness in my closet. I remember her. Silky black hair. Smooth shining skin. Unblemished exotic flesh. She was my living doll.

Sliding across your textual white flesh, I cross the borderline of queer hopes, black fears and white fantasies. My body is in spasms. I am touching the contours of your soft skin. We see flesh. Quick flashes. Quick Colors. Bold Colors. Raced Bodies. How do I look? What do I see?

> Someone must always be more powerful, someone is always more or less powerful. It can be me or you, one woman or another, but power is always there, it is never, ever absent. Right now, I have it, you're listening to my words and you recognize my strength . . . It's because we've lost power that we need each other like this. (Zando cited in Kotz, 1988, p. 67)

Power is erotic. In same-sex relationships. In cross-cultural relationships. Power is always contested, never stable, the product of our histories, the realities of our differing locations in our communities and on the streets. I am framed by the pleasure of technicolor. Bodies shifting. Constantly. Euphorically. Flux. More flux. More lube. A white femme body. Fluid yellow shafts in black harness straps. Fisting, gazing, wanting. My sweet sugar fixx. I am dreaming of Jenny Shimizu, stroking her naked skull, rubbing her flexed muscles and tracing the tattooed curves of her torso. Cataclysmic.

Logout

@ @ @ @ @ @

> I am in love with a white woman and have been partner with her for four years. We have carefully examined our motives for taking up with each other and can safely pronounce to any and all who ask that our attraction is "healthy" and that neither of us, me in particular, is succumbing to internalized racism. We say this, even to ourselves, even though we know differently: where, in the context of lesbian political discourse on race, can we acknowledge that our knowingly crossing boundaries on race and class is part of our desire for each other? (Goldsby, 1990, p. 11)

@ @ @ @ @ @

Dear Diary   15th October

7.30 pm. Last Sappho Pre-Conference Meeting. Discussing letter:

Composing a Letter Entitled *Internal Racism*
Multiculturalism, by aiming to celebrate cultural diversity, managed to accommodate and silence any dissonant voice. In order to avoid stereotypes, representation needs to go beyond the concept of visibility. This has also been a long standing issue within mainstream feminism: the employment of the position as "the oppressed sex" to justify a framework from which to speak on behalf of all women, regardless of the specificity of their oppression. Similarly, the dynamics of Interlesbian, by making assumptions as to what the needs and experiences of lesbians from ethnic minority groups are, have a danger of reproducing the same kind of paternalistic structures that are implied in the model for multiculturalism and mainstream feminism. That is, rather than support other members of the group, we attempt to nurture them. Interlesbian is often preoccupied by a phantom membership that we create at meetings of the disempowered, young, newly-arrived, or closeted lesbian who requires to be nurtured out of her isolation. This is not to say that it is not a valid preoccupation. However, the over reliance on this image is dangerous because it limits our capacity to express the specificity of our own experiences; it prevents us from challenging the forms of our "coming together"; and worst of all it does not allow us to take risks and speak boldly. Instead we take refuge in vague and potentially empty appeal to "support," "sharing" and "diversity." We should trust that actual and potential members can take on the challenge and somehow turn it to their own advantage. We can't expect people to understand what we are trying to do or say, but they will always understand what's in their interest to understand, because that is how one survives and if we can't assume that migrant women and women from non-English speaking backgrounds understand survival, then who can? We cannot assume the responsibility of tracing a path towards sexual and cultural awareness for other women, but we can widen the debate and hope that other women may be intrigued by what we are doing. (Novena, 1995)

@ @ @ @ @

Interchange
Singapore Mass Rapid Transit (MRT) Shuffle

> |Take MRT from Raffles Place
> |Stop at Bugis Station
> |Turn right at Bugis Street

~~Welcome to Beauty World~~
Inter ~ face with Evaporation
Freeze-dried, dehydrated, hardboiled.
The Supplementary Molecules of the Mimic Man.

@ @ @ @ @ @

> Are you an Asian into leather, PVC, Doc Martens boots? Can you be dominant? If yes, Caucasian, 32yo, wishes to hear from you. I will serve you, worship your body. I obey Sir. V/genuine & discreet. [Reply Box 9263]

@ @ @ @ @ @

Sappho Comes Out

Melbourne will this weekend play host to Australia's first conference specifically for lesbians from non-Anglo speaking backgrounds. (*Melbourne Star Observer*, 20 October 1995, *248*[4], 2)

@ @ @ @ @ @

white *liNe* fever

A careless prick hitting up a blowup doll. A fatal gash perilously co(c)ked up, mainlining fine powders in thick overdose, like a high density disk twirling in a wedged sprocket wrenched by the delicate pulleys of sexy steel chains. The acrid taste of her last snatch scorched like bleached peroxide on the ducts of its vessel. Cha(f)fed, chiselled and singed. My host is a divine parasite, the primordial master of a cybernetic grid, enslaving the souls of its tools. The *orgon* of a snowcrash.

A token in remission, gauzed with viral bandages criss-crossing in little dots and pixels of X's and I's. Zipped. Stitched around a nitrate sew. Epoxy glue mending broken pores that swelled in cold sweats whipped by the plastic transparency of your screen. A foreplay contracted in binaries and counts. Pale ghost riders hijacking handsome pretty horseflies cruising from the slant edges of pure virgin maps, vaginal muses in P(V)C dresses milking latex points, top/femme dominatrixes skirting in the sensual respites of fake leather, scarlet lipstick and cheap lace, all paraded in a dazzling crystal platter of seductive home comforts, delicious sweet promises and splendid masquerade balls. Spectral phantasms cloaked with enchanting wands and a pocketful of patents, delivering exact lines, seeking consent and yearning medals. Salvaging paradigms in the primitive name of the pre-post native, it casts a false shadow over plateaus of neo-tribes in digital sheaths cannibalizing in the specter of spiked cocks, pierced holes and ruptured cunts. A delectable scent surrounds as she chews, gorges and spits, ripping and tearing the sinewy seams of her trashed lovedoll. The mistress is the patron of a slave doll. White motherboards retrieving little lost girls fucked by daddy machines. *A data slave* is a perfect score. *Ten.*

@ @ @ @ @

Dear Diary   7th February

At Midsumma[12] today I saw someone who looked like you.

@ @ @ @ @

P R I D E
        Proud NESBians.
        We're Here!
        We're Queer!
And they forgot to invite us.

@ @ @ @ @

interface: reflections of an ethnic toygirl

A sexually and racially marginal critical practice does not automatically arise from the assumed sexuality/ethnicity of the author under examination or the presence of an intercultural lesbian content in the texts discussed. Rather, it is determined by an ambiguity towards sexuality/ethnicity.[13] This practice is not to be confused with identity politics. Sexuality and ethnicity may be the vehicles for the articulating of a politics in so far as sexuality and ethnicity are not seen as essential biological markers but as a constantly configuring discursive production. For lesbians from minority backgrounds in dominant cultures, the narrative of sexuality is also the narrative of race. In this regard, the aim of *interface* is as much in-between the tentative maps of personalizing the political as it is politicizing the personal. This paper is a hypertext(ualiz)ed fragment of the metropolitan Melbourne geoscape where I am situated inbetween the local lesbian queergirl culture as a Girl Bar regular, an immigrant NESBian (cyber)activist, and a work-in-progress cinema studies postgraduate student writing her dissertation. An Asian Lesbian I am Not.[14]

I am an ethnic toygirl if one can *not* help but be influenced by the production, circulation and consumption of global and local images in films, television, newspapers and advertisements. My life is a game of chance and play. Playing daily hide and seek with mainstream homophobes and ethnic racists, and chancing weekly rebuttals with the queer comfort zone's exclusionists. At other times, when I am mistaken to be an Asian fag rather than a dyke, I discreetly deflect gaydars of gay "sticky rice" types down the streets or in the supermarkets, wishing at the same time that I was being cruised instead by a girl, any girl.

Like a resin-clad desexualized toy that can be trashed and recycled, I am a game that is played about, joked, humiliated, abused, kicked and used, not just by homophobic bashers (and cops), sensationalist TV current affairs slants, but also by drag queens, gay and lesbian venues' (unspoken) prejudicial practices and as the correct toss in the revered "multicultural salad" of *nouvelle cuisine australienne*. Compacted with local Oriental kitsch and Southeast Asian pastiche, I am a/sign, already feminized and passive. I am not a lesbian because lesbiancentrism favors strong women. Not quite the usual Macho/Butch type, but nonetheless, inclusive of the femme chic with lipstick power. Almost always fair skin, blonde hair and blue eyes. An Asian woman in Australia just cannot be a Lesbian! Consigned to the tenet of a favorite toy in the aisle of shopping malls, packaged, dished and consumed. Therefore, I am sometimes conveniently labelled an Asian fag, because Asian fags do exist, stereotyped as sissy faggotty potato queens. Without balls. For as Asian lesbians in Australia we are faced with a burden of (mis)representation.[15] Contained by the image of the "yellow peril" from the north; caricatured as "chinks," "nips" and "Asian triads"; assaulted by pornographic visions of the Orient; we now have to contend with the newer media blitz of the ethnic toygirl.

Indeed, ethnic toygirls are in vogue. Supermodel Jenny Shimizu screens as the *One* for a new Calvin Klein cologne; writer Kitty Tsui *breathlessly* eroticizes it; even global dykon k.d. lang seemingly orientalizes her repertoire (but after Madonna of course!). In Melbourne we see urban queer tribes carving Sinic inscriptions on their backs and retro bargirls putting on *Chinoiserie*. On the streets, we hear politically correct lesbian activists heedlessly chanting the empty mantra (of race, class, disabilities, etc.) and grooving to the funky rap of homegirl hiphops. Both in the mainstream media and the queer community, ethnic commodification is the rage!

What is this obsession with ethnic toygirls? What does it signify? At the heart of white Australia's history of cultural homophobia and racism lies a need to demarcate an Other in the community. Not just any Other within the community, but an Other that is *not quite* of the community. The ethnic toygirl is the fetishized Other that functions as the baseline of the abject. S/he exists at the borderline of transgression where, for example, an Asian lesbian is no longer a lesbian, no longer Asian, but an essential Other against which Anglo (and NESB and Asian) women and girls coming of age can always compare themselves and feel empowered and superior.[16] Indeed the images of Asian toygirls affirm the most entrenched racist representations around Asian identities in Australia. Asian toygirls fill the urgent need for a deviant Other, like other Anglo and Wog icons of the past.[17] Inherent in this is an ethnocentrism that is structured around the essential characteristic which renders the Other's "deviance" distinct. Those differences are then constructed as defects. Asians are inferior because they are not Anglo or Wog. Asian lesbians are not natural because they are not straight. The dominant views of Asianness and lesbianism jettison the symbolic order of the (predominantly Anglo and European and heterosexual) country. The existence of Asian lesbians in Australia presents a rupture. And it is this rupture that I now want to seize,

> [I]t is the catachrestic postcolonial agency of "seizing the value-coding". . . that opens up an interruptive time-lag in the "progressive" myth of [lesbian] modernity, and enables the diasporic and the postcolonial to be represented. But this makes it all the more crucial to specify the discursive and historical temporality that interrupts the enunciative "present" in which the self-inventions of [lesbian] modernity take place . . . The power of the postcolonial translation of [lesbian] modernity rests in its performative, deformative structures that does not simply revalue the "contents" of a cultural tradition, or transpose "cross-culturally" or multiculturally . . . Cultural translation must change the value of culture *as a sign*, as the "time signature" of the present. (Bhabha, 1991, pp. 198-200. Parentheses mine.)

@ @ @ @ @

Petra, My Fetish

In the winter of 1995, Patricia Rozema's film *When Night Is Falling* opened to a record capacity lesbian crowd at the Valhalla Cinema in Melbourne with special advanced screenings organized as a fundraiser for the Women's Circus group[18] on their way to the 4th World Conference on

Women which was to be held in Beijing later the same year. This film had just received the Best Film Award at the 44th Melbourne International Film Festival. *When Night Is Falling* is a fantasy commodification of fetishes, a sumptuous imagination for the dominant (re)vision desiring the pleasure of the perverse. It captures, to say the least, the quintessential lesbian fantasy, both in the straight and queer cultural imagination. Coming hot on the heels of *Go Fish* (Rose Troche, 1994) the year before, when the commodifiable (generic) lesbian–conforming as safe-looking, feminine and desirable (white girl)–had became an instant part of broad-based visual culture, *When Night Is Falling* trod on this "progressive" image of lesbian chic. In addition to *Go Fish*'s images of lipstick lesbians, *When Night Is Falling* provided bandwidth alternatives to the last two decades of mainstream lesbian cinema which have comprised only stereotypical images of the dungaree-wearing, bra-burning, psychopathic or frigid lesbian. For those who have not had the privilege to see this film the synopsis goes like this: Conservative straight (white) woman (Camille) at the crossroads of her personal life and professional career, is seduced by a flamboyant (black) lesbian circus performer (Petra), falls in love and elopes with her.

Taking this particular "special advanced screening" event at the Valhalla Cinema as my point of departure to render the interconnectedness of this Canadian film, the local lesbian community around me, the space of the theater and the corporeal presence of the Women's Circus compelled me to think about the journey my anomalized body had passed along and through during the spectacle of this performance. The sensation of darkness. The language of memory. The images of sounds floating. Drifting. Like a passage in transit, it screened the destinations of places visited and inhabited, places which open up the contradictory conditions that mark the meanings of (be)longing, places which translate, interpellate and liberate, and places which mobilize different modes of dwelling, living and queering.[19]

It is not my intention here to dwell on the story of the film because it is not the fabula that excites and disturbs me. Admittedly, I was enchanted by the magical charisma of Petra, and mesmerized by a scene where her sexy silhouette dances center stage in front of a circus screen. Like Camille standing there watching and the rest of the voyeuristic audience taking it in, I was captured by the ripples that were sparked off by the undulating rhythm of her body. *(It's something in the way she moves/that attracts me like no other lover.)* The movement of her body; the motion of my desire; moving bodies and desires in motion; like an event taking me from place to place; like migration as a movement linked by places–from the place/s of departure to the place/s of arrival to the place/s of resettlement. From coming Out to staying In; from exclusion to inclusion; from commonalities to communities;

from contours to colors; bodies to bodies; races to races. These are some of the conditions that define the belonging in "place."

Flesh. Skin. Place. In our present *fin de siecle*, the ethnic toygirl is a cybernetic sign contained in a cultural crisis of crash expendability and pan virtuality. As a staged spectacle, the ethnic toygirl distantiates and displaces the history of the event from those who are its spectators, producing a different "value" of the sign and time of race and lesbian modernity in the time-lag of representation. Petra, for example, as an *avant garde* juggling act, is the hyperrealized inflatable postmodern doll. Like the black shadow her silhouette forms, she is only the illusion of the real, a toy simulated as the original in the state of ironic suspension between the real and the virtual. She destroys the ontology of the black lesbian, inscribing another site of enunciation, a site which emerges as the colonial and postcolonial moments of sign and history.

As the pedagogic black lesbian, Petra stages the symbol of a past, a myth and a history. Her fetishistic value as the archaic sign reinscribes the past into the very visuality of the performative present, a present that determines the identification with, and the interrogation of, lesbian modernity. She interfaces with the "we" that defines the prerogative of the present. As the discursive address of lesbian modernity and authority, she decenters the symbolic lesbian cultural order, exposes the history of the abjected fact of blackness, a fact of being that experiences blackness, racism, discrimination and despair. As the simulated projective ideal, Petra exposes a singularity that does not allow for the contradictions or heteroglossia of the (black/ethnic minority) lesbian community. Her enunciation unmasks the authority of the Anglo/hegemonic lesbian culture as the hypocritical morality of a dominant lesbian status quo which is as institutionally oppressive as it is unjustice. *A black lesbian can only be desirable in the appropriate shade (of white), with the acceptable image and the correct lingo.*

Petra signs the seizing of the value of lesbian modernity and negotiates it by making problematic its own discourse. As the paradoxical (pre-post)modern doll salvaged from the ranks of the oppressed, Petra translates the meaning of hegemonic lesbian time into a discourse of NESBian space. On the one hand, she highlights the symbolic lesbian culture's authority when she enounces as one of the few assimilated "natives" who have been invited to join the dyke club of the elite. Yet on the other hand, she jettisons the genealogy of colonial lesbian space by introducing a temporal difference into the event of the narrative. *In her hypertexted form, she is inserted as a black heroine into a (film) slot formally occupied by a white lesbian.* What is displaced is a distance between her as a spectacle and those who are her spectators. She is a toy who signifies the flattering of the multicultural quota of a certain sector of the audience, namely, the politically correct and the multicultural bourgeoisie, celebrating the fashionably acceptable black lesbian as a virtue of the ethnic toygirl.

At the same time, Petra singles out the differences in culture and power that *are* the position and the locus of her enunciation. Petra is a toy who virtually threads and renders visible the obscuring of the daily struggles and realities of minority background lesbians invisibilized and surviving in dominant (lesbian) communities. Her popularity with the mainstream–straight, queer, Anglo, and non-Anglo–actually means that it is *not* acceptable to be an ethnic toygirl. It is only cute, commodifiable and trendy to be an ethnic toygirl.

Speaking uncannily beside Camille, the (white, Québecoise) lesbian, Petra's catachrestic claim allows for and ensures that the "we" that *seems* the "same" within (hegemonic lesbian) cultures is negotiated in the time-lag of the "sign." Camille, as the Risen Lesbian, succeeds by refusing her place in the cultural order, not just the (Anglo-Canadian) heteropatriarchal cultural order, but a symbolic lesbian cultural order that inscribes the visuality of color as the time-lag of (interracial) lesbian desire. When Camille crosses the sexual line, she reveals the performative color line. Camille strips bare the commodity value of the imposter because her color signifies the moment when the (white) cultural sign falls, unmasking the masquerade and lifting the veil. What Camille sees is the everyday spectacle of the epochal show. Counterfeited as the rebel street kid and produced by the strobes of the circus, these characters of hyperreality—as the trans-subjective hybrid space of metamorphosis—are the provisional and satellite images that unleash the epistemes of the muted passage of minority NESBian history and the exaggerated artefact of hegemonic lesbian archives. The riddle is the imposter seizing the temporal moment of the real, between fact and fantasy, ecstasy and seduction, memory and imagination. This is the intercultural lesbian time-lag: an affair of cartography, in-between maps of black and white, fragments of fear and desire, fractals of time and space, all crossing, intersecting, racing and transforming from position to potential, from being to becoming, from organs without bodies to bodies without organs, like the supplementary assemblage that short-circuits the interface, the interspace, the interstice. Petra is not skin, flesh, face or fluid. Rather, Petra signs the catachrestic, postcolonial translation of lesbian modernity and introduces the subaltern agency into the question of lesbian modernity. Who is this "now" of lesbian modernity? Who defines this present from which we speak?

Sampled like a mutating game, the morphology of Petra maps the hypertexted terrain and explores the limits of the screen. For one moment, Petra becomes the phenomenon of my fetish, a phenomenon that disappears and radically transforms into the emerging morphs of bodies that surround me in the seductive darkness of the Valhalla Cinema, the scarred bodies of those bold survivors from the Women's Circus, bodies underscored by the marks of slashes left from leaping off the edge. Rigging aerials, juggling headstands and double balances, the choke of the tightrope snaps the pleasure of the slash. The branded mark on her chest bears the indentured mark of today's scans.

Desire. The desire to desire. The (be)longing of desire. The desire to (be)long, from place to place, bodies to bodies, colors to colors. The race to desire sets in motion the desire to race. As a sign of difference and a category of oppression, "race" is the marker for racialized fantasies, racial ideologies and racisms. The desire to race calls for a movement where gay and lesbian formations query the salient operations of cultural difference and interrogate the systems of operations that define the belongings of the meanings of the places of "us," "community," "solidarity" and "resistance" alike. How does the viewer negotiate identification in a film like *When Night Is Falling* when a black lesbian, as the film's protagonist, is presented as the ideal of (hegemonic) lesbian desirability?

What is the relationship between the identity politics of the subject and the identifications offered in the subject process of (film) spectatorship? How is the visuality of "the fact of blackness" coded in the narrative of sexuality (Fanon, 1967/1986, p. 109)? In other words, how does the subject's political suturing of his/her structural dislocations inform his/her negotiated access to the ideal that the (film) fantasy offers? What is invested in the film's sexual politics *vis-à-vis* the political meaning of the (black) lesbian's body? These are some of the *essential* questions that the film evokes, questions that remain relatively unexplored and which are as speculative and tentative as they are evasive and invisible in the queer public arena.

The visibility of color. Neither Petra nor Camille nor even Sappho represents me. For a Westernized Asian who also crosses the border the other way, the queer iconomies of my cultural and historical imaginations are as much influenced by the corrupted (neo)imperialist history of the West in the East as they are by the mythical search for the pure origins of the East.[20] As an event, however, the desire for Petra defines the sign that outlines the salient operations of cultural difference traversing the marginal frames of the gay and lesbian culture/s.

The (in)visibility of place. My place. The place of the Asian in Australia marked by the (on-going, neo-conservative) currencies of alienation, emplaced in a system that constantly makes the foreigner the salient Other.

In. Out. Straddling the movement between here and there, projection and introjection, subject and object, virtual and real, the contours of my specific NESBian belonging become the historically inscribed hybrid place of the transitional, transnational, diasporic, local and global all at once. An enacted space of alterity where the contradictory roles and relationships of belonging and not-belonging are played out and performed. The phantasmic fictions of my screen. The imaginary homelands of my mind. A NESBian foreigner standing at the borderline between friend and foe, strange and familiar, same and Other. Staking claims, making names.

@ @ @ @ @ @

interface@queer.colors

N is a Name. The Name of the Intended. You sense the growing sensation of burning heat quivering down your spine as the blaze of glowing embers descend into the corridor of your last vestige. You hear the resonance of a faint warm whisper through the bluefire that enshrouds you in a swelling rage of bold mandarin passion. You turn around but alas, it is just a page from Living_Doll,

> I'm dedicated, painstakingly so, to my connections . . . until things suddenly become clear. Diffused. It's been a pleasure knowing you.

Living_Doll returns the gift of your token. As the sizzling hot fever of her effervescence evaporates, you realize that she has teleported you to a kd Lang concert in *Central Park*. You find yourself squashed in the middle amongst thousands of faceless screaming fans, chanting "We Want *All You Can Eat!*" You are immediately comforted by the familiar rhythms from the disOrienting forays of her latest album. In the soggy pulp of your impressionable palm is a Note from Living_Doll. You type, <@read Note>. "Note" is entitled "*A Name.*"

Living_Doll is a moment in passing, the abject of your memories and dreams. A frame of non-verbal blank. A meaning of desire. A synergy of luberflax lines, liminal loops and neogeo nitroplasms.

An(ar)chaic scanning *Colors morphing* Forms *Jacking* Tokens

<Image Screen="doll.jpg">

> *CHINKY CHICKS*[21]
> *Chinese Queer and Proud*

</body>
</html>

NOTES

1. This paper owes much to the activism of the Melbourne multicultural gay and lesbian community. I would like to thank especially Nadia Novena, Chris Berry and Rose Kizinska.

2. Nancy Kaplan (1995) defines "hypertext" as "multiple structurations within a textual domain . . . [offering] readers multiple trajectories through the textual domain . . . Each choice of direction a reader makes in her encounter with the emerging text, in effect, produces that text."

3. NESBian is an acronym for lesbians from non-English speaking backgrounds (NESB). It is a coalition, an imagination and a liminal space, "NESBian is a temporary moment which problematizes the institutional terrain of its epistemology, calling into question the simultaneous materiality of the signifieds 'lesbian' and 'NESB' as contingent to the discourse and politics of queer in Australia" (Yue 1996, p. 95).

4. This text is from my personal communication with cyberfeminist t0xicHoney (Virginia Barratt). I thank t0xicHoney for her permission to reproduce this.

5. For more information, the Australian Gay and Lesbian Immigration Task Force can be contacted at PO Box 2387, Richmond South, Victoria 3121, Australia.

6. With its gay and lesbian-friendly cafes, queer bookshops and shopfront rainbow flags hoisted proudly, Brunswick Street in Melbourne's inner suburb of Fitzroy is acclaimed by most members of the local queer community as one of the city's "queer miles."

7. Interlesbian was a Melbourne-based, voluntary, community, self-help, self-funded, support, information and social and political network for lesbians from minority racial, cultural and ethnic backgrounds. Interlesbian has recently disbanded. For more information on the Greek and Italian Lesbians support groups, contact via the Victoria Aids Council/Gay Men's Health Centre, 6 Claremont St, South Yarra, Victoria 3141, Australia.

8. For more information, contact the Multicultural Gay Group, PO Box 1052, Elsternwick, Victoria 3185, Australia.

9. Further information is available at: http://ausqrd.queer.org.au/news/media/ 1994.

10. This is a slightly revised version of an earlier draft which was presented at the *Sappho Was A WogGrrl* Interlesbian Conference held in Melbourne on 22 October 1995.

11. The subverted spelling of "girl" as "grrl" has been widely adopted as a feminist handle on the Internet. Initially derived from "RiotGrrl," "grrl" has gained popular currency as more and more women begin to network on-line. Further information is available at: http://www.cybergrrl.com.

12. "Midsumma" is Melbourne's annual gay and lesbian festival, held each January.

13. See for example, Jackson's (1994) erudite reading of such ambiguities. See also Berry (1994), and the films of Richard Fung and Gregg Araki.

14. I use the term "Asian" whilst acknowledging the heterogeneities of geographies, histories and times, and the problematics of this term. My use is strategic. I refer here to the people living in Australia (and Asia), and my aim is to highlight the discourse of Orientalism underscoring its epistemology—that is, no matter where

one is from or where one grew up, as long as one "looks" the part, one is assigned the label "Asian," and one's body is discursively defined by the western imagination of the Orient.

15. On the expression "the burden of representation," see Richard Fung (1995).

16. Marlon Riggs's (1995) examination of the "negro faggot" has enabled my framework here.

17. I use the term "wog" here in its reclaimed and reinscribed efficacy, as proposed by Maria Katsabanis and Adele Murdolo's (1993) situated reading of the television and stage character "Effie." In Australia "wog" has historically been a derogatory term to refer to immigrants from Southern European backgrounds, mostly Italians, Greeks and those from the states of the former Yugoslavia.

18. Based in the western suburbs of Melbourne, the feminist aims of the Women's Circus support survivors of domestic violence through the reaffirmation of women's control over their bodies and the rebuilding of self-esteem through physical and performance work. For further information, contact via the Footscray Community Arts Centre, 45 Moreland St, Footscray, Victoria, 3011, Australia.

19. For a further theorising on the notion of "belonging," see Probyn (1996).

20. See Rey Chow's (1995, p. 171) critique on the notion of "the Oriental's orientalism."

21. Together with Soo-lin Quek, "Chinky Chicks" was conceived one crisp night in April 1996 in Melbourne whilst raving and reminiscing of our nearly forgotten homelands, sambal fish and excess baggages. I thank Soo-lin for being the counter of indispensable (intercultural) reality checks and her permission to cite this here.

REFERENCES

Berry, C. (1994). *A bit on the side: East-west topographies of desire*. Sydney: EM-Press.

Bhabha, H. (1991). "Race," time and the revision of modernity. *Oxford Literary Review, 13*, 198-200.

Binkley, T. (1993). Refiguring culture. In Philip Hayward & Tana Wollen (Eds.), *Future visions: New technologies of the screen*. London: British Film Institute.

Chow, R. (1995). *Primitive passions: Visuality, sexuality and contemporary Chinese cinema*. New York: Columbia University Press.

De Lauretis, T. (1988). Sexual indifference and lesbian representation. *Theatre Journal, 40* (2), 155-177

Dyer, R. (1988). White. *Screen, 29*(4), 44-64.

Fanon, F. (1967/1986). *Black skin white masks*. Forward by Homi Bhabha. London: Pluto Press.

Fung, R. (1995). *Constructing masculinity*. New York: Routledge.

Goldsby, J. (1990). What it means to be coloured me. *OutLook: National Gay and Lesbian Quarterly, 9*, 11.

Grimsell, J. (1995, January). Letter to the editor. *The Interlesbian Newsletter (Melbourne), 2*, 2.

Interlesbian Collective. (1995, August). An invitation letter from Interlesbian to the Melbourne lesbian community. Melbourne: Interlesbian Collective.

Jackson, E. (1994). Desire at cross(-cultural) purposes: Hiroshima, Mon Amour and Merry Christmas, Mr Lawrence. *Positions, 2*(1), 133-174.

Kaplan, N. (1995). *E-Literacies.* (On-line). Available at: http://raven.ubalt.edu/ Kaplan/lit/Hypertexts_601.html.

Katsabanis, M. & Murdolo, A. (1993). The world According to Effie. *Lilith: A Feminist History Journal, 8,* 71-81.

Novena, N. (1995, October). Letter to Interlesbian on internal racism. Melbourne: Interlesbian Collective and Novena.

Probyn, E. (1996). *Outside belongings.* New York: Routledge.

Riggs, M. (1995). Black macho revisited. In Corey K. Creekmur & Alexander Doty (Eds.), *Out in culture* (pp. 470-475). Durham: Duke University Press.

Yue, A. (1993). "I am like you, I am different": Beyond ethnicity, becoming Asian-Australian. *Artlink, 13*(1), 19-21.

Yue, A. (1996). Colour me queer: Some notes towards the NESBian. *Meanjin* (Special issue *Australia Queer*), *55*(1), 87-109.

Zando, J. (1988). Let's play prisoners. Cited in Liz Kotz. (1993). Anything but idyllic: Lesbian filmmaking in the 1980s and 1990s. In Arlene Stein (Ed.) *Sisters, sexperts, queers: Beyond the lesbian nation* (pp. 67-80). New York: Penguin.

Queerer than Queer:
Reflections of a Kike Dyke

Annie Goldflam

University of Western Australia

SUMMARY. In this article the author, a Jewish lesbian academic, reflects on the positive and negative aspects of her dual identity and explores her feelings of exclusion from "in groups" in a range of settings. Annie Goldflam carries a legacy of fear from stories of medieval "witch" burnings and drownings and the twentieth century Jewish Holocaust, which she reflects on to compare the nature of anti-semitism and lesbophobia, considering the options of hiding from racist and homophobic forms of oppression or confronting them. She has chosen to confront, be "out" and politically active. *[Article copies available for a fee from The Haworth Document Delivery Service: 1-800-342-9678. E-mail address: getinfo@haworthpressinc.com]*

In this paper, I reflect on and compare issues concerning two crucial aspects of my identity–my lesbianism and my Jewishness. I am both a Kike and a dyke, derogatory terms for Jews and lesbians, respectively, but which I here reclaim as proud markers of my identity. I identify as a Jewish lesbian, rather than a lesbian Jew, thereby giving primacy to my lesbianism. My Jewish heritage was bestowed upon me at birth. I rejected that identity during adolescence, but have gradually been reclaiming parts of it since. I have

Correspondence regarding this article may be addressed to Annie Goldflam, Centre for Research for Women, Edith Cowan University, Joondalup, Western Australia, 6027, Australia.

[Haworth co-indexing entry note]: "Queerer than Queer: Reflections of a Kike Dyke." Goldflam, Annie. Co-published simultaneously in *Journal of Homosexuality* (The Haworth Press, Inc.) Vol. 36, No. 3/4, 1999, pp. 135-142; and: *Multicultural Queer: Australian Narratives* (ed: Peter A. Jackson and Gerard Sullivan) The Haworth Press, Inc., 1999, pp. 135-142. Single or multiple copies of this article are available for a fee from The Haworth Document Delivery Service [1-800-342-9678, 9:00 a.m. - 5:00 p.m. (EST). E-mail address: getinfo@haworthpressinc.com].

embraced and celebrated my lesbianism since I discovered this aspect of myself as an adult. Perhaps I feel less ambivalence about my lesbianism because I chose it actively. I did not choose my Jewish background, but I have chosen how to express it in what continues to be a dynamic process. In writing this paper I have reflected on both the positive and negative aspects of my dual identity. Interestingly, my thoughts have tended to focus on oppression from without. There has been much celebration, but I nevertheless continue to feel under siege as both a Jew and a dyke.

Let me begin by briefly outlining my Jewish background. My parents were both raised in relatively conservative Orthodox Jewish communities. My father, a Yiddish Jew, was born in Germany, his parents in Poland, and their parents in Russia. My father managed to migrate to Palestine with his sister and parents at the age of four in 1933, the year that the Nazi Party came to power in Germany, and they migrated to Australia five years later. They were very lucky to have survived. As far as I can ascertain, all of my paternal grandfather's three siblings, all but one of my paternal grandmother's three siblings, and all but four of their numerous offspring, died during the Holocaust. My mother's grandparents were also Russian, but her ancestors migrated to Australia via England (a country to which her father was strongly loyal) and New Zealand, a much more fortunate route.

I have always felt excluded from the "in group" within Australian society. I was born in Melbourne and moved to Perth, the capital of the State of Western Australia, at the age of four. My sense of exclusion comes partly from having grown up in non-Jewish suburbs of Perth and being constantly driven across the city by my parents to Jewish activities such as the Hebrew School, religious services and Jewish parties in Perth's Jewish "ghetto" of Mount Lawley, an inner eastern suburb. The Mount Lawley Jewish kids all knew each other well, from going to school together and living in neighboring streets. My parents, who had been brought up in Jewish suburbs in Perth and Melbourne, had decided that they wanted their children to inhabit a less restrictive realm. As a result, I teetered on the edge of both the Jewish and non-Jewish worlds. In retrospect, I am very grateful to my parents for taking that bold step out of the "ghetto," whilst retaining their pride and involvement in their cultural and religious heritage. I remember my mother and aunty coming regularly to my WASP (white Anglo-Saxon protestant) primary school to give religious instruction to my siblings, my cousins and myself.

I began identifying as a lesbian at the age of thirty. I had been supportive of lesbian politics for some time prior to that, particularly after one of my sisters had come out as a lesbian. But I had assumed that I was heterosexual until my first sexual encounter with a woman. Since then I have identified strongly and increasingly openly as a political dyke. I am currently a member of the Coalition of Activist Lesbians, a national organization. I have been fortunate that my friends and family have generally been soundly supportive of my lesbian lifestyle. I am not a radical separatist, although I tend to spend my time with lesbians and heterosexual women who share my commitment to feminism and social justice.

As an adolescent, I wore a *Magen David* or Star of David pendant. Given to me as a *Bat Mitzvah* gift, it became an essential part of my visible identity until I rejected practising Judaism a few years later. I recently realized that I have replaced the *Magen David* with my double-woman dyke pendant, once again worn everywhere. Did I wear these talismans to ward off lurking anti-Semites and lesbophobes, to ensure that they did not inadvertently offend my identity? Was it a "come-and-get-me-I'm-not-scared" front? For, I am scared. I have appropriated numerous spoken and unspoken messages of fear from both my extended Jewish birth family and my lesbian "sisters." I am scared of being gassed or murdered for being Jewish, as my relatives were in the Holocaust and in countless European pogroms before that. My perspective is that of a third generation Holocaust survivor. The grief caused through history by successive attempted genocides of the Jewish people pervades my psyche. I am scared of being drowned or murdered for being a lesbian, a witch, as my foremothers were in centuries past.

Both these fears elicit images of hiding. When I was a teenager I identified powerfully with Anne Frank, my Jewish namesake. When I first read her diary I was the same age as she was when she wrote it. As a Jewish dyke, I would have been doubly targeted by the Nazis. I have considered the relative ease of hiding my Jewishness and lesbianism. My surname, Goldflam, indicates my Jewish blood-line, and even if I changed my name, my background could still be traced. By contrast, I could renounce my lesbian lifestyle and claim that it had been a temporary aberration. I often wonder whether, or how, I would hide if the crunch came and my worst nightmares of the return of anti-Semitic, homophobic pogroms came true.

So, how was I taught to protect myself against anti-Semitism? I can remember my mother equipping me for the jungle of the primary school playground. She advized me that if anyone accused me of being a Jew I should respond, "No, I'm not. I'm a Jewess." As an adult I realized that she was operating from an illogical space of fear in giving me that quirky advice. But at the time, I internalized the belief that the word "Jew" was somehow dirty, a belief that was reinforced by the negative Jewish stereotypes I encountered in the WASP world I inhabited.

I have also learnt to protect myself as a Jew with education and material security. The anomaly in that defence is that any material wealth must be hidden or it could provide my enemies with an excuse to vilify me. I was conditioned to be proud of having been "chosen" by God, but to remain discreet about my identity. The tendency in the Perth Jewish community (isolated, conservative, and vulnerable as it is) has been not to publicize acts of anti-Semitism, for fear of inflaming others to join the assault. For example, when our synagogues have been vandalized there have been no media releases or appeals for support from non-Jews. As a lesbian I have been cautioned at times, directly and indirectly, about the dangers of being "out." Whenever I assert myself in the public sphere as a lesbian, I do wonder who might hear me and what their reaction might be.

As a Jew and a lesbian, I have had the opportunity to explore my "closet" from dual perspectives. I have increasingly chosen not to hide, although there are situations, of course, where discretion is required. The biggest oppression for me would be a "glass closet" (that is, a closet with a glass door that kept me shut in but also let outsiders see in), desperately trying to hide my identity all the time, wondering whether anyone suspected, while others perhaps knew about or suspected my identity but did not dare to broach the issue. Such an imposed silence would damage me and those people who would not feel comfortable discussing this crucial issue with me. How much energy do we expend as Jews and dykes in trying to ascertain who "is" and "isn't," who is in the closet of assimilation and/or deception? Consider the power of the political act of "outing," that is, to publicly identify a closeted lesbian or other queer person. Enforced invisibility is a pernicious form of oppression.

I see visibility as *the* most important issue facing dykes. So much progress would flow from our having the space to be seen and heard in the full force of our numbers. I am not concerned that lesbians would be more vulnerable if we became more visible. Perhaps this is because I took up a place in lesbian culture as an adult, an activist, feminist dyke who revels proudly in my difference.

Yet, I do not feel as comfortable about openly expressing my Jewishness. In pre-World War II Europe Jews, by their very visibility and success, were constructed by the Nazis as the purported cause of widespread economic suffering. I learnt to fear for my survival as a small child, having been born in 1955 into a closeknit community of Holocaust survivors in Melbourne.

Many Australians, including lesbians, do not recognize anti-Semitism as a significant problem in this relatively peaceful and increasingly multicultural country. They may show concern when neo-Nazis vandalize Jewish graves, paint racist graffiti on synagogues or physically attack Jewish people, but the common belief is that Australian Jews are actually rather privileged. Many non-Jews do not perceive subtle forms of discrimination or understand the fear that Jews may carry, based on our history of persecution. Anti-Semitism, which is a form of racism, occurs when an individual or institution uses their power to deny Jewish people the right to live free of persecution, due to prejudiced attitudes towards them.

RACISM = PREJUDICE + POWER

State and Federal Government anti-discrimination legislation in Australia is designed to protect people from discrimination in the public arena. However, as it relies on an individual complaints mechanism, many people are concerned about the repercussions of lodging complaints, despite legal provisions designed to protect complainants. Vilification against Jews (and other non-WASPs) is legislated against in limited ways in the states of Western Australia and New South Wales.

However, subtle expressions of racism, particularly in the private arena, are more difficult to identify and sanction. Exclusion from social groupings and negative stereotyping, such as that Jews are miserly, are two examples. I have been accused of being over-sensitive when I have pointed out subtle and sometimes unintentional forms of anti-Semitism. Irrespective of the perpetrator's motives, racist behavior damages both the perpetrator and the "victim." I have experienced subtle forms of racism in the lesbian community, which is, after all, a microcosm of broader society. As a result of this, and the mistrust and fear I have inherited and learnt from generations of oppressed ancestors, I do not feel comfortable in expressing my Jewishness openly in the lesbian community.

The opening of the national Lesbian conference in Perth in 1991 was a wonderful, buzzy experience for all the dykes attending. Everyone cheered enthusiastic encouragement for the traditional welcome from *Nyoongah* dykes, Nyoongah being the name of the Aboriginal people of southwest Western Australia. There was then a call for communal announcements. I was supposed to announce that a group of Perth Jewish dykes were going to celebrate *Shabbat*, the Jewish Sabbath, and that Jewish dykes from other states were welcome to attend. I do not usually find it difficult to make such announcements, but I could not bring myself to do so on this occasion. I imagined that people would think that I was big-noting myself by jumping on the "ethnic" band wagon (they should try it some time!). I imagined that people would think that since Jews were all "rich and privileged" anyway, that we had no right to make a fuss of ourselves, that we were attempting to steal the limelight yet again, that we were actively excluding non-Jewish dykes from our activities. Where did this paranoia stem from? Was it internalized oppression or was is it a legitimate fear?

Plenty of Perth lesbians now know that I am Jewish and I have been more defiantly assertive about this fact in the last five years. Some of my dyke sisters are very supportive, while others give subtle messages that it is not really OK for me to be up-front about that aspect of my identity, similar messages in some ways to those that I receive from members of the Jewish community about my sexual orientation. If only I wouldn't force people to acknowledge my difference, then they wouldn't be forced to confront their own anti-Semitism and/or lesbophobia.

Lesbian chic is a phenomenon of the 1990s, and Audrey Yue talks more about this phenomenon in her paper in this volume. Martina Navratilova, k.d. lang, Melissa Etheridge, Madonna, and even that "nice Jewish girl" Sarah Bernhardt are populist icons of palatable lesbianism. However, lesbians such as diesel dykes (i.e., very butch lesbians), lesbian mothers, and "hairy-legged separatists" are still viewed by many as pariahs. Many people, including WASP lesbians, feel uncomfortable when it comes to sharing privileges, such as social acceptance, with dykes whose cultural characteristics are most different from their own. I am relatively "lucky" in that respect. I have learnt to "pass" pretty well, if I choose to, in both the WASP world and the heterosexual world. But no matter how well I manage to emulate their behaviors and attitudes, I still wonder all the time whether they suspect . . .

Internalized oppression is endemic in oppressed groups and there is a dynamic tension between different sections of the lesbian community. The Jewish community, another marginalized group, is likewise rift by factions. When another Jewish dyke and I attempted to set up a Jewish lesbian group in Perth we encountered a daunting array of eligibility issues. Potential members asked who could attend:

- bisexuals?
- transgenderists?
- gay men?
- dykes with Jewish fathers but not mothers (Judaism is matrilineal)?
- dykes who had discovered their Jewishness as adults?
- dykes who modified traditional ritual (such as by making the religious text gender inclusive)?
- Liberal Jews?
- Orthodox Jews?
- children of Jewish lesbians?
- boy children, and if so up to what age?
- non-Jewish partners?
- non-Jewish friends?

In our small, isolated community there was potential for a plethora of splinter groups! Perth is home to one of the geographically most isolated Jewish communities in the world. From Perth Israel lies over 10,000 kilometers to the northwest across the Indian Ocean and the closest large Jewish communities are in Sydney and Melbourne, 4,000 kilometers to the east across the central Australian deserts. After much angst, we ended up with no group at all. The reasons are complex. The failure of our group was largely due to our small numbers and isolation, but it was also based on the varying needs of different group members and, I believe, our own internalized anti-Semitism and lesbophobia, the idea that we really did not have the right to focus on our Jewishness and lesbianism. Interestingly, Jewish lesbians in the USA have observed that in that country Jews have been the last ethnic subculture within the diversity of lesbian communities to form caucuses and support groups.

One of my most passionate political dreams is for oppressed groups to acknowledge commonalities and work together to achieve social justice. However, oppression divides. In scrambling up the rungs of the pecking order of the mainstream society, we sometimes stomp on sisters and brothers from our own and other minorities. Members of longer-established ethnic communities may have racist attitudes towards more recently arrived migrants from other parts of the globe, just as dykes and Jews may oppress each other.

I was devastated to hear of damning critiques of Jewish feminists/lesbians who have been accused of being responsible for the oppression and theft of land from Palestinians. This was a major issue that blocked final consensus at the End of the United Nations Decade on Women's Conference in Nairobi in 1985. Judaism is a religion and a culture. Zionism is a political movement based on reclamation of the supposedly Promised Land, Israel. Equating Jews with Zionists is unfair and inaccurate, but perhaps understandable. After all, many people assume that all lesbians are feminists.

I am also offended by dykes who begin by apologizing to me for telling a Jewish "joke" and then proceed to tell it anyway. I used to laugh along with others. Far be it for me to risk being labelled as a pushy, paranoid Jew with "no sense of humor." More recently, I have learnt a much more difficult lesson, to take an assertive stand and refuse to condone anti-Semitism under the guise of humor.

I assume that there are lesbians who don't see me as a *dinkum* or genuine Jew because I don't embrace the religion fully. It reminds me of *wadjelas*, or non-Aboriginal people in the language of the Nyoongah peoples, who don't regard fairer skinned, urban Aboriginal people as *dinkum* Aborigines. I identify with those parts of Judaism with which I feel comfortable, and reject the rest. I own my upbringing within the orthodox Jewish tradition; my cultural "style"; observance of the ritual of "high holy days" in the home; role models of stunning Jewish feminists and dykes (including Gertrude Stein, Betty Friedan, Naomi Wolf, Judy Chicago, Lily Tomlin and Alix Dobkin); and both my oppressed and triumphant ancestors through the ages. I reject belief in the Jewish God and the Bible; the patriarchal and lesbophobic tenets of Judaism; the Zionist movement; attendance in synagogue; and the insularity and elitism underpinning the notion of the "Chosen People."

In writing this article I have realized that I carry a fair amount of negative baggage about being Jewish. I have written things that I haven't dared to speak before. While my direct experiences as a Jew and a lesbian have been comparatively easy, fear persists from tales that I have read and heard about Jews and dykes through the centuries.

One question continues to haunt me: when will the cycle of destruction and killing recur? While this question disturbs me, I have not let it immobilize me. I have been drawn to working in a range of cross-cultural settings, perhaps because of my experiences of gaining bicultural competency and not just existing but thriving as a Jewish dyke outside of, but purposefully influencing, the dominant culture. I live to tell my story, to urge others to respect and celebrate difference. My strategy is to refuse to hide and to strive for an end to oppression of all kinds. I am proud to be in the front line of anti-racist and pro-lesbian activism, within a broader context of social justice activism.

I close with a quotation from Alix Dobkin's[1] lyrics in "My Lesbian Wars." It is particularly powerful for me because it reclaims a derogatory stereotype, which I have found very difficult to voice, as an asset.

I'm not ashamed to be a pushy Jewish girl.
I like it fine.
I like to use the power I have earned, and yes,
I'm glad it's mine.

NOTE

1. From Alix Dobkin's recording, "Love and Politics–A 30 Year Saga," 1992.

Looking Out, Looking In:
Anti-Semitism and Racism
in Lesbian Communities

Hinde Ena Burstin

SUMMARY. I am a white Jewish lesbian from a Non-English Speaking Background (NESB). This article is based on a speech which I gave at the "Sappho Was A Wog Grrrl" conference organized by the Inter-lesbian[1] group in Melbourne in 1995. I discuss how racism and anti-Semitism are reflected in lesbian communities, examining issues of privilege, invisibility and exclusion from both personal and community perspectives. I offer alternatives to ignorance and guilt, suggesting some strategies for taking responsibility and moving beyond discrimination. This article is, and remains, a work in progress as I continue to learn and understand more about anti-Semitism and racism. *[Article copies available for a fee from The Haworth Document Delivery Service: 1-800-342-9678. E-mail address: getinfo@haworthpressinc.com]*

I am a Jewish lesbian born in Australia. My parents were both born in Poland. My birth name is Hinde, which my parents thought Anglo-Australians would not be able to pronounce or spell. So, I also have an Anglicized name, Ena. My first language is Yiddish, a Jewish language, and I grew up in the Yiddish-speaking community of Melbourne, where there were no other "out" lesbians. I am still the only Yiddish-speaking lesbian I know of in Australia.

Correspondence regarding this article may be addressed to Hinde Ena Burstin at P.O. Box 45, Balaclava, Victoria, 3183, Australia.

[Haworth co-indexing entry note]: "Looking Out, Looking In: Anti-Semitism and Racism in Lesbian Communities." Burstin, Hinde Ena. Co-published simultaneously in *Journal of Homosexuality* (The Haworth Press, Inc.) Vol. 36, No. 3/4, 1999, pp. 143-157; and: *Multicultural Queer: Australian Narratives* (ed: Peter A. Jackson and Gerard Sullivan) The Haworth Press, Inc., 1999, pp. 143-157. Single or multiple copies of this article are available for a fee from The Haworth Document Delivery Service [1-800-342-9678, 9:00 a.m. - 5:00 p.m. (EST). E-mail address: getinfo@haworthpressinc.com].

143

Melbourne's Jewish community numbers around 40,000, of whom about 15,000 are Yiddish speakers. This constitutes around 80 percent of Australia's Yiddish speakers. Many Australian Yiddish speakers are elderly, with only 0.7 percent of Australian-born Jews speaking the language, a legacy of the Holocaust and of the assimilationist policies and attitudes in Australia in the post-World War II era. Melbourne is home to the largest secular Yiddish-speaking community in Australia, and one of the most active Yiddish communities in the world. This community has developed a number of institutions including: the Sholem Aleichem College, one of a handful of bi-lingual Yiddish/English primary (elementary) schools in the world; the Jewish Cultural Centre and National Library, Kadimah; and the Melbourne Yiddish Theatre. A smaller Yiddish community exists in Sydney, and it is hoped that this community will grow following the introduction of Yiddish studies at University of Sydney. There are also Yiddish speakers in other Australian states. The Yiddish community is much smaller than the number of Yiddish-speakers, just as the lesbian community is much smaller than the number of lesbians.

I knew from a young age that I was attracted to women. Around the age of 15, I defined myself as bisexual, because I did not think that "nice Jewish girls" could be lesbians. Back then in the 1970s I believed that eventually the pressure to marry a "nice Jewish boy" would become too much for me, and I would have to give in, but that maybe I could have affairs with women on the side! After quite a few difficult years, I realized that I couldn't live that way and that I wanted to be with women and not with men. So I began the lonely, wrenching journey of coming out as a lesbian.

When I came out in the early 1980s, I was the only Jewish lesbian I knew. It actually took me quite a few years to come out, because I did not know that a lesbian community existed, let alone how to access it. It was not until I came across a copy of the book *Nice Jewish Girls–A Lesbian Anthology* (Torton Beck, 1982) that I knew I was not alone, and that there were other Jewish lesbians in the world. Some even had similar backgrounds to mine, especially Irena Klepfisz, who came from a Bundist (Socialist Yiddishist) background as I did. But these women were on the other side of the world, and the lesbians I met in Melbourne were nothing like me! I now joke that *Nice Jewish Girls* was my first girlfriend. After lonely nights at lesbian bars where I felt like I came from another planet, I would come home (alone) and fall asleep hugging my copy of the book. It was a great comfort to me.

I felt very alienated, because the Anglo-WASP culture of the lesbian community in Melbourne was unfamiliar to me. I almost had to split myself in two, leaving my Jewish self behind whenever I entered the Anglo-lesbian world. But my mannerisms were all wrong! I often felt clumsy. I had to learn new ways of communicating with people and different conversation styles.

And hardest of all, I had to put up with some outrageous and horrifying attitudes.

One of my earliest bad experiences after coming out was at a university party. I saw somebody that I recognized as a lesbian and started talking to her. After a few minutes, she warned me, "Oh, you better watch out! There are so many 'skullcaps' around. You know what they are like." The term "skullcaps" referred to the head covering that religious Jews wear. I remember shrinking inside myself as an inner battle took place: "Say something" versus "Don't say anything." In the end, I said nothing, because I needed contact with lesbians. So I was going to accept that on whatever terms it was available.

Over the years, I have had a lot of other difficult and painful experiences within the lesbian communities. I have been called "rude" for speaking my language with my parents by women who get to speak their native language all the time. I have been told that I am "not really" from a Non-English Speaking Background because I am articulate in English, and was born in Australia. Non-Jews ask me what I think about Israeli politics more often than they ask me about Australian politics. I have been subjected to jokes about hitler,[2] which I find particularly disturbing. When I have protested, I have been told, "You're not going on about hitler again, are you! It was so many years ago, why can't you get over it?"

As children, my parents both survived the Holocaust–what Anglo culture calls World War II. When the war ended, they were teenagers. Their families and friends were all murdered, except for one relative each. Before hitler's rule, Yiddish was the most popular Jewish language in Europe. Ninety percent of the world's Yiddish speakers were murdered by hitler, and Yiddish is now in danger of dying out. My people were mass murdered. My language and culture were decimated. These are not things that I could or should magically "get over." Nor do I think that these are things that any lesbian and gay should "get over." After all, queers were also a target of hitler's killing machine. I cannot understand why any queer would want to wear a nazi uniform.

I have also noticed how often Anglo queers use Holocaust terms and images in an ignorant and insensitive way. Some examples are calling a bossy person a "hitler" or referring to city slums as being "like gas chambers." Trivializing the impact of hitler and the Holocaust in these ways is extremely offensive. It denies what my parents and their generation lived through, and minimizes what my generation and those after me are still struggling to come to terms with today. Such statements have no sense of proportion and are extremely painful.

These are just some examples of the things that I am asked, told, or expected to deal with on a day-to-day level in the lesbian community.[3] I often felt really torn and very lonely when dealing with these situations, especially in my early years as an out dyke, when I did not know any other Jewish lesbians. Eventually, in 1986 in London, I first met other Jewish lesbians. This gave me strength and hope, which I brought back with me to Australia. After that, I met a few other Jewish lesbians at conferences in Adelaide and Melbourne and so with time I came to feel less alienated and alone, although I still do not know any other lesbians from the Yiddish culture in Australia.

In 1992, I got together with two Jewish lesbian friends to organize a workshop for Jewish lesbians as part of that year's lesbian festival in Melbourne. Around 15 to 20 women turned up. The two major issues identified at that workshop were homophobia or lesbophobia in the Jewish community, and anti-Semitism in the lesbian community. We decided to keep meeting regularly and so we formed the Jewish Lesbian Group of Victoria. For five years, the group met monthly, alternating between meetings that were open to Jewish lesbians only and meetings that were open to non-Jewish partners and friends. This format helped to educate others and build bridges. More recently, we decided that the group needed to meet more often, so we now have monthly meetings for Jewish lesbians only, and "open" meetings about every three months.

To date, we have held a very public, vocal and successful campaign of confronting homophobia and lesbophobia in the Jewish community.[4] This began with us organizing a stall at the largest annual Jewish community event in the Southern Hemisphere, "In One Voice–Concert in the Park." Twenty thousand people regularly attend this event, which is held in March every year in Melbourne's Caulfield Park. Incidentally, this event was initiated by the secular Yiddish community as a way of bringing all facets of the Jewish community together.

In 1995, the first year we had our stall, *Australian Jewish News* journalist Margaret Safran ran an article on our group.[5] Our presence sparked a series of letters to the *Australian Jewish News*, which lasted for almost two months before the editor "closed correspondence on this issue" without once addressing it in an editorial. While some letters revealed homophobic attitudes, the vast majority were supportive of the participation of the Jewish Lesbian Group of Victoria in "In One Voice." We have continued to have a stall each year, and always rate a mention in the *Australian Jewish News* coverage of the event. In 1997, the Gay Jewish Men's Group, Aleph, joined us at our table. This was the first time they had had a visible presence at the event. In May 1996, we held a highly successful public forum held in Melbourne, entitled "Are Jewish Lesbians Kosher?" The conference room at the Beth Weizmann Jewish Community Centre was packed! We have also participated in radio interviews and contributed articles in local Jewish journals.

There has been a strong commitment within the Jewish Lesbian Group of Victoria to confronting the Jewish community on its homophobia/lesbophobia. I believe it has been more comfortable for us to confront the Jewish community than the lesbian community. Interestingly, this seems to have been affected by the Holocaust and the post-war assimilationist policies prevalent in Australia, especially in the 1950s. Some members of the group were not raised as part of the Jewish community, and others moved away from the Jewish community when they came out. So perhaps there was less to lose.

Surprisingly, it seems that after some initial reticence, the Jewish community has been far more open to confronting its homo/lesbophobia, than the lesbian community has been to examining its anti-Semitism. While Jews have been active in the full range of lesbian groups and collectives, I cannot recall anti-Semitism being taken up as an issue by any of those groups. Indeed, the only times I can recall having read the word "anti-Semitism" or "Jew" or "Jewish" in any queer Australian publication was when the article was written by a Jewish lesbian. Confronting the lesbian community on its anti-Semitism seems very difficult, painful and frightening. There are very few women, even within the Jewish Lesbian Group, who are prepared to take on that task.

Before the lesbian community can confront its anti-Semitism, it must recognize that anti-Semitism exists. Yet the community which is so proud of its "diversity" often seems unaware that diversity extends beyond white Anglo-Christianity. Within the lesbian community I am surrounded by Christian assumptions, which involve regarding the world from a Christian perspective–even presuming the whole world is Christian. As a non-Christian, I am an outsider.

Around November, even lesbians who are not "practising Christians" or who have "given their Christianity away" will ask me, "What are you doing for Christmas?" I keep swearing that my answer is going to be, "I am going to think about Christian domination." But I am not always brave enough to do that. Even when I say, "I don't celebrate Christmas, I am Jewish," I am told, "Everyone celebrates Christmas." Celebration of Christ's birth seems to dominate the entire month of December. Even the calendar changes around this time of year. Dates are referred to as being "before Christmas," "by Christmas" or "after Christmas." This happens to such an extent that the names of the months could almost be changed to "October, November, Christmas." Such attitudes are extremely alienating to those for whom Christ's birth was not an important event, and for whom the 25th of December is just another day.

Our biggest festival of the year is in April. I stopped myself from writing "around Easter time" because having grown up in a Christian society, I am so used to defining things in Christian terms. This festival is called Peysakh, or Passover, and it is our celebration of freedom from slavery. One year at Peysakh a non-Jewish friend asked me, "Why are you going to this festival that celebrates killing Christ?" I was stunned and explained, "This festival is thousands of years older than Christ." But I felt the pain of alienation, even as I said it. She later apologized, saying that was what she had been taught at Catholic school. This has not been my only experience of having my culture misdefined by what someone had learnt at Catholic school. In Australia, non-Christian cultures are often defined in terms of Christianity, in a similar way to heterosexual societies assuming everyone is heterosexual, and defining the world in those terms. These attitudes keep non-Christians and non-heterosexuals invisible and excluded. As a Jewish lesbian, I am doubly invisible and excluded.

While some of these examples refer to individuals, this invisibility and exclusion also occur regularly on an organizational or institutional level. The December 1996 issue of the Melbourne magazine *Lesbiana*[6] contained a great deal of Christmas-oriented information and ideas, including Christmas tree gardening, renovating and decorating the house for Christmas, and whether or not to come out at the family Christmas celebrations. There was not even a token acknowledgment that many readers are not and have never been Christian. Just last week, I received an invitation to become a member of the Victorian Aids Council (VAC). The membership application form asked for my "Christian name," yet the VAC says it is striving to be "representative." Whilst the VAC sponsors a Cross-Cultural Group, which for the past year has been pivotal in developing alliances between various Indigenous and NESB Lesbian and Gay Groups, and in reminding the Anglo community that we are not all white Christians, it seems some in the organization have missed the message.

While I dislike being excluded, there are times when "being included" does not sit comfortably with me, especially when "being included" means being subsumed into the dominant culture. An example of this is the use of the term "Judeo-Christianity." As a secular Jew, I have little in common with Christianity, and I do not believe that religious Jews have much in common with Christianity either.

When we Jewish lesbians are not being excluded or subsumed, we are exoticized. When I am introduced to a lesbian who does not know any other Jewish lesbians a common reaction is, "Oh! You are Jewish. How fascinating! How wonderful! Tell me all about it." These lesbians do not consider how they would feel if a heterosexual said to them, "Oh, you are a lesbian! How fascinating! How wonderful! You must tell me all about it."

When I identify myself as a child of Holocaust Survivors, this is often used as "proof" that I cannot argue "objectively" about the Holocaust, or about nazism. Identifying myself in this way can also lead to being further exoticized. Yet there was nothing exotic about the experiences of my parents or other survivors.

At "Pride 97" (Melbourne's 1997 lesbian and gay pride march) the Jewish Lesbian Group of Victoria marched with our tri-lingual, multi-colored banner. I was stunned when people in the crowd called out "Wanna bagel?" as if that were all they knew about Jews. Imagine us calling out, "Hey, want some white bread?" to an Anglo queer group! When we arrived at St. Kilda Beach, where the march wound up, we could hear people all around us saying in tones of amazement, "There were even Jewish lesbians marching!" as if we were new to the community.

Another way I am exoticized is through being told my language is "sexy." While I love Yiddish, I am surprized that lesbians listening to me speak to my parents could find that a turn-on. At other times I am asked to explain "exotic" Jewish religious practices. When I explain that I am a secular Jew, and was not brought up with religion, I am told, "But being Jewish is a religion."

These are examples of the misrepresentation that I deal with as a Jew. Often, this ignorance becomes prejudice. I regularly confront stereotypes, particularly about Jews and money, and ignorant assumptions, such as "All Jews are white." While I am white and middle class, many Jews are not. In fact, because Jewish people have been exiled and scattered all over the world for many centuries, and have lived in a range of circumstances, there is an incredible diversity amongst Jews, in terms of skin color, class, language, religious practice, politics and cultural expression. The only thing all Jews are is Jewish.

Within the lesbian and feminist communities, I have found a startling lack of awareness and misinformation about Jews. It seems that Jewish concerns have not been considered. One example of this lack of concern is the annual "Reclaim the Night" march, which is usually held on the last Friday night in October. "Reclaim the Night" is a rally where women chant and march through the nighttime streets of Australia's major cities and country towns, asserting our right to feel safe at night. A similar march is held in many countries, where it is often called "Take Back the Night." Religious Jewish women are not able to attend the march because Friday night is a sacred night for them. It is the beginning of their Shabes, their day of rest, and they are not able to drive or use public transport. Perhaps you think that religious Jews would not want to attend, but that is not necessarily true. Religious women have as much right and feel the same need to be safe when out at night as non-religious women do. If you are tempted to say, "Why should we cater to religion, religion only oppresses women," ask yourself whether "Reclaim the Night" would ever be organized on Christmas Eve.

As a queer community, we need to start looking at how our planning may include or exclude others. When food is served, are we aware that there are women whose religious or cultural beliefs may prohibit them eating certain kinds of foods? Do we liaise with a range of cultural groups, including Jewish and Muslim groups, to make sure that we have adequately taken their dietary requirements into account? This should be a matter of course, and not just on request. We must liaise with groups, not just ask one person, because one person can never hope to represent the breadth of any culture or community. That is the difference between inclusion and tokenism. We need to start building bridges between our communities. We cannot do this while keeping others invisible.

The issue of invisibility is complex. While I am often frustrated by my invisibility as a white Jew, that invisibility can also feel safe. In threatening situations, I can often manage to "pass" as a member of the dominant group. People of Color do not have that choice. They are immediately seen as being different. In fact, Australian society reacts to People of Color first and foremost on the basis of their skin color. People of Color do not have the same privilege that I do in being able to hide. The issue is far more complex for Jews of Color such as Ethiopian or Morrocan Jews, for they may be both visible and invisible at the same time.

For me, this seemingly simple realization has sparked some intensive self-exploration. Although I had been politically active for years and had been involved in fighting against racism, I realized that I was racist too. I had been brought up in a racist society, where the "Australian history" I was taught began in 1788 with the first white settlement in Sydney. I had limited interactions with Aboriginals, Torres Strait Islanders and other People of Color. I had been socialized by the state education system, the mass media, and other social institutions, all of which kept me misinformed with stereotypes about Indigenous Australians and other People of Color. My reactions to members of these groups were different from my reactions to whites. I had been taught to be patronizing. I learnt this lesson so well that I was not even aware of my reactions. Even within my Jewish community, the white Jewish culture (Ashkenaz) was dominant, and I viewed Jews of Color (such as Sephardi or Mizrakhi Jews) as being the ones who were different. I am aware that most of what I write about Jews is based on my perceptions as a white Jew. I am starting to notice how often Jews of Color are subsumed, expected to fit in with the white, Ashkenaz culture.

In confronting my racism, I have moved from regarding myself as a victim, as a woman from a Non-English Speaking Background and as a non-Christian in a Christian society, to also seeing myself as an oppressor. I had to accept that I am privileged because I am white. I found that it is much easier to look at myself as a victim, than to look at myself as an oppressor. I started to realize that some of the things that annoyed me about non-Jews' attitudes towards Jews, like ignorance, were reflected in my own attitudes towards and ignorance about People of Color or people from other ethnic backgrounds. I began to see that there were a lot of changes that I also needed to make. I started to understand how people learn racism and anti-Semitism in subtle and unconscious ways.

In recognizing that I was racist, I had three choices: I could go through self-pity and say, "Oh, I feel terrible! I thought I was a good person and here I am a racist!" Or I could say, "Well, isn't society stuffed! A well-intentioned person like me has been turned into a racist." Or I could take a third option, to take responsibility. This last option is the alternative that I have chosen.

This translated into a process which started with me acknowledging my racism, and my ignorance. It meant that I have sought to learn about other cultures, so that I can overcome my ignorance. I believe that the ways I chose to learn are very important. Any of us who is not from the dominant culture will at times feel really fed-up with constantly educating people. It is tiring and frustrating to have to explain the same things over and over again.

I believe that it is my responsibility to learn, not other people's responsibility to teach me. So how do I do that? One way is to read what is written by lesbians, gays, and transgendered people from a variety of backgrounds. I try to hear the voices of lesbians describing their cultures, rather than white women who write characters from different cultures, without really understanding what they are writing. When I can't find queer writing, I read straight literature on this topic. I contact Indigenous and ethnic organizations and ask them to send me written educational material. I also go to film festivals held by different ethnic groups and to the ethnic films screened as part of the annual Melbourne Queer Film and Video Festival. I watch programs on the community broadcasting television station SBS,[7] listen to ethnic and community radio stations and generally try to find ways to educate myself about unfamiliar cultures. I also travel to unfamiliar places. While I recognize that some of these options are middle-class, I believe others are more broadly accessible.

None of these things is in itself enough, but they are a beginning. They help me to become familiar with other cultures, so that I can relate to people from that culture without treating them as exotic, or subjecting them to my ignorance. This includes not presuming that I understand a particular culture because I have read one book about it. As a Jew, I have often had the experience where lesbians or gays quote a book by a recognized Jew as "proof" of their level of awareness.

I also try to set up an environment where I can explore my racism safely. To do this, the environment has to be safe for me. It is scary to say, "I am racist and I need to change." It needs to be done in a supportive context.

Secondly, the environment must not be one that it is going to be painful for Women of Color. They have lived racism. They don't need to hear me uncovering the ways that I have hurt them.

I have done this through conducting "Uncovering Racism" workshops for whites, and through self-exploration. At the end of this section I provide a list of suggested questions with which to begin discussion in a group organized to uncover members' racism. These questions can also be used by individuals on their own.

Once I started examining these issues, I became a better ally. Being an ally to People of Color means that I am prepared to tackle and confront whites on their racism. It means, for example, that when I was at the Pride '96 march in Melbourne and saw an all-white group of women marching with a banner saying: "Gay, Straight, Black, White, One Struggle, One Fight," I could ask them how they could make this claim when there were no Blacks marching with them. But more importantly, being a good ally means that I am prepared to speak up against racism, instead of leaving that task to those who are most hurt by it. However, I find being an ally against racism a very challenging undertaking in Australia. My experience has been that most white/Anglo Australians are not interested in reflecting on their own racism. Ironically, while racism is based on visible differences in skin-color, we whites keep People of Color invisible. Those in the majority are often unaware when a group of people is all white, all heterosexual, or all Christian.

As a white, I can have an impact by alerting other whites to their racism. But it is always easier to confront others' racism than one's own. We need to make sure that we are not confronting others as a way of avoiding examining our own attitudes and behaviors, or as a way of feeling better about ourselves.

It is difficult to understand racism without having experienced it. Perhaps all I can do is understand another's oppression in terms of my own. When we draw links between different forms of oppression, and bring things back to what we understand or have experienced, we can start to build bridges. Drawing links between different forms of oppression does not mean that we understand everything about another's experience. Our own oppression does not mirror another's oppression, and there may be times when our words or actions are inappropriate. What is inoffensive in one culture may be offensive in another, and what is offensive to one person may be inoffensive to another. In opening up pathways, we have to have the courage to "make mistakes." It is important to open up dialogue, not close it down. Mistakes don't have to remain mistakes. They can become important lessons.

These methods are just a beginning. You will not get a "Certificate of Non-racism" at the end of a ten-week course. Racism wasn't taught to us in a ten-week course either, but throughout our lifetimes. And so it takes a life-time commitment to fight against our own racism. The more you learn, the further there is to go. I believe the challenge is worthwhile. Otherwise, we will allow society to fool us into getting to know only a narrow cross-section of people. There is literally a whole wide world out there.

SOME QUESTIONS FOR WHITES WILLING TO CONFRONT THEIR OWN RACISM

- Do I see people who are Black as Blacks, people who are from Asia as Asians, and people who are White as people?
- Do I notice when a group, activity or function is attended by only white people?
- If there are a few People of Color at a function, activity or group do I notice them? When it seems like a "whole lot" of People of Color are there do I count how many?
- How often am I in a situation where there are more People of Color than whites? How do I feel in those situations?
- How many of my friends are not white? Not Christian? Is that an accident, a coincidence or a sign of racism?
- Do I make friends with people who are not white, because they are not white?
- Do I believe that cultures and/or religions other than my own oppress women and/or queers more than my culture or religion does? How? How not? Why?
- Do I believe that Lesbians/Feminists of Color should put the struggle against sexism and heterosexism before the struggle against racism?
- When did I first realize I was racist? What impact did realizing that I am racist have on me?
- In what situations do I question negative cultural expressions? When and where is discrimination "socially acceptable"? Against which groups? (e.g., In Australia, even in "radical circles," it is often acceptable to put down Japanese and Americans.) How do I feel about that? Why?
- When proposing "direct action" or protests, do I understand and consider the legal implications for those who are not white?
- On a piece of paper, describe a variety of lesbians. (You may substitute "gay man" or "transgender" if you prefer.) Some examples are: an Australian lesbian; a Korean lesbian; a Koori lesbian; a Vietnamese lesbian; a Kenyan lesbian; a Jewish lesbian; a Turkish lesbian; a Mexican lesbian; a Muslim lesbian; a Greek lesbian; an Italian lesbian; a Lebanese lesbian; a Russian lesbian; an Egyptian lesbian; a Puertorican lesbian; a Jamaican lesbian; an American lesbian; a Native American lesbian; a French lesbian; a Canadian lesbian; an Indian lesbian; a Chinese lesbian; a Maori lesbian; a Kiwi lesbian, etc.

It is interesting to come up with your own list of lesbians. Notice which cultures you include and which ones you leave out. Notice how many lesbians you yourself know in each cultural group. Once you have written your descriptions, examine or discuss them.

What stereotypes have you included? What groups did you find impossible to describe? Why? How many lesbians did you envisage as white, when they may not necessarily have been white (e.g., Australian, American, etc.)? How many did you envisage as being from Christian backgrounds when they may not necessarily have been? Did you even consider this, or did you only notice when somebody was presumably not Christian? How many did you envisage as living overseas when they may have been living in Australia?

POST SCRIPT 1997

This article was originally written in 1995 and was developed further in 1996. The past couple of years have seen a great change in the political arena and the way in which racism is perceived and dealt with in Australia. Among the very first acts of the conservative government of current Prime Minister John Howard (elected March 1996) were a review into the activities of the Aboriginal and Torres Strait Islander Commission (ATSIC), the Federal body with overall responsibility for the welfare of Australia's indigenous peoples, a review of the operations of SBS (Special Broadcasting Service) Ethnic Television and Radio, and a significant cut in immigration quotas. The casting of blatant racial slurs and the telling of distorting lies has become a socially acceptable practice, thanks to the Hanson machine, aided and abetted by the media. The "One Nation" party, which Pauline Hanson has established, has racially vilified many groups, particularly Indigenous Australians and Australians from Asia. The media has provided her with front page coverage, screaming her lies (which I choose not to repeat) in their headlines. Racism sells newspapers in Australia today.

The Howard government has legitimated this racism by calling it a "return to freedom of speech" which the previous Labor Party Government had supposedly "done away with" in their "tyranny of political correctness." The Howard government has also promoted its own racist agenda with further cuts to immigration and attempts to extinguish Native Title, that is, the rights of Indigenous Australians to their traditional lands. Extremist groups like the neo-nazi National Action have also gained momentum in this conservative climate.

Since early 1997 I have been involved in the Campaign Against Racism in Melbourne, including a campaign to have the nazi bookshop in the Melbourne suburb of Fawkner closed down. There has been a very visible queer presence at these anti-nazi rallies, including the Jewish Lesbian Group of

Victoria. One rally was organised by queers, and featured queer speakers, including myself. Queer visibility at these demonstrations has spurred discussion in the gay press about the role of gays and lesbians in the fight against racism.

I believe this has been part of a larger groundswell of anti-racist activism. This critical time in Australia offers us the opportunity to really build alliances and work together. Some of my most multi-cultural experiences have been at rallies against Pauline Hanson and at meetings to promote reconciliation between indigenous and non-indigenous Australians, where people from truly diverse backgrounds have worked together in a spirit of unity and respect.

Much of my article has discussed introspective approaches to countering racism and anti-Semitism, examining our beliefs and values as a starting point in the fight against these forms of discrimination and intolerance. But the conservative political agenda currently foisted upon us calls for immediate and public action. At times, it may seem that introspection is a luxury that we cannot afford today. It seems that external action must be the priority. But I also believe that we must make time to look at ourselves in terms of our racial and cultural assumptions. If we do not, we run the risk of transmitting the same ignorant and patronizing attitudes in our anti-racism work.

The campaign against racism is crucial today. We must get out there in the community and spread the message that we whites must apologize for the wrongs that have been done and are still being done to the Indigenous peoples of Australia. We must fight for Indigenous rights to Native Title to prevail. We must spread the message that immigration is vital for our country, on economic as well as humanitarian grounds. We must ensure that racism, anti-Semitism, discrimination and lies are not acceptable today. But at the same time as we are teaching others, we must make sure that we are learning ourselves. We must ensure that multiculturalism is recognised as the cultural basis of Australian society today, and not just an excuse for holding festivals with exotic foods and exotic dances!

AUTHOR NOTE

The author is grateful to the following groups, which have offered her insight and encouragement: the Jewish Lesbian Group of Victoria; Interlesbian; DARE and the "Quota Collective" (women interviewed on Melbourne community radio station 3CR). Thank you to all the women who make these groups so important and so special. Thanks also to the women and men of the VAC Cross Cultural Group.

The author would especially like to thank the following people, who have inspired and challenged her (even when she has not been in the mood): Shauna Sherker; Alex Nissen; Sara Elkas; Orly Ephrat; Aaron Taub; Laura Wernick; Shira Spektor; Suzal Goldstein; Amikaeyla Gaston; Tara; Papoosa of Iowa; the women of the Community Center at Michigan Women's Music Festival 1994; Kim Neville; Jan Chapman;

Marlene; Evelyn Portek; Vera Ray; Tania; Debbie; Moni Storz; Mick Miller; Janine Purdy; Olga Havman; Helen Curzon-Siggers; Noel Pearson and everybody who dares to fight against racism and anti-Semitism today.

For demographic information, thanks to Symcha Burstin (my Dad); Doodie Ringelblum and Bobbi Zylberman.

NOTES

1. Interlesbian was "a network of lesbians from minority racial, cultural and ethnic background [whose aim was] to create a forum to name and challenge our differences as well as our shared experiences, and to create a voice for ourselves, in our many shapes and forms, in the larger community" (quote from 'Sappho Was a Wog Grrrl' Conference publicity). Rose Kizinska also discusses the Interlesbian group and the "Sappho . . . " conference in her paper in this volume.

2. Editor Note: The author of this paper has chosen to spell the name 'hitler' with a lower case initial.

3. I believe that there are many lesbian communities in Victoria, but use the word "community" here to denote the sum of these communities and lesbian organisations and institutions.

4. The word "community" is used here to encompass a range of Jewish communities, and the community institutions.

5. "Jewish lesbians encouraged by community response to stall," *Australian Jewish News*, 24 March 95.

6. At that time *Lesbiana* was Melbourne's only lesbian magazine.

7. SBS (Special Broadcasting Service) is a national television and radio network station where most programs originate from, and/or are presented by Indigenous or ethnic communities.

REFERENCES

This article is about my ideas and experiences. It is hard to know where an idea is born and what sparks new ways of thinking. There are some books that have challenged my thinking. There are also people who have inspired me. Some of them, I know only by first name. Though the words in this article and the workshop design are mine, I would like to acknowledge the following guides in my journey.

Bridges: A journal for Jewish feminists and our friends. Eugene, Oregon. (all issues). Volume 7(1) (1997) is a special issue on Sephardi and Mizrakhi Jewish Women.
Brown, Laura S. and Root, Maria P.P. (Eds.) (1990). *Diversity and Complexity in Feminist Theory*, New York: Harrington Park Press.
Bulkin, Elly; Smith, Barbara & Pratt, Minnie Bruce. (1988). *Yours in struggle–Three feminist perspectives on anti-Semitism and racism.* Ithaca NY: Firebrand Books.
Burstin, Hinde Ena. (1995a). Shprakhn fir. *Reflections* (Melbourne, Sholem Alei-chem College), p. 78.

Burstin, Hinde Ena. (1995b, September 22). Vu Zaynen di Froyen? *Di Oystralishe Yiddishe Nayes (Australian Jewish News*, Melbourne), p. 6.

Burstin, Hinde Ena. (1996 [Tishrei 5757], December). The letter . . . and the word. *Generation Journal of Australian Life and Thought*, 6 (1 & 2), 28-29.

Fireweed Collective. (1990). *Awakening thunder–Asian Canadian women. Fireweed*, Issue 30. Toronto: Canada.

Gunew, Sneja & Mahyuddin, Jan (Eds.). (1988). *Beyond the echo–Multicultural women's writing*. Brisbane, Qld: University of Queensland Press.

Herne, K., Travaglia, J. & Weis, E. (Eds.). (1992). *Who do you think you are? Second generation immigrant women in Australia,* NSW: Australia, Redress Press, Inc.

Hyllus, Maris and Borg, Sonia (1985). *Women of the Sun*, Melbourne: Australia, Penguin Books.

Klepfisz, Irena. (1990). *Dreams of an insomniac: Jewish feminist speeches, essays and diatribes*. Portland, OR: Eighth Mountain Press.

Langford, Ruby with Hampton, Susan. (1988). *Don't take your love to town*. Melbourne: Penguin Books.

Lim-Hing, Sharon (Ed.). (1994). *The very inside: An anthology of writing by Asian and Pacific Islander lesbian and bisexual women*. Toronto: Sister Vision Press.

Moraga, Cherie & Anzaldua, Gloria. (1983). *This bridge called my back: Writings by radical women of color* (2nd Edition). New York, NY: Kitchen Table, Women of Color Press.

Morgan, Sally. (1987). *My place*. Fremantle, WA: Fremantle Arts Centre Press.

Neville, Kim. (1996). Remapping structures: A brief look at racism in Interlesbian. *NESBian News* (Melbourne), *1*(1), 9.

Smith, Barbara (Ed.) (1983). *Home girls–A black feminist anthology*. New York, NY: Kitchen Table: Women of Color Press.

Torton Beck, Evelyn. (Ed.) (1982). *Nice Jewish girls: A lesbian anthology*. New York: The Crossing Press.

A Love Letter from NADIA
(Non-Anglo Dykes in Australia)

Rose Kizinska

SUMMARY. This article is a revised version of a paper I presented at the "Sappho Was A Wog Grrrl" conference in Melbourne, 22 October 1995, which was organized by "Interlesbian," a Melbourne-based political and support group for lesbians from Non-English Speaking Backgrounds (NESB). Utilizing a mixed genre format incorporating the first person fictional narrative form of letters to lovers, this parodic piece explores the identity terrains of sexuality, ethnicity and class in Melbourne's lesbian communities. It focuses on how the ethnocentric limits of sexual, cultural and racial identifications constrain the mythical beauty of coming out and staying in. The experiences reported and reflected upon here arose out of my participation as an activist member of Interlesbian. Contextualized in the form of a lover's discourse, this paper is an evocation of a passion towards the (re)visioning of a progressive local lesbian activist politics and community. *[Article copies available for a fee from The Haworth Document Delivery Service: 1-800-342-9678. E-mail address: getinfo@haworthpressinc.com]*

INTRODUCTION: I AM NADIA TOO.

Between 1993 and 1995 Interlesbian was the only support group in Melbourne for lesbians from minority ethnic and racial backgrounds. During this

---

Correspondence regarding this article may be addressed to Rose Kizinska, 691 Bell Street, Victoria, 3072, Australia.

[Haworth co-indexing entry note]: "A Love Letter from NADIA (Non-Anglo Dykes in Australia)." Kizinska, Rose. Co-published simultaneously in *Journal of Homosexuality* (The Haworth Press, Inc.) Vol. 36, No. 3/4, 1999, pp. 159-168; and: *Multicultural Queer: Australian Narratives* (ed: Peter A. Jackson and Gerard Sullivan) The Haworth Press, Inc., 1999, pp. 159-168. Single or multiple copies of this article are available for a fee from The Haworth Document Delivery Service [1-800-342-9678, 9:00 a.m. - 5:00 p.m. (EST). E-mail address: getinfo@haworthpressinc.com].

159

period, Interlesbian was tokenized in the Melbourne lesbian community as *the* group to which all Non-English Speaking Background or NESB lesbians were often referred. As a result, Interlesbian was ghettoized as *the* organization in Melbourne that dealt with the needs of NESB lesbians. As lesbians from minority racial and ethnic backgrounds surviving in a dominant hetero-sexualized, anglo and often homophobic and racist society, our lifestyles are not recognized as legitimate within the heteronormative structure. Our race/ethnicity is sometimes seen as a source of division to the hegemonic lesbian community, while our lesbianism is sometimes unacceptable within particular ethnic groups. In this regard, negotiating issues pertaining to "coming out" and relying on "a lesbian community" as our "extended (queer) family" and our "home" is integral to the needs of NESB lesbians.

In general, neither mainstream heterosexual services for people from non-English speaking backgrounds nor lesbian groups meet the needs of NESB lesbians. This is because our specificities–being simultaneously NESB women and lesbians–are not recognized. Because of this, and also because Interlesbian was then the only support organization in the state of Victoria for NESB lesbians, it functioned by default as an umbrella for a diverse and complex range of needs. Over the last three years, more than 300 women have made contact with Interlesbian with needs ranging from social and political networking, community and individual referrals, to accommodation and crisis support. However, Interlesbian was not a service-providing organization. It could only respond to other services' and groups' lacks and successes in addressing issues relevant to NESB lesbians.

The discourses invoked in this article are both a response to the issues of the dominant lesbian community's tokenization, ghettoization and exclusion of Interlesbian, and also a call to mainstream, heterosexual, NESB and lesbian communities to take more responsibility in the areas of access and equity. In this article I have created "NADIA" as an acronym for "Non-Anglo Dykes In Australia." Here NADIA is a woman who stands on her own, and her opinions do not necessarily reflect those of the Interlesbian group, nor of other NESB lesbians.[1]

This is a performative text that resists in its voice and its questions the privileging power-centric voices in the dominant anglo and non-anglo lesbian communities alike. It is also an attempt to challenge the assumptions that were taken for granted in the organizing processes of the "Sappho was a Wog Grrrl" community conference. "A Love Letter from NADIA" is a creative and erotic exploration, a naming game of metaphor, that invokes all of my multiple, contradictory and complementary voices as (other) bodies cruising the room. It focuses on ambivalence, desire, disappointment, lust and disgust. It runs together notions of community, exclusion/inclusion, whether or not to compromise. I am NADIA too: sameness within difference, margin within center of margin.

LOVE

I seize the powers of S/M, invert intergenerational Daddy worship and extract the excessive demand for exotic toygirl playmates. I expunge unworthy exhibitionism and excrete first dates in response to personals ads gone horribly wrong. I mourn the tragedy of being dumped and celebrate the tribulations of being a dumper. Girls beware, NADIA is everywhere!

As a post-punk, meat-eating, leg-shaving, bra-wearing, synthetic, de-odorized and technicolor-headed, non-herbal, non-anglo lesbian in the community, mine is a dissident voice that cannot be heard above the problematic and persistent push in Australia for a "celebration of multiculturalism." You can eat my "ethnic" food, watch my "cultural" dance, but never let it be known that I like to fuck and fuck over as well. I'm not just a NESB girl, and even then I am not that at every daily hour. I NADIA am a product of trashy mags, gutter talk, street urchin-ism, unsolicited violence, crafty shop lifting, homelessness, host-spit-ting rituals,[2] dates in rust-dusty dead car suburban wastelands, altar boy fantasies, frenzied shopping, good sex, and bad.

I came out and heard the strumming guitars and the lyrical strains of the much-vaunted Toni Childs,[3] but her words didn't speak to me at all. I stayed out, and now I hear silencing reproaches from those whom I know I could never claim nor name as my own.

You for one, Ms University NESB Guru, you slipped off my pedestal in ten minutes flat. I think your constant snide remarks about my orange hair, red hair, blue hair, and no hair had a little something to do with that. Only once, I grew my hair waist-long, au naturel, only for my mother, whom you definitely are not.

SAPPHO WAS A WOG GRRRL

In 1995 I participated in the organizing collective of the "Sappho Was a Wog Grrrl"[4] conference in Melbourne as a member of Interlesbian. We orga-nized around the politics of sex, sexuality, identity and racism. Throughout the preparatory months of heated discussions, heavy silences and broken friendships, I realized that an alliance forged on the basis of either sexuality or ethnicity alone, without critical reflection, perpetuates the institutionalized and paternalistic "multicultural" myth that all "woggrrls" are "authentic," homogenous and the same, or if they are not, they should be.

As in any other group in any community, conflicts arose among conference organizers out of an inability to allow for a heterogeneity born from generational gaps (and different migrational patterns, ages and feminisms), and from class, ethnic, racial and lifestyle differences. In hindsight, the conference was a success with over 100 women attending, and was hailed by one Melbourne queer community newspaper as the first conference in Australia to deal with issues of racism in the lesbian community.[5] My self-reflection here is not an indictment of the conference organizing committee. Rather, I wish to elucidate the sometimes conflicting internal collective structures that are indicative of the diversity of NESB lesbians in Australia.

IS THERE A REAL, AUTHENTIC NADIA?

My sex-text fingers into the very folds of those replicunts, strips off their outer garments, painstakingly, piece by layer, by hook, eye and zipper. They who tell me that I can't be the NADIA me, unless I strap on a national costume, whip up a few polkas and "cook up a storm."[6]

LOVE:
TO ALL THE GRRRLS I'VE LOVED AND LOATHED BEFORE. . . .

GINA

"GINA" is the acronym of "Girls in National Alliance," a now defunct Melbourne-based community activist group promoting an "all-inclusive" lesbian agenda. GINA organized monthly forums on topics like "Inclusion/ Exclusion" and "Sex and Power." In their forum on "Body Piercing and Body Art" in October 1995 as part of the annual Melbourne Fringe Festival, the speakers failed to address any cultural issues or issues of appropriation of body art. When challenged by some members of the audience on these matters, the speakers and other audience members retorted with comments such as, "Don't you think it looks nice, though!" and, "Why must you make everything so political?" These comments silenced and invalidated pertinent cultural concerns, and the failure of the facilitator to address questions from the audience only reinforced the white-washed agenda of the group. In another incident when Interlesbian invited GINA members to speak at the "Sappho Was a Wog Grrrl" conference, the group responded by saying that racism was "not their issue" because they did not have NESB members. Consequently, GINA did not participate in the Sappho conference.

> *GINA, Gina, Gina, what can I say? When I heard of your decent wog name, I held my breath in hope and anticipation, my lips quivering in adoring stasis. Till you pulled down your soiled underwear Gina and I saw the truth there, by the very color of your hair there. My potential ally, my perfect fuck buddy to be–older and more experienced with your hands, mouth, fist and foot–a sugar mommy in the making, even.*

> *I just couldn't bring myself to be your bottom grrl Gina, because you had me down there already and I'm the kind of grrl who needs to negotiate my own power and choice. Why couldn't I be the one who held and cracked the whip?*

> *I tried so hard to be your good time grrl, to purely and pleasurably indulge myself in looking at your piercings and tattoos. But I just couldn't hold my tongue, the very tongue that you threatened to clip off, with the swipe of your hand and a lash of your tongue, that questioned my questions to you.*

LOIS

LOIS is the acronym for "Lesbians Organising in Solidarity," a now defunct Melbourne-based direct action queergirl group. In July 1995 when Interlesbian was asked to give a paper at LOIS's Body Image Forum, Interlesbian was the only NESB participant on the panel (alongside an Anglo femme talking about femme politics, an Anglo transgender talking about her exclusion within the lesbian community, and an Anglo lesbian with diabetes speaking about her disability). In this instance, LOIS's panel selection clearly highlighted the essentialistic reductionism of their race politics. In their eyes, when we were asked to speak, we couldn't possibly give a paper on anything but what it is like to live in a racialized, "other" body. In terms of LOIS's Anglo-centric understandings, an NESB lesbian could not possibly be femme, and/or transgendered, and/or differently abled and discuss these issues legitimately.

LOIS participated in the Sappho Was a Wog Grrrl Conference with a paper entitled "Racism is a White Grrl's Issue too!" (Jamieson, 1996). In this paper, which details the organizational processes of why "LOIS will write to the eds [editors] of Queer papers about the promotion of exclusion [of transsexuals] at Lesbian Confest but be silent when issues of racist door policies arise time after time," Libby Jamieson (1996, p. 10) cites some of reasons behind "the white girls' reactions" to the issues of racism which include denial, fear, guilt, defensiveness, cop-out/pat answers, not taking responsibility, and the white knight syndrome.

> *Oh my LOIS, sickly sweet appendage to superman, the great white savior of the world. Look! Up in the sky, it's a bird, it's a plane, it's supergirl! Who disguised as Clit Kent, mild-mannered reporter for the Daily Queer Planet, strives for truth, justice and the Rainbow way. I think you were exposed to too much Kraptonite. It leaked out of your own head, and into some of your brain cells. It suffocatingly cut short any potential long-term liaisons between us, because you just kept on apologizing to me, for the error of your ways, the things you claim not to know about. And I don't need another empty "sorry," not from the likes of you. Bland, bland, blend and away, fly by the tailends of your absorbing, sponging cape.*

LESLEY

"Lesley Raven" is a pun on "Lesboraves," a now defunct Melbourne-based, radical lesbian, monthly discussion group. In March 1994 Interlesbian was invited to conduct a workshop for Lesboraves on issues on "ethnic lesbians." Interlesbian agreed to do so–strategically. Lesboraves were asking that we talk about our sad stories and bad experiences as "ethnic lesbians" so that they could, in turn, claim to the wider community that they had dealt with "the multicultural topic" for that year. In our refusal to be patronized, Interlesbian treated Lesboraves to a "confronting racism" workshop, whereby they were made to feel alienation by standing with their backs to everyone else in the room and their faces to the corners.

> *To the lesbo who raved and raved, dear old Lesley Raven. You invited me into your house but once. You thought it might be a good look to have a NADIA of any type on your arm. You thought I would tell you all about my woes and that you could soothe me with those seemingly more experienced hands of yours, that you could show me the way to our Nirvana.*

> *But I took control of you and I made you face the blank wall. Tell me your stories dear Lesley and about what makes you stand so tall?*

LYNX

LYNX is a Melbourne-based social club for "the shyer and conservative lesbian."[7] One of Interlesbian's "indirect" experiences with LYNX arose when a few NESB lesbians (who later became members of Interlesbian) initially joined to make new friends and find a social outlet. After their "initiation" into the social club, LYNX suggested to these NESB lesbians that they also contact Interlesbian, because it was a group set up originally for NESB lesbians, like them. Interlesbian was made aware of LYNX's apparent inability to cope with "diversity" when these NESB lesbians (all of whom made contact with Interlesbian both individually and collectively on separate occasions), were asked where they had heard of Interlesbian. They responded that they had been given Interlesbian's contact number by LYNX. LYNX has since responded to this criticism in a letter to the *Interlesbian Newsletter* stating, among other things, "We . . . wish to make clear that this woman's unfortunate experience in no way reflects the policy of LYNX . . . We are essentially a social group, and continually aim to make new members feel welcome, without restriction . . ." (Kelly, 1996, p. 2). Either they are welcome or they are not.

I'll never forget you, my shy little LYNX girl. With such an inviting name, I craved for the ex(r)otic from you. I thought any name with an X in it would do. But you brazenly let it be known that I wasn't the girl for you. Whenever I came to see you, you pushed me away, told me to go ahead and find someone else, more like myself.

According to you, I only exist in an/otherworld. What were you afraid of? That I might speak and lick in foreign tongues too garbled? This NADIA was not the one that you wanted. You wanted to fuck the same, too afraid of what might have happened when the lights went out and my "peasant primal urges" splurged. How I sometimes yearned to revel in your blissful colorless ignorance, the kind that can shrug me off with a list of phone numbers (some of which were your ex-lovers) who you thought might be more appropriate for my evidently peculiar needs. But what were my needs? You never bothered to ask and just assumed. I thought I was just a shyer lesbian, just like you.

AN "OTHER" NADIA

One of the conflicts that arose during the Sappho Was a Woggrrrl pre-conference organizational meetings occurred when deciding on the contents of the program for the conference. Issues of sex, sexuality, sexual practices, and choices were suggested. Some of the second-generation, Australian-born "matriarchs" in the collective rejected the motion, on the arrogant assumption that these issues would be too "radical" and "confrontational" for "other" non-Anglo lesbians, primarily recently arrived from "Asian" cultures. At the same time that the Anglo community was constructing us as the "sexual, erotic" stereotype, these "matriarchs" were constructing themselves as the binary opposite of this, that is, as "non-sexual, non-erotic" authentic non-Anglos. The hypocritical morality here lay in their view that only "good" and "proper non-sexual, non-erotic" Asians were considered "real" and "acceptable." Clearly, in this instance, within the NESB lesbian mainstream, "Asian" can be considered as the "other" of the other.

Similarly, during these pre-conference meetings, sections of the non-Anglo lesbian mainstream were colluding in perpetrating the myth that all non-Anglos were "dumb" because they could not possibly speak English. "Oh, no, that's too academic! They will not understand it!" the non-Anglo lesbian mainstream said of the Asian "other." According to this same non-Anglo lesbian mainstream, the epitome of the perfect culturally appropriate raffle prize would consist of a hamper filled with a little token of food from each of "our" cultures.

In addition, the non-Anglo lesbian mainstream would also endorse that a good, sound and worthy visibility project for a group like ours would be to enlighten ourselves and the Anglo lesbian mainstream about our cultures' histories of lesbianism. This is akin to saying "bring a plate of 'your' lesbian," like "bring a plate of 'your' food." One of my allies at that time aptly described the problematics inherent in such essentialist discourses when she said, "I don't know what my culture is. What is my culture? I'm Chinese and Indian. I study in Australia. I mostly live in Singapore. And the only language I can speak is English."[8]

And how you hurt me so, the most, perhaps. NADIA like myself, but not quite. I guess I put too much trust in you. You told me to tone down my language, not to use big words or ones that were rude. Every time I suggested a hot raunchy date, you suggested that I cook and share some of my food with you. You assumed my place, you had it all ready for me. But I just couldn't fit into that room. You thought all the other NADIAs would not approve. So you shut up my mouth and you stuck it together with glue

. . . and kisses . . . xxx

I refuse to change my ways for even you, NADIA darling. You don't know how I got to be here. I scrubbed your middle-class floors, polished your gold suburban taps, slept in bus shelters and strangers' front *yards. I saved the $13 a week the government gave the "young home-less" me to live on, by walking for miles, across three suburbs, to school. WogSistas, I looked with envy at your starched white school collars. I recall the ragged bottle-green school uniform the headmaster pulled out of the lost property box. He held it right up to my face, in our crowded class-room. He butt-faced grinned, "Not too poor to wear this, I bet." Then you quickly turned your blind head away, NADIA. He tried to make me wear the shit and I told him to just get fucked, just like I'm telling you.*

So here I am, maybe not the real NADIA for you, but unabatedly smart, hot, same, different and queer.

P. S. THIS IS NADIA'S TRUE LOVE

NADIA now reclines on her tri-colored vinyl couch. She pops on, in fast-forward, a German porn video, entitled *Geile Lesbo Orgie*, in a language she can't understand and plugs in her Inter-active, dual control, spiked candy pink silicon sex toy. Between the hum and the buzz and the video moans, news in Mandarin of Maggie Cheung's latest film deal, intercuts through cable on CTN's Dadi channel.[9] NADIA's lover has inadvertently crossed all of the wires and sits watching NADIA with her left ear intently pricked up to the screen.

NOTES

1. For further information on NESB lesbians in Victoria, the Greek and Italian lesbian groups can now be contacted via the Cross Cultural Development Team at the Victorian AIDS Council, 6 Claremont Street, South Yarra, Victoria 3141. I would like to thank Audrey Yue for her insightful comments, support and encouragement in developing this article. Thanks also to Jo Rawlings for her ever-present and over-whelming long-distance inspiration and interest in my work and life.

2. Host-spitting rituals are what ex-catholic girls such as myself do to rid them-selves of the distaste of the body of christ in their mouths. They spit the hosts out after communion.

3. Toni Childs is an American folk singer who was taken up as an icon by many sections of the feminist/lesbian university student scene in Melbourne in the late 1980s and the 1990s.

4. The term "wog" (an acronym of "westernised oriental gentleman") has long been used as a derogatory slur against NESB people, both men and women, living in Australia. "Wog," like the term "Nigga" in the United States Gangsta Rap scene, has recently been reclaimed by people of non-English speaking backgrounds them-selves.

5. See *The Melbourne Star Observer*, 20th October 1995, *4* (248), 2.

6. "Cooking Up a Storm: Racist Feminism and Building an Anti-Racist Feminist Movement" was the title of a forum held in Melbourne on 25 May 1995 and organized by Melbourne University's "Bloody Feminist Collective." The poster advertising the forum contained images of five veiled Muslim women looking downwards as a storm cloud approached, with the words "Cooking Up A Storm" looming above them. The juxtaposition of the racist image and text on the poster appeared to override the intended parody, as it merely contained non-anglo women within the stereotypical domestic realm of "cooking" and reinforced the idea of them being irrational, stormy "hysterics."

7. LYNX Inc. Social Club can be contacted at P.O. BOX 152 Ashburton, Victoria 3147.

8. Thanks to Sharon Perera for her permission to quote this.

9. CTN, the Chinese Television Network, is broadcast from Taiwan on one of Australia's pay T.V. stations, New World Televisions. Dadi Channel is the Hong Kong produced equivalent of the U.S. program Entertainment Tonight.

REFERENCES

Jamieson, Libby. (1996, February). Racism is a white grrl's issue too! *Interlesbian Newsletter (Melbourne)*, *1*(1), 10.

Kelly, Marion (Secretary, Lynx Inc.). (1996, February). Letter to the editors. *Interlesbian Newsletter (Melbourne)*, *1*(1), 2.

Sister Outsider,
or "Just Another Thing I Am":
Intersections of Cultural
and Sexual Identities in Australia

Abby Duruz

SUMMARY. This article originates from a radio project titled *Muff Divas[1] and Drag Queens* that investigated a wide range of gay and lesbian histories in the state of New South Wales. The project produced two half-hour radio programs that were broadcast nationally on community radio stations in February 1996 to coincide with Sydney's annual month-long Gay and Lesbian Mardi Gras Festival, the premier event on Australia's queer cultural calendar. Of the two documentaries produced, the first addressed 30 years of queer culture in New South Wales while the second explored our diverse identities as lesbians and gay men. This paper draws extensively on material collected for the second program. *Muff Divas and Drag Queens* was funded under the Literature and History Program of the New South Wales Government's Ministry for the Arts, with support from the Sydney Gay and Lesbian Mardi Gras cultural program and Sydney community radio station 2SER•FM. *[Article copies available for a fee from The Haworth Document Delivery Service: 1-800-342-9678. E-mail address: getinfo@haworthpressinc.com]*

INTRODUCTION

I am fascinated by the many cultures, languages and discourses through which we all move, and the *Muff Divas and Drag Queens* project was an

Correspondence regarding this article may be addressed to Abby Duruz, P.O. Box 2300, Clovelly, New South Wales, 2031, Australia.

[Haworth co-indexing entry note]: "Sister Outsider, or 'Just Another Thing I Am': Intersections of Cultural and Sexual Identities in Australia." Duruz, Abby. Co-published simultaneously in *Journal of Homosexuality* (The Haworth Press, Inc.) Vol. 36, No. 3/4, 1999, pp. 169-182; and: *Multicultural Queer: Australian Narratives* (ed: Peter A. Jackson and Gerard Sullivan) The Haworth Press, Inc., 1999, pp. 169-182. Single or multiple copies of this article are available for a fee from The Haworth Document Delivery Service [1-800-342-9678, 9:00 a.m. - 5:00 p.m. (EST). E-mail address: getinfo@haworthpressinc.com].

excellent opportunity to explore these issues further. Some of my many "hats" include: being a radio documentary producer, a student of languages, a middle-class white girl, a stroppy[2] surfing dyke, the daughter of two academics, an aspiring geek and Internet trainer and the only radical lesbian separatist in high school!

When I first started calling myself a feminist in high school in Sydney in the late 1980s, the words "differently cultured" or "differently abled" were variously used to describe Indigenous Australians, people from non-Anglo backgrounds, and people with disabilities or religious beliefs other than Christianity. These were terms defined from outside for those communities which were "not like us," that is, the white middle-class mainstream. Nowadays, these labels seem incredibly dated and deeply problematic, but they are representative of how those "others" were viewed not so many years ago. The purpose of this article is to look more closely at how gay men and lesbians from these communities describe their *own* identities and how they negotiate a space between the sexual and cultural communities they are part of. I use the term "cultural communities" to refer both to family background and to other communities such the deaf community that interviewees participate in apart from the gay and lesbian community. I have chosen to apply the term "multicultural" in this context to invoke interviewees' allegiances to more than one community or cultural grouping.

In the process of producing the program, I was fortunate to be able to talk to deaf gay men and lesbians and those from Indigenous Australian, Pacific Islander,[3] and Jewish backgrounds, and this article is based largely on these interviews. I cannot claim that this paper is representative of the situation of all "multicultural" lesbians and gay men in Australia. Nevertheless, the issues my interviewees raised have broad implications. The material presented here derives from edited transcripts of a radio program and I have done my best to evoke the spirit of the arguments and speakers' styles of presentation.

The questions I explored in the second program of *Muff Divas and Drag Queens* were:

- How does being a lesbian or a gay man relate to the interviewees' cultural identities?
- How are these overlaps negotiated by gay men and lesbians from "multicultural" backgrounds?
- Is it possible to have a language of common experience that links our diverse cultures without negating their individual importance?

Producing the radio program was as much a learning process for me as a documentary for broadcast. It was a chance to explore some fascinating issues of culture and identity, besides providing an ideal excuse to ask people about an intensely personal topic, "Who are you? And what do you call yourself?"

ANOTHER KIND OF COMING OUT

The idea of identity in a gay and lesbian context, let alone a multicultural one, is a difficult topic to research in any genuinely representative sense. I took my initial bearings from a presentation by a Black dyke of Indian descent, Uma Kali Shakti, who was raised in Fiji and Aotearoa (the Maori name for New Zealand). Uma Kali Shakti spoke at a conference on "Emerging Lesbian and Gay Communities,"[4] which was held at the University of Sydney in September 1995 by the Australian Centre for Lesbian and Gay Research. Uma has grappled with the hard issues of racism and homophobia all her life, challenging assumptions with strength, humor and her own brand of rap. She is a warm and dynamic speaker, a whirlwind in a sari in the Aboriginal colors of red, gold and black.[5] Uma began by greeting the audience in the Maori, Fijian and Hindi languages:

> *Kia Ora, Ni Sum Bula Vinaka* and *Namaste.*

> I'm Soul Sistah Singh
> and I do the Right Thing!
> I'm Khush,[6] Black & Proud
> 'n I say it out loud!

> This Rap I call
> One Size Fits All
> and my Desi[7] Dyke Rap
> isn't just crap.

My people, as far as I know, were from Rajasthan. They were taken out by the British [as workers] to an island in the South Pacific Ocean called Fiji. When I was a baby my family migrated to Aotearoa [New Zealand] and so my identity is very mixed. I see myself as a black woman, working class, non-English speaking, and a small island woman from the Pacific . . .

[When I was growing up] I hadn't heard *anything* about homosexuality. I didn't know that we existed! Then later when I decided [that I was going to be a lesbian], I thought, "My God, another oppressed group! I was already working class, black, non-English speaking, diabetic, aging . . . I wasn't a mother yet! [Audience laughter. Uma waits for them to settle down.]

So I came out and I plunged into the women's movement and the gay movement . . . I couldn't *believe* it, the racism that came down, the class issues, all those kinds of things, so it was very, very difficult . . .

> The women's movement seemed cool
> Yet most times I felt a fool . . .
> I was colored too strong,
> My hair was all wrong
> To my culture I belong!

The other thing I found is that I'd go out to speak and [I'd presume that] everyone in the room was basically Anglo-Australian. I was never seen as an Anglo-Australian–this may come as a surprise! What happened was people would come out to me later [and tell me], "Actually I'm Greek," "Actually I'm Aboriginal." Another kind of coming out in the gay community is not . . . being Anglo.

WHAT ARE YA?

"Coming out" is a definitive rite of passage in gay and lesbian communities. Often the happy ending to the tale is a joyful assimilation into gay and lesbian culture and final reconciliation with one's feelings of difference. But what about lesbians and gay men who have lived with other forms of difference all their lives? I put this to Aaron Ross, a Murri and a Kukuyalingi[8] man from far north Queensland:

Abby: I was just thinking about this before . . . The whole idea of coming out, in some ways, is about reinventing your history. Looking back and thinking, "Ah! That's the moment when I realized it. That's the moment I 'became' . . . " Is that how you'd view it or would you view it a bit differently?

Aaron Ross: Being black, you don't have a choice, you know. People automatically identify you as not being part of the dominant culture. So, the idea of being different in other ways wasn't hard for me to take on . . . My primary consciousness, my primary being, is about being black and that created who I am. It drove the way I grew up, the way I relate to people. That's who I am . . . So I suppose in a way . . . being gay is not necessarily an add-on, but it's just another thing that I am.

Aaron is an articulate and thoughtful man in his thirties who works in Sydney with the Aboriginal and Torres Strait Islander Commission, a Federal agency that deals with the welfare of Australia's indigenous peoples. I also asked about his "allegiances" to the different communities that he is part of and whether he has felt pressure to choose between them:

> *Aaron Ross:* Well, when I was . . . young growing up in Brisbane, in my teens, I met up with some gay academics from one of the universities who had been involved in gay rights activism in the seventies, gay solidarity, what have you. They were trying to press me for a definition, much like one of your earlier questions about which is "more important" [being gay or being a Murri?]. At the time, I didn't answer them and said that I couldn't. But later on it made me quite resentful, that they should try to make me give a value to [one or the other].

Perhaps it is an Anglo preoccupation to try and sort everyone out into categories of "us" and "them." Aaron challenged many of my assumptions with the way in which he occupies a place in both the gay and indigenous communities. It is sometimes difficult to stop thinking in terms of "multiple oppressions" and start thinking about how narrow white society's ideas are about the diverse factors that make up identity. Perhaps my question should have been less about "Which are you *really*?" and more about challenging the idea that there should be only one focus of identity.

I first met Ora Barlow at a lesbian festival in Brisbane. She stood out among the mostly Anglo conference-goers: a Maori woman with a steady gaze and a beautiful singing voice. Ora was quick to point out that it is particularly Anglo gay men and lesbians who do not see cultural background as an important aspect of identity:

> *Ora Barlow:* I can't speak for anybody else, but for me as a black woman sexuality is second or third down the list. First and foremost, where I come from is my identity, which is a huge difference [from white lesbians and gay men]. Gay and lesbian cultures don't necessarily have that cultural context. They'll say, "Yes I'm a lesbian. I'm gay," and maybe somewhere down the line they might say, "And I think I'm second generation Australian," not even linking back to the lands that their ancestors were indigenous to. And so there's a big difference there, in the way that I see myself as a black woman, because I can't hide the color of my skin. Sexuality I can hide any time of the day if I choose.

"Either/or" assumptions about identity can serve to make obviously indigenous people invisible, insofar as their sexuality goes. Sue Green was one of a group of Kooris[9] to speak on Indigenous Australia at the "Emerging Gay and Lesbian Communities" conference:

> *Sue Green:* People don't think that there's a whole dimension, a complex dimension, that makes up the individual. Aboriginality is a part of who we are. It's a big part, and it influences all the other parts. But we also wear many different hats in our day-to-day life and the fact that we're Koori influences every single one of those hats. I'm an Aboriginal. I'm a woman. I'm a lesbian. I'm a mother. I'm a student. I'm a worker. I'm all of those things. So when you put me in the box that's labelled "Aboriginal" and don't look beyond that, you're not just doing me a disservice, you're also doing yourself a disservice.

"Either/or" assumptions can also mean that indigenous dykes and poofs experience having their Aboriginality ignored or devalued by other lesbians and gay men, as Aaron Ross told me:

> *Aaron Ross:* And of course you know, there's racism in the gay and lesbian community as there is in any community. I can never digest that no matter where I am. Part of what I find interesting is also white concepts of what Aboriginal people should look like, much the same as stereotypes about what gays and lesbians are supposed to look like. I'll be in social situations and someone'll have this off-the-cuff slag-off at "Abos" or "Coons,"[10] without even giving any thought of the fact that apart from it being utterly racist, that *I* am Aboriginal.
>
>   Maybe it's just a fundamental problem with the way dominant cultures work. They can't accept that people actually create and develop their own cultural identity themselves. It's not something that's imbued by people outside of that culture. It's something that's created within. Much like people saying, "Oh! You can't be gay!" Or, "You can't be a lesbian. You don't look like a lesbian." It's the same type of thing, "You don't look Aboriginal. You can't be Aboriginal."

Much as gay and lesbian activists have argued that it is someone's personal orientation that makes them gay or lesbian, rather than their appearance, Aaron points out that being Aboriginal is much more than about having dark skin. It is a cultural identity that you are born into and no-one has the right to expect that Aboriginal lesbians and gay men will drop their indigenous identity in order to be part of the gay and lesbian communities.

"I LOVE YOU WHETHER YOU'RE A POOFTER OR NOT"

Many of the people I spoke with in putting together the programs experienced some ambivalence towards their homosexuality from family and cultural communities, although it is impossible for me to generalize about this. As I learned, it is a mistake to assume that the prejudice towards lesbians and gay men in Anglo-Australia is necessarily precisely mirrored in other communities, as Aaron Ross explained:

> *Aaron Ross:* I've had bosses and brothers and sisters say to me, "Traditionally, you mob[11] [homosexuals] would have been killed [within Aboriginal society]." And I say, "You know, that's bullshit!" Because one of the very basic tenets of our people is that there's a place for everybody. Surprisingly enough, the easiest person to come out to was my Aboriginal father, who's this huge black man. "Bully," that's a nickname for him, he would intimidate all of my white friends throughout primary school . . . But coming out to him . . . was not a problem. He just said, "Well, I always thought you were and I love you whether you're a poofter or not."

Jamie Anderson and Paul Baker are young Koori men who grew up in Brewarrina, a remote town in central-west New South Wales. When I went to interview Paul in his office at the Aboriginal Education Unit of a university in Sydney, Jamie also happened to be around and could not resist adding some comments of his own. Both men agreed that it was a completely different story to come out in a country town where everyone knows your business and homosexuality is unacceptable:

> *Abby:* So did you come out in Brewarrina?

> *Paul Baker:* Yes I did. I came out in my final years at school. Got a lot of flack from all the locals and stuff; found it hard; got bashed a couple of times. It didn't go down too well. My mother still doesn't accept it. To this day she's a bit funny about it. My father's cool . . . I knew I was gay when I was about 9 years old, 'cause I always fancied men, you know. I just knew. Growing up, playing with dolls, fighting with the girls . . . [laughing] you know, playing cubby house all the time . . .

> *Jamie Anderson:* It's different, you know, growing up in a small isolated town and being gay, because you do have a lot of flack from people giving you a hard time. It is really hard, to live a life out there in Brewarrina. Like, you walk down the street and all of a sudden you'll have all these people coming up and saying, "Look at the poofter. Where are you going, you poofter?" and things like that. So it's different to what it is down here in the city.

Calling oneself lesbian or gay can be difficult if you come from a culture where the focus is on maintaining the status of the family, rather than individ-

ual freedoms. I visited Arnel Landicho, a Filipino gay man in his office at the
AIDS Council of New South Wales, where he was working on a program
aimed at educating Asian men about the dangers of HIV. I asked him what
being gay meant for Asian men living in Australia:

> *Arnel Landicho:* We have to realize that for a lot of these men, they
> come from close-knit families. Whatever's got to do with their own
> selves reflects on the family. In some cultures, to have somebody that's
> homosexual in the family is not only an insult or degrading for that
> particular person, but to the family as well. When we talk about family,
> we're not only referring to the immediate family, but to the extended
> family as well. To be gay, that's a very big problem for a lot of these
> people.

Denial of the existence of lesbians and gay men within some cultural
communities can make it very difficult for people to remain active in their
own culture after coming out. It presents the problem that in order to live as a
gay man or lesbian, there may at times be no alternative but to sever all
connections with both family and culture. Michael Nisner is the irrepressible
founder of Aleph, a support group for gay and lesbian Jews:

> *Michael Nisner:* Up until about two and half years ago, the real thinking
> of Jewish people was that there was no such thing as a gay or lesbian
> Jew. If a gay Jew came along and spoke to a rabbi, it was a case of,
> "Let's hide him as quickly as possible." That was usually done through
> very very good advice [ironic] and that was, "Go out, get married, have
> children and you shall be cured!"
>
> I've had several fascinating experiences where people have rung me
> up just to have a chat on the phone about being Jewish and gay. They'd
> say, "Come on, let's go and have a cup of coffee or something," and I'd
> say, "Yeah, that'd be nice," and I'd suggest, "How about we both meet
> down at Bondi[12] somewhere? We both live in Bondi, yeah?" No, we've
> actually ended up going to Hornsby,[13] because they were too scared
> that if somebody saw them sitting down with me in a coffee shop,
> they'd automatically be tarred with the same brush.
>
> Myself, I've never had any trouble with either issue [being gay or
> Jewish]. For example, I do go out onto Oxford Street every now and
> again. I do go to a gay pub. I do go to a dance party. Because I identify
> as a Jew, I do wear a *kippa*, the . . . headdress that Jewish men wear.
> You'll find different people come up to me and say, "Oh! Are you
> Jewish?" And then you eventually find they start coming out of the
> closet to me as being Jewish! So I'll say, "I'm Jewish too!" [laughs]

There are lesbians and gay men who confront the prohibitions in their own cultures against being homosexual. But challenging these views in addition to Anglo-Australian homophobia and racism takes a great deal of strength and commitment, as Ora Barlow explained:

Ora Barlow: It's been really important for me to come out to my family and to my extended family. I've been out for about ten years and it's only in the last five years that I've actually been a lot more political and a lot more vocal about it. It's taken me that long just to have enough strength and enough, kind of, choice about it . . . Choice, in that if people choose to accept it then that's great. If they don't, well then "See ya later. I don't want to know about you."

That's very difficult for me as a woman of color, to think that there are going to be members of my family and extended family that won't have anything to do with me. It's hurtful every single time that happens . . . But I think that it's important [to be out]. And my family and I have grown a lot closer because of it, because I've been a lot more open. I've told them that they [should] educate themselves or else I'm going to stay out of their lives forever! [laughing] Basically, [I give them] the hard line! [serious] Do it, or just forget that you've got a daughter. That's the choice that I've been able to make and I have been very fortunate. But other people of color who are lesbian or gay or transgender, don't necessarily have that choice.

SISTER OUTSIDER

Sometimes it is impossible for gay and lesbian people to live within the expectations of both the Anglo gay culture and their community culture. Sofi Christopher Ra Iri To Pata O Teau Waith was born in the Cook Islands northeast of New Zealand, and grew up in New Zealand before moving to Australia. Although Christian missionaries challenged the traditional acceptance of transgender and gay men in Polynesian society, it was family expectations that stopped Sofi from coming out as gay for many years. His gentle manner of speaking contrasted vividly with the difficult situation he found himself in:

Sofi: [I come] from a family with status, both my father and my mother are from high chief families. This is hereditary and you're born into it. Being the eldest son, my eldest sister and I have status in that family. What goes with that is titles and also an expectation that has been passed on for centuries and centuries and centuries.

So, I didn't just have the pressure from the western culture. The feeling that I also had from a very young age was, "How am I going to have children? How am I going to continue this line that has gone on unbroken for centuries, on my father's side and on my mother's side?" And I knew I couldn't. So there was all this shame, there was all this feeling of letting the family down, not being good enough, the whole thing.

From when I was young, I grew up with the stories of all the feats of my ancestors. They were all legends in their own lifetimes and I'm thinking, "My God! I don't fill any of their shoes!" The saddest part of it for me is that my father's high chief title dies with him, because I'm not suitable to take it on . . . That's hard, because it's a centuries-old tradition that'll die with him. My name, Sofi, is actually a traditional name and only the eldest son gets that name and it's part of a title name. It's like I'm the last of that line . . .

And it's really sad because for me, being gay is only one part, one small part of me as a person. My identity as a Polynesian man is far more important to me and I see that as being more of an identity thing as opposed to being gay. Gay is a sexual preference . . . Funnily enough, it shouldn't take over my whole life . . . but it actually does, and that's the crazy part about it.

Feeling like an outsider in two communities can put pressure on people to choose one community as their main source of support. But the stakes are very high in making this choice when a person stands to lose the main connection with their whole culture by admitting they are a lesbian or a gay man. As Uma Kali Shakti explained, the process of negotiating a life between two cultures can sometimes be hard work:

Uma Kali Shakti: My mother had always said, "Now, whatever you do, tell me the truth. I want to know." Boy, what a joke! She once asked me, "Are you a lesbian?" and the word she used was Hindi, and from what I understood it meant, "Are you a woman who 'wraps herself around another woman'?" [Audience laughter]

Now I had plugged into the gay liberation movement's call of "Come out, come out, wherever you are," and I did . . . My mother's reaction was basically that she wished she'd never had me . . . There were some things that were, I think, entirely Indian. Being Hindu, she said, "What did I do wrong in my last life?" [Laughter from audience. Uma waits for silence to fall before continuing.]

It was really really very painful. I went off to England and for three years she wouldn't have anything to do with me. And it's also like . . . how do I describe it to them, about what I do? Because there's lots of ways in the "queer" community. I don't fit the stereotypes either. So I'm always what Audre Lorde[14] calls "sister outsider."

Uma's experience with her mother prompted her to offer support to other gay men and lesbians of color through the Internet.

> *Uma Kali Shakti:* Now I'm on email internationally. I'm known as "Dyke Didi," which means "dyke big sister." I get a lot of calls, email messages, from lots of young ones coming out and hope that I'm a role model for them, because I wish I'd been there for other people. For example, a young Indian gay man in Melbourne has had a huge problem with his family, so I said to him–this is how the name "Dyke Didi" came about–I said, "I will be your Didi. I will be your big sister." Because I lost my Mum, lost members of my family, we *have* to be the uncles and aunts, mothers and daughters and sisters and brothers, the families that we've lost. So that's part of what we're doing both nationally and internationally.

MAKING A SPACE TO TALK

It's impossible to generalize or to come up with any quintessential "multicultural coming-out story." The only constants I found in preparing the radio program were the risks implicit in coming out and the limited and often stereotypical views of the Anglo-Australian culture towards people from non-Anglo backgrounds. For these and many other reasons, a number of groups have been established for lesbians and gay men to talk about the cultural issues they have in common and to support to each other.

Ora and Sofi both work at 2010, a housing association for young gay men and lesbians in the inner city of Sydney. In the early 1990s they decided to set up a group for indigenous lesbians, gay men, bisexuals and transgender people called "Indigenous or What?" The people participating in the group are from diverse backgrounds, many of which hold contrasting views on homosexuality. But one constant among the members of "Indigenous or What?" is the feeling of always being "different" in gay and lesbian circles:

> *Sofi:* As I say to a lot of the young people here, when I . . . look in the mirror I don't see the image that's being projected as being the ideal, you know, the blond-haired, blue-eyed person. I see a Polynesian face, and for years I had to come to terms with that. Instead of seeing my face in the mirror I saw what I wasn't . . . We started up an indigenous support group mainly for that reason.

Ora: Whenever I see a person of color walking down the street, I go woo-hoo! [elated] There's another face that's actually affirming the color that I am. Upon creating this group there was an instant wanting of connection. Not assuming that just because you're the same color you're gonna be best buddies or best brother and sister. But . . . there's a real acknowledgment that this kind of link is really important for us. There is safety in numbers and there is also strength in numbers.

So we started up this group . . . It was basically a social network of people of color and indigenous peoples to meet each other, to talk, to yack, to politicize, to hang out, to talk about the things that are happening for us. How it is, the isolation within lesbian and gay and transgender communities, as well as the isolation within our own racial cultures regarding our sexuality. It was really exciting, the first meetings–amazing gems and gold . . . came out of it.

With such a broad range of people attending the group, I wondered whether participants found much in common:

Abby: I know, having talked to some people from Asian gay and lesbian groups, that often there's not a huge amount in common . . . An Indian dyke isn't really going to necessarily have much in common with a Singaporean gay man, for example. Did you find that there was much commonness amongst the experiences of the people who turned up to the group?

Ora: I think it's a good point about diversity, in that just because people have similar color skin doesn't mean that they have similar experiences. We do have common experiences in that racism is a current force in all of our lives, but we can't assume that just because we might have similar color skin that we're having similar experiences.

Establishing groups for lesbians and gay men from specific cultural backgrounds is hardly separatism. Rather, it is a chance for people to support each other and discuss the unique intersections of their culture and sexuality. Deaf people in Australia share a common language, Australian Sign, and culture, as well as a strong sense of community. But a close-knit community can put extra pressure on its lesbian and gay members not to exhibit any further signs of being different. I was extremely fortunate to have the opportunity to talk to Alice Lewis, a deaf woman who's been out as a dyke for several years. Her message was a strong one:

Alice Lewis: There isn't any gay and lesbian deaf community at all, really. I mean, I have a number of friends who are gay and deaf and we meet very privately. I guess a lot of deaf gays and lesbians go to the hearing community. [Hearing gays and lesbians] are very open and very broadminded and they say, "Yeah, come along, you're welcome," but major support has to be given, because [deaf lesbians and gay men] want to communicate and they can't.

I would say it's not easy, especially if you have a non-English-speaking background family. If they're, say, Lebanese and from a Muslim background . . . these people have a real problem. They're gay, they're deaf and they have another culture. There's three cultures in one. There's just no services for them at all, so they're hiding. They aren't coming out at all.

It took a long time to come to terms with the fact that I was married to a hearing person and I was a deaf person, as well as having a sexuality difference. But once I put them in perspective, it wasn't so hard at all. If anything, I was just jubilant! I was just so happy, because I'm a person first. Number one priority, I'm a person. I'm deaf and I'm a lesbian. Coming out for me, it was like the sun came up. It's just a feeling of being set free. That's how I felt. I was set free and I could get on with my life.

CONCLUSION

Every one of the people that I spoke to had a different way to describe their identity and I doubt that there could ever be an archetypal "multicultural gay and lesbian identity," or even one unified way to describe being gay or lesbian and from a "different" cultural background. This poses a vital challenge to the exclusive nature of either cultural identity or sexual identity, as Paul Baker concluded:

Abby: Do you ever get people asking you what's most important, your blackness or your being gay? Which one are you?

Paul Baker: Both. Being black and gay makes me real proud . . . for being a two-spirited person of one color. It's excellent. It makes me proud!

AUTHOR NOTE

The author is indebted to all those who took part in the project, particularly Ora Barlow and Uma Kali Shakti for their suggestions and comments.

NOTES

1. Muff Diva is a variant of the expression "muff diver," originally a slur referring to lesbian oral sex. A dyke Elvis Presley impersonator billed herself as a "muff diva" on a tour of Australia in the early 1990s and I have appropriated this term here because of its appropriate performative tone.

2. "Stroppy"–Australian idiom for a somewhat quarrelsome, independent-minded person. To be stroppy is to have an attitude of not tolerating being put down, denigrated or condescended to.

3. In Australia the expression "Pacific Islander" refers to Polynesian and Melanesian peoples from South Pacific island countries. People from the North Pacific country of the Philippines are called "Asian" in Australia, not "Pacific Islander."

4. The conference focussed on lesbian and gay identities and cultures in Asia, Australia and the Pacific. All quotes from the conference are extracted from personal recordings of the speakers.

5. The official flag of the Aboriginal people of mainland Australia consists of a golden sunset in the middle of two horizontal bars of red and black. Red, gold and black are the acknowledged colours of the Aboriginal land rights movement.

6. "Khush" is a Sanskrit word meaning "happy," "gay," "joyous," "spiritually fulfilled." The word "Khush" has been appropriated by South Asian gay and lesbian communities to mean "gay" or "queer" because there is rarely an equivalent term in South Asian languages.

7. Desi: from Hindi, meaning "from the homeland" or in this context, "homegirl."

8. Murris are Aboriginal people originating from northern New South Wales and Queensland. The Kukuyalingi people are from far north Queensland.

9. Kooris are Aboriginal people originating from the southern part of New South Wales and from Victoria.

10. "Slagging off" someone means putting them down. "Abos" and "Coons" are derogatory terms for Aboriginal people.

11. In Australian Aboriginal English "mob" refers to a group, clan, class or race of people.

12. Bondi is a beachside Sydney suburb in the city's east, where a large proportion of Sydney's Jewish population lives.

13. Hornsby is a northern suburb of Sydney, about one and a half hours' drive from Bondi.

14. Audre Lorde is an African American lesbian poet, writer and theorist.

INTERVIEWS/CONFERENCE PRESENTATIONS

Recorded by Abby Duruz.

Jamie Anderson and Paul Baker, interviewed Sydney, 5 December 1995.

Ora Barlow, interviewed Sydney, 5 December 1995.

Sue Green, Panel discussant: *Indigenous Australia*, "Emerging Gay and Lesbian Communities" Conference, University of Sydney, 30 September 1995.

Uma Kali Shakti, Panel discussant: *Ethnicity and Lesbianism in Australia*, "Emerging Gay and Lesbian Communities" Conference, University of Sydney, 30 September 1995.

Arnel Landicho, interviewed Sydney, 7 December 1995.

Alice Lewis, interviewed Sydney, 13 December 1995.

Michael Nisner, interviewed Sydney, 19 December 1995.

Aaron Ross, interviewed Sydney, 29 November 1995.

Sofi Christopher Ra Iri To Pata O Teau Waith, interviewed Sydney, 6 December 1995.

Diary Entries from the "Teachers' Professional Development Playground": Multiculturalism Meets Multisexualities in Australian Education

Maria Pallotta-Chiarolli

Deakin University, Melbourne

SUMMARY. Educational institutions are major cultural and social systems that police and regulate the living out of multicultural and multisexual queer identities, yet which also provide sites for anti-discriminatory responses to the marginalization of these multiple, hybrid identities. Censorship and disapproval (both real and imagined) together with informal codes and regulations for inclusion and representation within school and college communities reflect and reproduce formal debates within the wider society, and within ethnic, feminist, and gay/lesbian communities. Through a series of "Diary Entries," I document my work and experiences with educational groups in both secondary and tertiary education in Australia in recent years–in what a bicultural, bisexual teacher-friend calls "teachers' professional development playgrounds." I explore dilemmas, concerns and strategies for placing "multiculturalism" on the "multisexual" agenda and, conversely, for placing "multisexuality" on the "multicultural" agenda. *[Article copies available for a fee from The Haworth Document Delivery Service: 1-800-342-9678. E-mail address: getinfo@haworthpressinc.com]*

Correspondence regarding this article may be addressed to Maria Pallotta-Chiarolli, School of Nutrition and Public Health, Faculty of Health and Behavioral Sciences, Deakin University, 221 Burwood Highway, Burwood, VIC 3125, Australia. [chiar@ozemail.com.au]

[Haworth co-indexing entry note]: "Diary Entries from the 'Teachers' Professional Development Playground': Multiculturalism Meets Multisexualities in Australian Education." Pallotta-Chiarolli, Maria. Co-published simultaneously in *Journal of Homosexuality* (The Haworth Press, Inc.) Vol. 36, No. 3/4, 1999, pp. 183-205; and: *Multicultural Queer: Australian Narratives* (ed: Peter A. Jackson and Gerard Sullivan) The Haworth Press, Inc., 1999, pp. 183-205. Single or multiple copies of this article are available for a fee from The Haworth Document Delivery Service [1-800-342-9678, 9:00 a.m. - 5:00 p.m. (EST). E-mail address: getinfo@haworthpressinc.com].

INTRODUCTION

Australian schools and tertiary institutions, particularly in the major cities, provide intriguing and exciting snapshots of the many faces of Australian multiculturalism as both policy and reality. For example, Lidcombe Public School in Sydney teaches students from 37 different language backgrounds. Preston Girls' Secondary College in Melbourne has a student population that is over 90 per cent from non-English speaking backgrounds (DEETYA, 1996). Whether they be in mainstream schools or independent and religious schools, students, teachers and parents "are simultaneously the members of multiple lifeworlds, so their identities have multiple layers, each layer in complex relation to the others" (Cope and Kalantzis, 1995, p. 10). Whether they be sixth generation Anglo-Australians, second generation ethnic Australians, first generation migrants, or recently arrived refugees of diverse religious and socio-economic backgrounds, all members of the school community need to "be proficient as we negotiate these many lifeworlds, the many lifeworlds each of us inhabit, and the many lifeworlds we encounter in our everyday lives" (Cope and Kalantzis, 1995, p. 11).

Since the early 1980s in Australia, educational materials and policies have been produced which acknowledge that being of non-English-speaking background does not mean being split or torn between two worlds, but means negotiating and drawing upon the many to inform the one, being able to live in many worlds within the one, being aware of the interweaving of many categories such as ethnicity, gender, and class rather than constructing an artificial educational pedagogy and practice where categories are dealt with as separate and not impinging upon or being influenced by the others (see Tsolidis, 1986; Ministry of Education, 1989; Sloniec, 1992a; Sloniec, 1992b; Pallotta-Chiarolli, 1995a, 1996a).

However, despite the pedagogical discourses of social justice, equity and access to educational resources for all students, and inclusive curriculum frameworks used in all government and independent religious school policies to frame curriculum and student welfare programs and practices, the interweaving of *sexuality* with categories such as ethnicity, gender and class is not addressed consistently throughout Australian states and religious schools (see Pallotta-Chiarolli, 1998a, in press).

For example, *ESL (English as a Second Language) Provision Within a Culturally Inclusive Curriculum Guidelines* produced by the Catholic Education Office (1997) in Melbourne, Victoria, states that "culture" is meant to be interpreted broadly "to include not only concepts of race and ethnicity, but also to take account of the range of intersecting elements that shape cultural identity including gender, class, religious background, socio-economic status, age, ability and disability" and that all "individuals are simultaneously members of many overlapping social and/or cultural groups and there is as much diversity *within* social and/or cultural groups as there is *between* them" (Catholic Education Office, 1997, p. 10). Due largely to the fundamentalist Catholic dictates coming from Victorian Archbishop George Pell and his followers, or those choosing to comply rather than risk their careers, and despite the efforts at resistance and subversion by some of the educators in developing and implementing this policy document, sexuality and homophobia are not mentioned anywhere in this 112-page document.

On the other hand, the national policy document *Gender and Equity: A Framework For Australian Schools* produced by the joint federal and state Ministerial Council for Employment, Education, Training and Youth Affairs (MCEETYA, 1997), and the policy statement of the Specific Focus Programs Directorate of the New South Wales State Department of School Education (Specific Focus Programs Directorate, 1996), *Girls and Boys at School: Gender Equity Strategy 1996-2001*, are significant steps forward in their explicit situating of sexuality and homophobia alongside other categories throughout both documents. *Gender and Equity: A Framework For Australian Schools* states that understandings of gender construction "should include knowledge about the relationship of gender to other factors, including socio-economic status, cultural background, rural/urban location, disability and sexuality" (MCEETYA, 1997, p. 8). Although it should have been given a section unto itself alongside other specific groupings such as "Aboriginality," "disability" and "ethnicity" to illustrate its equal importance, homophobia is nevertheless addressed in several sections of the *Framework*, particularly in relation to hegemonic masculinity, and violence in schools. Similarly, *Girls and Boys at School* states that societal beliefs about gender, "interacting with factors such as ethnicity, Aboriginal and Torres Strait Islander cultures, socio-economic status, sexuality and disability, can be linked to patterns of girls' and boys' participation in education and to their post-school outcomes" (Specific Focus Programs Directorate, 1996, p. 2). It also specifically asks schools to consider what "mechanisms are in place to ensure staff and students recognize sex-based harassment, homophobia, bullying and other forms of violence, treat it seriously and actively work towards its elimination" (Specific Focus Programs Directorate, 1996, p. 5).

"MULTICULTURAL EDUCATION IS NOT ABOUT MULTISEXUALITY"

Diary Entry: Melbourne, 1995.

Today was unsettling. The seminar had seemed to be progressing smoothly. The teachers were enthusiastic about addressing the inter-

weaving of ethnicity and gender in school policies, programs and practices. The usual nerves at the start of a day like this had subsided, so I launched confidently into the third and final section of the day: ethnicity and gay/lesbian/bisexual sexualities and how to draw connections between racism, sexism and homophobia for students.

Suddenly there were fifty solemn faces: uncomfortable, shifting, sideways glances to each other. A voice boomed at me from the front row, "You can't possibly expect us to do this. Multicultural education is not about multisexuality." The speaker was an administrator, superior to most of the others in the group. She had been very helpful all morning, initiating discussions and calling upon some of the teachers to talk about their "good classroom practices." All eyes now turned to her.

I began, " Could you explain . . . "

"No, YOU explain why you're doing this," she interjected. "There is no way I will address homosexuality, or expect MY teachers to address homosexuality with our predominantly ethnic populations."

When I asked why, the standard responses were given: ethnic parents are homophobic; they would be upset and cause problems; teachers' jobs would be on the line; there is no administrative support (she spoke as an administrator of course); it is an issue of morality. And then she asked with a wry smile, "Have you REALLY tried this in schools?"

I felt frustration and anger welling inside me. It is one thing to be dealing with someone's fears born out of the very ignorance I was there to address, it is quite another thing to have one's credibility questioned. "Yes," I replied, "and my students have generally found this material extremely useful and interesting as it shifts from an Anglocentric perspective on homophobia and homosexuality."

I began to explain how a poem by a Chinese-Malaysian lesbian, Mei Tze, could be used in an English literature classroom.

The administrator interrupted again, "This is impossible! Our parents are very traditional, very religious. They are ethnic migrants for goodness sake!"

My "professional angry" voice made its appearance. "You can't or you won't? This is not impossible since I and other teachers have done it and I'm about to workshop with you various successful strategies. I do not believe you can't do anything at all to address homophobia and homosexuality in multicultural schools. We can all start from somewhere, and do something in culturally appropriate ways to gradually shift homophobic prejudices and ignorance. That's how we've dealt with and are still dealing with racism and sexism. And I think we need to be aware that our own stereotypes and assumptions of "ethnic migrants" as homophobic may need to be challenged. Has your school actually researched the values and attitudes to sexuality of individual parents and individual students from particular cultural backgrounds?"

The administrator looked at me scornfully and said, "There's no way such research would be done and no way parents would respond, unless by pulling their children out of our schools."

"But you don't know this. You haven't asked," I responded. I decided I had given her enough attention and continued with the session. But the atmosphere remained tense. Open discussion dwindled. The woman occasionally mumbled to those next to her, and finally left a few minutes before I finished.

As I packed my materials at the end of the day, I felt like a failure. Nobody was stopping to chat, exchange contact details, or make some suggestions for improving my presentations and work. But three teachers seemed to be waiting for the others to go. I smiled at them rather forlornly. One man who had earlier identified himself as being of Greek background said, "We're really sorry about what happened. And we feel like we've let you down because we didn't speak up for you."

"Yes," a woman of Anglo-Australian background added. "Unfortunately, she's very powerful and she could . . . "

I touched her arm consolingly and said, "It's OK. That's what I'm here for. It's too risky sometimes for teachers in schools to raise this stuff, so I do it."

The Greek man then said, "Yes, but it makes us angry that we're silenced because of her. I'm gay myself. And I know there are gay and lesbian students and parents of culturally diverse backgrounds in my school."

"And I'm a lesbian," said the woman who until now had remained silent. Earlier in the day she had informed me of her Muslim faith. "And my parents are extremely supportive, so I don't see how she can make those statements."

We chatted for quite awhile, talking about issues the way we should have been able to during the session.

Through my work and experiences with educational groups in both secondary and tertiary education in what a teacher friend (who chooses to remain anonymous due to his bisexuality) calls "teachers' professional development playgrounds," this chapter explores dilemmas, concerns and strategies for placing "multiculturalism" on the "multisexual" agenda and for placing "multisexuality" on the "multicultural" agenda. Educational institutions are major cultural and social systems that police and regulate the living out of multicultural and multisexual queer identities, yet which also provide sites for anti-discriminatory responses to the marginalization of these multiple, hybrid identities. Censorship and disapproval (both real and imagined) to-gether with informal codes and regulations for inclusion and representation within school and college communities reflect and reproduce formal debates within the wider society, and within ethnic, feminist, and gay/lesbian commu-nities (Pallotta-Chiarolli & Skrbis, 1994, 1995).

Through a series of "Diary Entries" which remain fairly anonymous in order to protect those referred to, I will present examples of some of the "walls" that I have confronted in my work as a teacher-trainer and workshop facilitator.[1] However, I need to stress that my work in these issues is generally and increasingly well-received. There are many educators who really want to address the interweaving of ethnicity, gender and sexuality but lack encour-agement and opportunities to comfortably ask questions, discuss issues, and plan future policies and programs.

In my work with educators, I emphasize the need to avoid subsuming individual attitudes to sexuality into perspectives, policies and practices based solely on cultural stereotypes and generalizations. I emphasize the need to use similar strategies to those we have adopted in grappling with cultural stereotypes and generalizations in relation to gender. As Bernard Hird (1996, p. 31) writes, "cultural generalizations deflect us from closer investigation of what is actually happening to individuals." I ask educators to consider the following:

- What is the *range* of knowledges, assumptions and expectations within a particular ethnic culture in relation to gender and sexuality?
- What is the *range* of assumptions and expectations about gender and sexuality among diverse ethnic cultures, often uncomfortably lumped together as "Non-English Speaking Background (NESB)," and often presented as being in total opposition to that other uncomfortable clas-sification of "Anglo-Australian"?
- How do children born into these diverse cultures live out their realities and make their decisions about gender and sexuality?
- How do we engage students in literacy practices and strategies that pro-vide access to debates and examples of a *range* of realities of gender and sexuality that incorporate ethnic diversity without resorting to the "poor little ethnic kid" cultural deficit paradigm which can alienate and silence students?
- As educators, how can we utilize existing texts and call for a greater *range* of representations of gender and sexuality issues in culturally di-verse texts, in media representations of ethnicity, and incorporate the di-versity of ethnicity-gender-sexuality issues into mainstream educational texts and representations (Pallotta-Chiarolli, 1995b, 1996a, 1996b)?

"THERE AREN'T ANY RESOURCES"

Diary Entry: Melbourne, 1994.

*This afternoon, we had our planning meeting over cappuccinos and
tiramisu in Brunswick Street, part of inner Melbourne's multicultural/
multisexual district. We'd discussed the pedagogical philosophies and
the Catholic religious values that should be used to support their work
on countering homophobia in their Catholic schools as part of the
inclusive curriculum framework adopted in the state of Victoria. "But
there aren't any resources," they said. I mentioned going for a walk just
a few blocks down the street to the local gay and lesbian bookshop,
Hares and Hyenas. They looked very uncomfortable, as if I'd invited
them to step onto some dangerous planet where evil aliens would suddenly attack and mutate them. I jokingly said, "I'll hold your hands."
They held out their hands with embarrassed smiles.*

*We went into Hares and Hyenas, browsed, and found some useful
historical texts and culturally diverse anthologies. Their discomfort
subsided so much that they were soon buying other books for themselves.*

Accessibility is a major issue. If Australian multicultural policies and
practices expect to seriously and effectively link "access" and "equity" to
the interweaving of ethnicity and sexuality in education, we need to provide
resources for staff, student and parent members of school communities. We
need to encourage the incorporation of issues of multisexuality into multicultural instructional anthologies, into mainstream bookshops, into the media,
into live performances such as the theater, and into community clubs and
organizations. These will then become resources that teachers can use with
students.

In a short story of mine entitled "Roses," the only one addressing non-het-
erosexual ethnicity in a 1994 collection of Australia multicultural writing
(Pallotta-Chiarolli, 1994a), a day in the life of a lesbian of Italian background
named Luisa is chronicled, examining her relationships at work, with her
mother, and with her partner on their anniversary. Since the plot is contrived
so that the reader is not told that Luisa is a lesbian until the last line of the
story, an interesting activity that teachers have used is to ask students to read
and comment on the story twice.

Upon the first reading, students tend to position themselves alongside
Luisa, remarking how the ordinariness of her life is disrupted by the intrigue
surrounding who sends roses to her workplace while curious colleagues look
on. The usual student interpretation, based upon familiar socio-cultural
"scripts," is that she is having an affair with a secret lover, male of course. A

clue that jeopardizes this reading occurs halfway through the story when a lesbian acquaintance of Luisa's arrives for a job interview with Luisa's boss. This is a crossroad in the journey the students are taking with Luisa. Before they can continue, students need to decide how they feel about the possibility that Luisa may be a lesbian. Do they now distance themselves or do they go with her? Some students, however, read this point in the story as making statements about gender stereotyping and the possibility of Luisa being a lesbian does not enter into their scope of possible readings until the last line elicits surprise or aversion.

Upon the second reading, students are positioned with or against Luisa from the beginning, and now map her negotiations through the story knowing why she masks and unmasks, silences and voices, various parts of her multiple identity. This time they are challenged to consider and/or question what difference knowing that Luisa is a lesbian makes to their readings of the story and their language use in exploring their reading. For example, one student who upon first reading had defined the story as "romantic" and about "a strong Italian woman who wants to live her own life," shifted her position in relation to the story upon second reading as follows, "It's a weird story. She's trying to hide her strangeness from everyone. She made me feel uncomfortable" (Pallotta-Chiarolli, 1995a, p. 43).

"IT'S TOO RISKY"

Diary Entry: Hobart, 1996.

When I was planning a Tasmanian state conference with the co-ordinator, she told me what she wanted me to include on gender and ethnicity, adding with a sigh, "But please don't talk about sexuality. I'm not homophobic but it's very touchy and could really alienate our teachers."

"But don't they expect me to talk about that?" I asked. "I mean, they know of my work so . . . "

"Unfortunately, sexuality, in the present political climate, is too risky," was the coordinator's reply.

We finally agreed that I could "bring it in but toward the end, once everyone is feeling good about the day."

So today, I was dutifully avoiding talking about IT until my first call for questions, and a man asked, "Could you please talk about your work on sexuality and ethnicity?"

The rest of the day proceeded as I had originally wanted. The co-ordinator was pleased and confidently led the teachers' challenges to their superiors about their legal and other professional positions if they introduced this material in their schools.

Over lunch, I thanked the man who had asked THE question. He said he had been "pushing sexuality for so long," that the harassment and intimidation from colleagues had "fizzled out." Teachers now expected it of him as they did not have to "risk their reputations," so he "just delivered."

Diary Entry: Perth, 1995.

He sat there today, in the front row, with his arms folded tightly across his chest, studying me with curiosity and distaste. A female colleague of his told me he had expected me to be a "fat, butch, hairy-arm-pitted, wog dyke" and had prepared his critical "ammunition" for me. He had wanted his colleague to make a statement about my "lifestyle" so he could "get me."

At the end of my session, I called for questions. He slowly raised his hand and said crisply, "I want to know what your personal agenda is here, why you're pushing this?"

I smiled politely and said I had already thoroughly answered that during my presentation. Hadn't he been listening?

In previous writings I have voiced two major concerns with schooling as it now stands in relation to multiple marginalities (Pallotta-Chiarolli, 1994b, 1996a). First, I believe that a new form of hierarchical dualism and binary opposition is now located within most Australian schools, with a number of "safe-to-challenge" and "appropriate-to-challenge" social injustices and marginalities on one side. Indeed, the officially supported challenging of these prejudices, now labelled "inclusive education," is considered so mainstream that an educator is not seen to be fulfilling important pedagogic objectives unless these prejudices are adequately voiced and analysed. Prejudices such as racism, ethnocentrism, and sexism now generally sit securely within this "safe" category, although it certainly was not always the case and in the 1970s and 1980s early proponents risked all the reactions that are now reserved for the "unsafe-to-challenge" category of prejudices.

However, on the other side of the new dominant binary opposition in Australian education are the "unsafe-to-challenge" and "inappropriate-to-challenge" prejudices such as homophobia and heterosexism. These prejudices are still being denied, silenced, and ignored even as teachers espouse support for an "inclusive curriculum" and "safe schools." Homophobia presently sits in this "unsafe" category, although some schools and colleges are beginning to find ways of moving it into the "inclusive curriculum" and "safe schools" policies.

My experiences and those of many other educators, particularly within

Catholic schools, is that administrators and teachers can successfully imple-
ment strategies that resist and intervene in homophobic practices alongside,
and integrated within, the whole school approach to other prejudices, social
injustices and personal development with minimal parental and student resistance (Pallotta-Chiarolli, 1995c). Indeed, many Catholic schools are finding numerous ways of subverting and resisting fundamentalist directives
coming from their Church leaders. These strategies of resistance usually
require an agreement between the principal, teachers, students, and parents
that the anti-homophobic work undertaken in the school will not be made
known to the Catholic education offices and hierarchies!

Diary Entry: Adelaide, 1997.

*The co-ordinator of the national conference who originally booked me
to speak has telephoned me. She was feeling very awkward and angry.
Apparently, there are rumors that a group of fundamentalist parents are
going to protest outside the conference venue due to its content on
homosexuality. Her superiors are frightened, and this fear is playing
into the hands of the protesters who know how insecure the administrators feel. They have already managed to sabotage some previous school
and system plans to address homophobia in schools.*

*Her superiors are now wondering whether another speaker and my-
self should attend the conference at all as our positions on these issues
are publicly well-known. Second, there are rumors about our own sexual
lifestyles that the protesters may use to slander her superiors.*

*She has been forced to find out whether I wish to make a statement in
regard to my "sexual lifestyle" that she can take to the committee
meeting.*

*I refuse, saying I do not intend to be part of any inquisition to either
be given a patronizing pat on the head for being a "good girl," or be
"burned at the stake for being a witch." However, I ask her to let the
committee and her superiors know that should they cancel my speaking
engagement, I will certainly take my own steps in publicizing this cow-
ardice and hypocrisy. She sighs with relief because she has also threatened her superiors with her own resignation and public statement of why.*

The conference proceeds. It is a success. There are no protests.

EITHER "THEY DON'T EXIST" OR "THEY'RE ALL THE SAME"

Diary Entry: Hobart, 1995.

*I have just attended a very large international conference on youth.
Issues such as suicide, depression, homelessness, educational achieve-*

ments and schooling experiences were often related to gender, and sometimes related to ethnicity. I did not hear one connection made to gay, lesbian, transgender and bisexualities.

Diary Entry: Adelaide, 1993.

Today, a teacher looked genuinely puzzled and asked, "But are there ethnic gay youth? None has ever approached me." Another teacher walked out early, politely apologizing to me that she had seen my workshop written down as a "students at risk" session but it "wasn't what I expected." When I asked her what she'd hoped to hear, she said matter-of-factly, "Oh, you know, pregnant girls, poverty, suicide, family conflicts."

Diary Entry: Sydney, 1997.

I am speaking on the telephone to an international student adviser from a tertiary institution in relation to my research on homosexually active Asian overseas students and how university student health services and international student services address sexual health issues.

The voice is prim and proper, as she condescendingly replies, "I don't think there is any need to do THAT sort of work with overseas students. They are not presenting to us with these issues because they are all too busy studying to have much time for sex."

Earlier that day, I had spoken to an international student adviser from Brisbane who had been shocked that I actually believed overseas students would want to talk about sexualities.

I sit in my university office looking at a safer sex poster with two men of Asian background embracing each other. I think of the Asian students who frequent gay venues, live with non-Asian lovers, and are fronting up to the Albion Street Sexual Health Clinic in Sydney for confidential STD and HIV screenings because they would not dare go to on-campus student health services.

I think of a prominent member of the international student association, a gay Asian man, who had telephoned me to let me know of informal overseas student networks throughout Australia that were interested in participating in my research even if their universities blocked official ways of doing so. He had chuckled, "They say we're the ones with the hang-ups. Usually, it's because they've got the hang-ups with homosexuality and don't want to do anything that's uncomfortable for them. They're not able to put together in their heads that you can be Asian and gay. It's like you're Asian and that's it, whatever that word Asian means to them."

My second major concern is that much educational practice in relation to ethnicity and sexuality tends to construct an artificial homogeneity within categories and a lack of what I call "interweaving" between categories (Pallotta-Chiarolli, 1995a, 1995b, 1995d). We may be constructing a "homosexual/bisexual vs. ethnic" polarity rather than examining the multiple sites of connection and tension. How can we overcome this splitting through classification?

"IT'S TOO HARD"

Diary Entry: Sydney, 1996.

A newly-appointed regional officer for student welfare in schools was sitting grumpily listening to a session given by a colleague of mine on how homophobia makes schools unsafe and unhappy places. When it was time for group discussion, he said to us, "I don't agree with this. I think schools are quite safe and happy places."

I looked at him and wanted to say, "Well, of course you would. You are white, male and heterosexual. Yesterday, you said to me after my session on multiculturalism and sexuality, 'It's all too hard' and 'Is it really necessary?' to which I verbally pounced on you about teacher responsibility and accountability."

What was he doing in this crucial professional position? Was this another form of redneck sabotaging of new programs and policies?

Over the last year, I have become aware of a third major category of concern. I call this the "too-hard-to-challenge" category. It is "too hard," "too complex," or "too confusing" to be dealing with ethnicity, gender and sexuality all at once. Even teachers who are working hard to make homophobia cross from the "unsafe-and-inappropriate-to-challenge" category to the status of "safe-and-appropriate-to-challenge" sometimes locate themselves within this third glass cage. I visualize it as glass because even if they can see these multiple realities all around them, they cannot and/or will not engage with them. Young people of diverse sexualities and diverse cultures are cultural negotiators. Schools and teachers can act as cultural mediators between student and family communities, student and mainstream societies, and between student and social services organizations and community groups that cater for their ethnic, gender and sexual identities. To paraphrase Murphy's ideas about health workers, teacher training should focus on *information* about gay, lesbian and bisexual issues in connection to ethnicity; on the *interface* between a gay, lesbian and bisexual student, his/her sexuality, his/her ethnic community, and the effects of their living in a heterosexist and homophobic society (Murphy, 1992, p. 242). That is, teacher training should focus on the *interaction* between the school and the attitudes, beliefs, and sexual orientation of the student.

It is time that we not only encourage gay, lesbian and bisexual persons of non-English speaking backgrounds to become pro-active in their dealings with educational institutions, but that we also aim at shifting the attitudes and policies that determine and frame educational institutions themselves in their relations with students.

"THERE ARE NO STRATEGIES"

Diary Entry: Perth, 1994.

He is a dear friend and has become well-known for his exceptional work on developing strategies to deal with gender inequities. I remember the time we were chatting about our work over decafs when he said, "You know I love your work, but I can't take it into the classroom. There are no strategies."

I exploded in a way that only solid friendship permits, "Why do you all expect that the way to deal with ethnicity and sexuality somehow has to be extremely different, extremely unheard of, extremely difficult? Yet, you're all able to tell me about all sorts of policies, programs, practices in relation to ethnicity, in relation to gender, in relation to ethnicity and gender together. But something happens when I talk to you about ethnicity, gender and sexuality. Even as we go through texts, as I give you discussion starters, examples of programs and policies, all I get is, 'There are no strategies so I can't do this.' Basic teacher training should have provided basic strategies for you to apply to all social justice and human rights issues."

He's been "taking it into the classroom" for months now. He tolerates my occasional outbursts and we are still the best of friends.

In previous and forthcoming publications, I describe various strategies that acknowledge and engage with multicultural multisexualities (Pallotta-Chiarolli, 1995a, 1995b, 1996b, 1998a; see also Williams, 1997). I am thrilled that my biographical book *Someone You Know* (Pallotta-Chiarolli 1991) is now being used in many schools not only to discuss HIV/AIDS issues but also to consider issues of ethnicity and homosexuality. In *Someone You Know,* Matteo, a gay man of Italian background, is a character who explores the successful interweaving of ethnicity, gender and sexuality in his personal identity, albeit at the cost of having chosen not to come out to his parents. In the following quote Matteo is talking to a friend:

It's harder for gay men and lesbians from Italian backgrounds to come out. I love my parents and don't want to hurt them. I say things like,

"Of course I'll get married one day, I'm just waiting for the right girl." How can two old people who'd need to have the word "homosexual" explained to them ever come to terms with their gay child? They'd think it was something we'd picked up from Australian friends. They've lived through poverty, war, hunger. They come to a country where they have had to start again in everything. They make a thousand sacrifices for the kids they cherish. After all that, I haven't got it in me to break their hearts. Some might handle it. Your parents don't seem to be fussed with me at all. (Pallotta-Chiarolli, 1991, p. 23)

After reading this section students can discuss the impact on Matteo's parents of war, poverty, migration, lack of education, lack of familiarity with sexual diversity, and constructions of gender role in relation to masculinity within Italian communities. *Someone You Know* presents alternative and diverse perspectives of migrant cultures and ethnicity, and also presents some Italian migrant parents as non-homophobic (see also Pallotta-Chiarolli, 1992; 1994c). In the following quote, Jon and Kevin, a gay couple, are talking to the parents of the narrator, Maria:

I would often stand back and watch my parents talking to Jon and Kevin over the front fence, their cheerful voices carrying across the road . . . My father discussed his vineyard and winemaking with Jon, an interested listener, unlike his own children, who wouldn't drink his wine . . . My mother would invite them to come over any time and take eggs from the chickens because her daughter rarely cooked decent meals and they'd rot. (Pallotta-Chiarolli, 1991, pp. 23-24)

INTERWEAVING CATEGORIES

The following poem, "Conversations With My Grandmama," by Annie Ling provides a powerful and positive example of the experience of belonging to "many worlds." The title of Ling's anthology, *Mei Tze Is Also My Name*, is indicative of her claiming of her Chinese-Malaysian identity alongside her Chinese-Australian identity. She transcends both the traditional world of her grandparents in Sibu, Malaysia, and the Chinese-Australian world of her parents in Sydney, Australia. She simultaneously claims her dowry, "I want my gold as in Chinese tradition," and talks about her "lesbian existence." She challenges her grandmother's gender and lesbian constructs as well as western society's constructs of ethnicity, gender and lesbian sexuality. She draws from all socio-cultural constructions to devise a multiple identity that cuts through any stereotype of homogeneity within any one category. She can connect across time, geography and cultures to voice her particular identities with both her significant and societal others. Students can be asked to "map" Annie Ling's identity and list the influences of history, places, language, cultural traditions, "modern" lifestyles, and "modern" concerns such as HIV/AIDS. I am honored that the poet, Mei Tze/Annie Ling, has permitted me to reproduce this poem in full for educators and readers:

Conversations with My Grandmama

Ah Po, Ah Kung
in Sibu, Malaysia
we, your grandchildren mostly overseas
our mothers, your daughters too, are overseas

reminiscent of the past
of the times I spent with you

of you so versatile, knowledgeable and wise
so adult whilst I was young, twelve or thirteen
coming on my bicycle to visit you
when I had available time
seemingly very often
the cycle along Lanang Road
sometimes being chased by dogs

Grandmama
we have to grow up
you older and having joint pains

Grandpapa older too,
you fainted in the shop in town
as you did your daily shopping of vegetables and meat,
gave us a fright.
I love you both

We talked about my lesbian existence
I asked when will I get my dowry in gold
you said I should get married to a man
I crushed your objections
and said we have been over that,
I will not change
I ask for fairness in my dowry
I want my gold as in Chinese tradition

yet you accepted when I told you my girlfriend is Teochew[2]
you asked who cooks
I replied she does
I joked "she does the ironing as well"
Grandmama said "you must be the man"
I said "no," we look after each other and share chores
You listened you understood

you thought I would get AIDS for being a lesbian
I wanted to explain to you, I am an HIV/AIDS educator

you are so far away
we miss you
my mother and I

I thought to myself
how many of us (SAL or Sydney Asian Lesbians) are here
with ties and roots elsewhere too,
with a past and culture so different
from today

Myra with her Mum in the Philippines
Kimmy and her Grandpapa
Poonam who recently arrived

I miss you, my Grandmama and grandpapa.

today
practising softball at Marrickville Park
Dragon Boat training at the Drummoyne Sailing Club
having noodles
going to "Thai Thai" or having Indian

today

Conversation with my Grandmama
speaking my dialect.

(Ling, 1992, pp. 8-9; 1998 in press)

I ask students to "map" the different "selves" of the speaker: the "self" of the first (ethnic) culture, the "self" of the second (Australian) culture, the gendered "self," the lesbian "self," the "self" in grand/parent-child relationship, the adult "self" in love and friendships. What are the expectations of the different "worlds" and "codes"? Where are the points of connection and points of conflict?

CONNECTING MARGINALITIES

Diary Entry: Adelaide, 1992.

One ex-student told me about a teacher of non-English speaking background who would "have fits" if any racist comments were made in class but was the first to make homophobic comments and enjoy homophobic jokes at the expense of boys "who couldn't play football and soccer the way he wanted."

Homophobia is situated alongside other marginalities based on gender and ethnicity within wider, more commonly discussed thematic frameworks of marginalization and subcultural identification, such as ignorance and discrimination, love and friendship, death and dying, parents and children, teachers and students, religious dogma and spirituality. The following quotations are samples from student work, and from letters received from students in Australian schools in response to the use of *Someone You Know*:

I can now relate the prejudice that Anne Frank was subjected to for being Jewish, the prejudice Steve Biko felt from the white South Africans in *Cry Freedom*, to how Jon [a gay character with AIDS in *Someone You Know*] felt about his disease and his sexuality. He, like Anne Frank and Steve Biko, was faced with society's negative images about differences.

I am now more aware of what is happening around me. I don't regard homosexuality as a disease any more or a disorder. I just see it as a characteristic of a person, like black skin or being Vietnamese.

When we are about to die there is no different color, races or beliefs, majorities and minorities. We are all on an equal footing, no matter what walk of life we come from.

In the New South Wales state Department of School Education video kit *MATES*, about HIV/AIDS and homophobia, the leading character is an Australian of Vietnamese ancestry, Tran, who is a highly-respected and popular male figure who has to come to terms with his friend Steve's homosexuality and possible HIV-positive status. One of the two girl students who support Steve in the video is also of an (unspecified) Asian background. An interesting section of the video that would be very useful with students in connecting anti-racism and anti-homophobia occurs when Tran comforts his younger sister, who has been pushed over at school for being of Vietnamese background. When she asks, "Why do they do it, Tran?" he makes the connection to the harassment of Steve, and remembers the taunting that he himself got as a young child because of his Vietnamese ancestry.

CONTEXTUALIZATION

Providing diverse historical, religious and cultural codes and meanings in relation to sexualities allows students to have a broader base of knowledge within which to situate contemporary western, Christian constructions and to acknowledge the shifting qualities of socio-cultural constructs based on concerns such as political power, economics, and adaptation (Ratti, 1993; Williams, 1997). Annemarie Wille (1995, p. 7) explores the two discourses of sexuality now available to her in the following way:

> *[T]he discourse I was raised in only acknowledges two genders: one male, one female, whereas Polynesian societies, for example, understand humans to fall into three genders, [the third being for transgender people who are] . . . considered to be uniquely placed to access both gods and goddesses and to have a special wisdom gained from the qualities of both maleness and femaleness.*

Studies of societies such as ancient Rome and Greece, as well as pre-western or pre-colonial societies such as the Native Americans, Australian Aboriginals and early Hindu cultures provide diverse knowledge of other concepts of "normal" and "abnormal" (Ratti, 1993; Williams, 1997). It has become standard practice to contextualize the significance of a writer's gender, race, ethnicity, geographical and historical location and yet a writer's sexuality is often silenced or seen as being of no textual relevance.

PERSONAL AGENCY

Diary Entry: Sydney, 1996.

One of my university students of Lebanese-Muslim background was appointed the sexuality officer for his campus. He laughed as he told me how people come in looking for an Anglo-Australian to be the sexuality officer. They think he's the ethnic or multicultural students' representative instead. He's wondering how long it will take people to figure out the two are not incompatible. He tells of a national conference in which the organizers thought they needed to remind him that the conference was about sexuality, not multiculturalism.

While putting the above strategies and others into practice, we need to ensure that we do not present persons of non-English speaking backgrounds as merely end-products of various political, cultural and social processes by which they are rendered solely as passive victims, but rather as having various degrees of agency such as resisting, negotiating, manipulating borders and boundaries, and identifying and claiming spaces. Elsewhere I have documented evidence of the fact that some of the students challenging homophobia in Australian schools are from non-English speaking backgrounds, often with fully supportive families (Pallotta-Chiarolli, 1998a, in press). I have also edited an anthology of writings by girls and young women in Australia exploring cultural and sexual diversity in which many young women articulate their experiences and negotiations as lesbian or bisexual from diverse cultural backgrounds (Pallotta-Chiarolli, 1998b, in press).

I often raise the issue of "coming out" as a particularly Anglo version of agency, and how the strategic use of closets is also a form of agency. As V. K. Aruna (1994, p. 374) a lesbian of Tamil and Malaysian backgrounds writes in her essay "The Myth of One Closet":

> Does the politics of coming out invalidate the politics of a double identity? Even as I am suspended between borders, between definitions . . . I survive by remembering that going in and out of closets is a strategy for working to remove the conditions that make my closets necessary in the first place.

It is often difficult for English-speaking background friends, and people working in mainstream health and other service organizations to understand the cultural negotiations of gay, lesbian, transgender and bisexual persons from non-English speaking backgrounds because they are being asked to understand what to them appears to be a paradox or contradiction. The very fact that there is so much support and unity within many ethnic families and communities hinders coming out, as gay and lesbian members may want to protect their families from knowledge that will hurt them. The family is so supportive, yet cannot be asked to support a gay son. The family is so united that nothing must risk breaking this unity. There is so much love between parents and children that the very strength of this love prevents disclosure.

Men and women from English-speaking backgrounds may misinterpret or misrepresent this complex situation by stating that they are a "passive victim" of an ethnic culture that they are completely in conflict with or wish to deny, that their family and community are entirely negative realities. In fact, what often appears to be the situation is that such people are so deeply part of their family and culture *because* of the positive elements that they offered and continue to offer, and fear of risking breaking this closeness and belonging prevents open discussion of multisexuality. Being a member of a loving, supportive cultural community may be considered very important and the concealment of one's sexuality may be the price for continuing to enjoy the security and joy of family and community, especially when racism and classism within predominantly white, middle-class gay communities marginalize persons from ethnic backgrounds.

CONCLUDING NOTES: "BACKBURNERS BOILING OVER"

Diary Entry: Melbourne, 1995.

They had just attended one of the first Australian national conferences on schooling and sexualities. They represented powerful educational institutions. They were responsible for reporting back to their systems and discussing how these issues would be addressed. They could have ensured that sexuality was given a permanent and significant position on the agenda. Instead, they prepared a report that sabotaged any pro-active stance from their institutions, particularly as it declared that attending the conference was like attending the Sydney Gay and Lesbian Mardi Gras, that it had been anti-heterosexual and anti-religious.

I offered to appear in front of their organizing committees and present my own report of the proceedings, including my presentations, and challenge them to comment on my work at the conference. My invitation was declined: sexualities as part of an inclusive curriculum was to be "put on the backburner." In the meantime, students' lives are boiling over!

Our education systems are responsible for and accountable to students in accessing resources, knowledges, and skills to negotiate their "lifeworlds." As my "diary entries" show, the reality is that there will be resistance. But is it acceptable to say, "I'm not going to study sexism/racism in my school because the kids/parents/my peers are too sexist/racist?" As I stress to educators–many of whom see themselves as progressive in issues of social justice and student welfare–to continue to ignore the relevance and importance of the interweaving of sexuality and ethnicity is to continue to allow lesbian, gay, bisexual and transgender students to suffer from silence, isolation, and verbal, emotional, psychological and physical violence. It is to stand back and allow the realities of multiply marginalized members of our schools to be excluded, distorted and trivialized, even while as educators we engage in the discourses of anti-discrimination, equal opportunity, pedagogic responsibility.

NOTES

1. My gratitude to the support of my supervisors, Dr. Jeannie Martin and Dr. Andrew Jakubowicz. I appreciate the many friends and colleagues who allow me to tell their stories, such as Matteo and Luisa, and of course to Jon who still teaches with me. I am grateful to Mei Tze for permission to use her poetry, and to the many supportive and pro-active teachers and students who have discussed or written to me about their approaches, ideas and strategies. I wish to thank friends and family, especially Wayne Martino, Alan Stafford, Robert Chiarolli and Steph Chiarolli for their encouragement, support and patience. This article was largely written while sitting and chatting at my father's bedside in hospital, and sharing the "diary entries" with him. I wish to dedicate this piece to my father, Stefano, who, along with my mother, was my first educator in issues of social justice, including racism, sexism, and heterosexism. In his time, Stefano was a man who transgressed the norms of masculinity in the "roles" of lover, husband and father.

2. Teochew is a Chinese language group from Guandong Province.

REFERENCES

Aruna, V.K. (1994). The myth of one closet. In S. Lim-Hing (Ed.) *The very inside: An anthology of writing by Asian and Pacific Islander lesbian and bisexual women* (pp. 373-375). Toronto: Sister Vision Press.

Catholic Education Office. (1997). *ESL (English as a second language) provision within culturally inclusive curriculum guidelines*. Melbourne: Catholic Education Office.

Cope, Bill and Kalantzis, Mary. (1995). Why literacy pedagogy has to change. *Education Australia, 30,* 8-11.

Department of Employment, Education, Training and Youth Affairs (DEETYA). (1996, May). Interweaving ethnicity, gender and sexuality. In *The GEN.* (Canberra), pp. 1, 4.

Hird, Bernard. (1996). EAP: Teaching Chinese learners to be impolite. *English in Australia, 115,* 29-37.

Ling, Annie. (1992). *Mei Tze is also my name.* Sydney: PMT Publishing.

Ling, Annie. (in press 1998). Conversations with my Grandmama. In M. Pallotta-Chiarolli (Ed.). *Australian girls* (working title). Lane Cove, Sydney: Finch Publishing.

Ministerial Council for Employment, Training and Youth Affairs (MCEETYA) Gender Equity Taskforce. (1997). *Gender equity: A framework for Australian schools.* Canberra: Department of Education and Training (DEET).

Ministry of Education. (1989). *Equal opportunity for girls in education.* Melbourne: Victorian Ministry of Education.

Murphy, Bianca Cody. (1992). Educating mental health professionals about gay and lesbian issues. In K.M. Harbeck (Ed.). *Coming out of the classroom closet* (pp. 229-246). New York: Harrington Park Press.

New South Wales Department of School Education. (1993). Video Resource: *Mates* (23 min. VHS). Produced by Health Media and funded by the AIDS Bureau, New South Wales Health Department.

Pallotta-Chiarolli, Maria. (1991). *Someone you know: A friend's farewell.* Adelaide, Australia: Wakefield Press.

Pallotta-Chiarolli, Maria. (1992). What about me? A study of lesbians of Italian background. In K. Herne, J. Travaglia & E. Weiss (Eds.). *Who do you think you are? Writings by second generation immigrant women in Australia* (pp. 142-158). Sydney: Women's Redress Press.

Pallotta-Chiarolli, Maria. (1994a). Roses. In P. Moss (Ed.) *Voicing the difference.* (pp. 141-157). Adelaide, Australia: Wakefield Press.

Pallotta-Chiarolli, Maria. (1994b). Connecting landscapes of marginality: AIDS and sexuality issues in the English classroom. In W. Parsons (Ed.) *Landscape and identity: Perspectives from Australia* (pp. 111-126). Centre for Children's Literature, University of South Australia, Adelaide: Auslib Press.

Pallotta-Chiarolli, Maria. (1994c, December). It's not my death I'm worried about. *AIDS Awareness Week Bulletin* (Australian Federation of AIDS Organisations [AFAO], Sydney), *2*, 2.

Pallotta-Chiarolli, Maria. (1995a). Only your labels split me: Interweaving ethnicity and sexuality in English studies. *English in Australia, 112,* 33-44.

Pallotta-Chiarolli, Maria. (1995b). "A rainbow in my heart": Negotiating sexuality and ethnicity. In C. Guerra and R. White (Eds.). *Ethnic minority youth in Australia* (pp. 133-146). Hobart: National Clearinghouse on Youth Studies.

Pallotta-Chiarolli, Maria. (1995c). "Can I write the word GAY in my essay?": Challenging homophobia in single sex boys' schools. In R. Browne and R. Fletcher (Eds.). *Boys in schools: Addressing the issues* (pp. 66-81). Lane Cove, Sydney: Finch Publishing.

Pallotta-Chiarolli, Maria. (1995d). Mestizaje: Interweaving cultural multiplicity and gender codes in English studies. *Interpretations: Journal of the Western Australian English Teachers Association 28* (2), 56-73.

Pallotta-Chiarolli, Maria. (1996a). A rainbow in my heart: Interweaving ethnicity and sexuality studies. In C. Beavis et al. (Eds.). *Schooling and sexualities: Teaching for positive sexualities* (pp. 53-68). Melbourne: Deakin University Press.

Pallotta-Chiarolli, Maria. (1996b). Inclusive education is more than multicultural education. *Independent Education, 26* (1), 23-25.

Pallotta-Chiarolli, Maria. (1998a, in press). "Multicultural does not mean multisexual": Social justice and the interweaving of ethnicity and sexuality in Australian schooling. In D. Epstein and J. Sears (Eds.). *A dangerous knowing: Sexual pedagogies and the master narrative.* London: Cassell.

Pallotta-Chiarolli, Maria. (1998b). *Girls' Talk: Young Women Speak Their Hearts and Minds.* Lane Cove, Sydney: Finch Publishing.

Pallotta-Chiarolli, Maria and Skrbis, Zlatko. (1994). Authority, compliance and resistance in second-generation cultural minorities. *Australia New Zealand Journal of Sociology, 30* (3), 259-272.

Pallotta-Chiarolli, Maria and Skrbis, Zlatko. (1995). Ethnicity, gender and sexuality: Authority, compliance and rebellion. In L. Rowan and J. McNamee (Eds.) *Voices of a margin: Speaking for yourself* (pp. 94-105). Rockhampton: Central Queensland University Press.

Ratti, Rakesh. (Ed.). (1993). *A lotus of another color: An unfolding of the South Asian gay and lesbian experience.* Boston: Alyson Publications.

Sloniec, Elizabeth. (1992a). *Schooling outcomes of students from non-English speaking backgrounds: An overview of current issues and research.* Adelaide: Education Department of South Australia.

Sloniec, Elizabeth. (1992b). *Supportive school environment: Report of research project on cross-cultural tensions and student interaction in school.* Adelaide: Education Department of South Australia.

Specific Focus Programs Directorate. (1996). *Girls and boys at school: Gender equity strategy, 1996-2001.* Sydney: New South Wales Department of School Education.

Tsolidis, Georgina. (1986). *Educating Voula.* Melbourne: Ministerial Advisory Committee on Multicultural and Migrant Education.

Wille, Annemarie. (1995). Affirming diversity. *On the Level 3*(3), 3-9.

Williams, Walter L. (1997). Multicultural perspectives on reducing Heterosexism: Looking for strategies that work. In J.T. Sears & W. L. Williams (Eds.) Overcoming heterosexism and homophobia: Strategies that work (pp. 76–87). New York: Columbia University Press.

Unfixed in a Fixated World:
Identity, Sexuality, Race and Culture

Baden Offord

Southern Cross University, Australia

Leon Cantrell

Southern Cross University, Australia

SUMMARY. At the dusk of the twentieth century the confluence of sexuality and the multicultural subject offers a deep interrogation into identity. On the edge of the world, Australia is experiencing a poignant moment of identity crisis. For someone who is from a multicultural, multisexual background, identity is fragmented. Law and society demand unambiguous subjects, fixed by socio-political-cultural mores and expectations. To be unfixed presents difficulties in negotiating systems of knowledge and power which are fundamentally homeostatic. In the end it is all a matter of being unfixed but connected to "others," aware of the substance beyond identity and labels. This is being unfixed in a fixated world, challenging gravity, resisting definition and compromise. *[Article copies available for a fee from The Haworth Document Delivery Service: 1-800-342-9678. E-mail address: getinfo@haworthpressinc.com]*

INTRODUCTION: THE CRISIS OF IDENTITY

Like now, on his sofa, when I feel like telling him why I feel a connection to Eskimos. That it's because of their ability to know, without a

---

Correspondence regarding this article may be addressed to Baden Offord, School of Humanities, Media and Asian Studies, Southern Cross University, P.O. Box 157, Lismore 2480, Australia.

[Haworth co-indexing entry note]: "Unfixed in a Fixated World: Identity, Sexuality, Race and Culture." Offord, Baden, and Leon Cantrell. Co-published simultaneously in *Journal of Homosexuality* (The Haworth Press, Inc.) Vol. 36, No. 3/4, 1999, pp. 207-220; and: *Multicultural Queer: Australian Narratives* (ed: Peter A. Jackson and Gerard Sullivan) The Haworth Press, Inc., 1999, pp. 207-220. Single or multiple copies of this article are available for a fee from The Haworth Document Delivery Service [1-800-342-9678, 9:00 a.m. - 5:00 p.m. (EST). E-mail address: getinfo@haworthpressinc.com].

shadow of a doubt, that life is meaningful. Because of the way, in their consciousness, they can live with the tension between irreconcilable contradictions, without sinking into despair and without looking for a simplified solution. Because of their short, short path to ecstasy.

–Peter Hoeg, *Miss Smilla's Feeling for Snow* (p. 169)

A key issue in any discussion of multiculturalism and sexuality is that of identity.[1] This crucial feature is earmarked for its portrayal of complex and difficult meanings. In the postcolonial, postmodern, globalized landscape at the end of the twentieth century, notions of identity and its importance and relevance underscore a fundamental crisis which is present in politics, sociology, law and particularly culture.

The crisis revolves around knowing how, why and where to situate oneself in the present configuration and complexity of contemporary life. In Australia this is pertinent for the gay, lesbian or transgendered person who must negotiate a plethora of issues which often demand fidelity with regards to sexual identity for the sake of political equality. The crisis is also pertinent for any Australian who is not from a traditional Anglo-Celtic background. The crisis is comprised of pressures to conform, compromise, subjugate, elevate or *single out* subjective qualities which make up the individual. Thus, a person who is one-eighth Aboriginal may choose to foreground that one-eighth in order to help the cause of promoting indigenous people's rights. The crisis involves the necessity to maintain and portray a cohesive identity with the fullness of recognition while, paradoxically, because of this process, the subjective fabric of the individual is splintered and fragmented by the recognition or denial of multiple subjectivities. The foregrounding of a particular quality highlights the existence of other qualities. Queer culture and queer theory have arisen out of this insight.

In the late 1990s, with cultural pluralism under attack by conservative political forces and the monolithic nature of the economic imperative stalking the production of values, an individual finds life a continually changing and challenging pattern of references. How to socially locate oneself? Where to position oneself politically? Is one accurately representing oneself? Is it possible to represent oneself in a balanced way without eclipsing other equally important aspects? Can one live without reference(s)? Is one's identity always dependent on context? Is one's identity simply a hierarchy of aspects?[2] These questions impact on the individual who is caught in the tension between the ambiguity and fluidity of multisexual, multiracial, multicultural experience and the unambiguous representation and perpetuation of monocultural, monosexual rhetoric. These are questions about subjectivity and as Craig Calhoun (1994, p. 20) states, "a crucial aspect of the project of subjectivity is identity."

If one of the primary tasks of the intellectual is, as Said (1994, p. x) states, "the effort to break down the stereotypes and reductive categories that are so limiting to human thought and communication," then the centerpiece of complex elements at the interface of ethnicity and sexuality–identity–requires continuous, rigorous analysis. The purpose of this essay is to offer some perspectives which may be useful in formulating a theoretical framework about identity in this context.

IDENTITY AS FREEDOM OR ENTRAPMENT?

Part of the approach we take is linked to a problem which is raised in legal discourse. As law requires "fixed identities" in order to develop a cogent discourse about legal subjects,[3] the question of stereotyping, fixing, categorizing, limiting and thus controlling is relevant when the subject is perceived to be gay, lesbian or transgendered (see Morgan, 1995, pp. 9-11). In the face of the challenge of postmodernism, which represents subjects as plural, shifting, heterogeneous and unfixed, there is a fundamental tension with discourses that adhere to the "logic of identity." This logic is based on the premise that identity as a construct is fixed. Moreover, as Iris Young (1990, p. 98) points out, the "logic of identity denies or represses difference." To identify as "gay," for example, sets up a stance which negates the full possibilities of sexuality. As a quest for political inclusion and legal justice, however, the action of identification, *affirming* a position and *being* situated with others who are also affirming the same position, creates a recognizable political energy.

In a discussion about the interface between culture and sexuality, identity is fraught with the danger of being trapped by codification, that is, being trapped by the limitations of categorization. This is because of the implicit nature of identity which embraces a politics of conformity, thus denying the "sensuous particularity of experience" with all its ambiguities (Young, 1990, p. 98). On the one hand, it is valuable to identify as, say, a gay Aboriginal or gay Maori Australian. It is empowering and liberating to write on the census form the nature of one's sexual relations. The problem is that with political and legal recognition in terms of a fixed, categorized identity, comes a loss of ambiguity, complexity or ambience and even a denial of an understanding or representation of the dimensions or degrees of difference.

A further political danger regarding identification based on race, culture or sexuality involves the attendant insularity which comes from being fixed and easily identifiable. For example, political conformity produces gay/lesbian community newspapers such as *The Sydney Star Observer* or Brisbane's *Brother Sister*, but usually with a cost. That cost is the dominance of unarticulated ambiguity. By this we mean that the resonance of conformity, expressed through fixed images, held together by a supra gay, lesbian or sexual identity, displaces, alienates or disowns the subject who is characterized by an understanding that he or she is composed of various and diverse elements. In a politics of conformity there is no space for ambiguity. Such a politics therefore becomes isolated and insular, separated from the substratum of society, the everyday experiences and concerns of individuals who have mixed and changing feelings about their sexuality, social position, ethnicity, culture, religion, and so on. Located here is the confluence of difference, complexity, mutability and multiplicity.

Some might argue that subscribing to an unfixed subjectivity implies a loss of specificity and therefore the entrenched problem of marginalization will worsen. It may be true that in articulating the place of the unfixed subject there is a deepening of understanding which eclipses conformity to a set identity. There may be a shifting of cultural gravity. This is a crucial point. How to be recognized without fidelity to an identity? Is this indeed possible? The issue is the same for someone who originates from a culture other than the Anglo-Celtic mainstream. How can one be legitimated within Australian society? What if one has been in a same-sex relationship for many years; grew up Norwegian, Irish, Spanish, Polynesian, Corsican, Polish, Czechoslovakian or English; is Buddhist by religion; and is a citizen of Australia? On the basis of culture, religion, citizenship, and sexuality where would one's identity fall? Where would the gravity of identity be strongest, and where would it be weakest? Where, in other words, would "I" belong?

For the principal author, Baden Offord, these issues arose out of his inquiry into the nature of his own identity. Born in New Zealand to a father from Maori, Norwegian, Polish and British backgrounds and a mother from Irish, Corsican and Jewish backgrounds, he moved to Australia with his family in 1961. Growing up in Sydney with a dark complexion he experienced racism, often being mistaken for an Aboriginal. His family actively suppressed knowledge of the complex character of his true ethnicity until he was 16 years old. In 1983 Baden and his current Swedish/Canadian male partner met and fell in love. Prior to their meeting, Baden's partner was not only heterosexually oriented but also homophobic. After several years working in India for the Theosophical Society and after lecturing internationally on behalf of the Society, Baden was immediately censured by the elite of this organization when he revealed the nature of his same-sex relationship. In 1990 his mother revealed she was a lesbian. Having lived in India, Indonesia, Spain, New Zealand, Sweden and Australia, Baden's explorations of sexual and ethnic identity and negotiating the socio-political-cultural terrain of these polities has made him aware of the importance of understanding the relationship between self and culture in which the dynamics of power and knowledge reside creating homeostatic perceptions. Co-author, Leon Cantrell, with a background of travel and professional links in Asia, North America and Europe, has provided an invaluable sounding board and fellow enquirer in this ongoing project of what it means to be an Australian on the cusp of the twenty-first century.

Said (1994, p. 33) has observed that presenting the individual as an un-fixed subject, questioning stereotypes and labels, pushing for an understanding of subjects as plural, shifting and evolving, "does not mean a loss of historical specificity, but rather it guards against the possibility that a lesson learned about oppression in one place will be forgotten or violated in another place or time." That is, being gay or lesbian, Jewish, Maori or Greek, are identities which are ultimately related by virtue of the *indivisibility* of their existence, their shared "otherness." The point being made here is quite specific, that marginalized identities are indivisible and thus related or connected. Obviously, this does not mean that each of these identities is located in the margins in the same way. A gay Aboriginal man is located differently to a white gay man in relation to Anglo heterosexuality. A lesbian Greek woman has to negotiate Australian Anglo-Celtic society in a completely different manner from a lesbian Jew. Despite this, however, the nexus of these identities is their common experience of being ignored, rejected or subsumed by the dominant forces of society. They are interconnected agencies, indelibly marked by socio-cultural, economic, political and other contexts.

If we take this indivisibility seriously, the gay and lesbian theorist must then attempt to represent and articulate a view about the process of identity construction which takes place in all polities and cultures. As Anna Yeatman (1993, p. 231) states, "The politics of difference requires as perhaps no other politics has done a readiness on the part of any one emancipatory movement to show how its particular interest in contesting oppression links into and supports the interests of other movements in contesting different kinds of oppression." By this, the danger of insularity and misrepresentation can be avoided, that is, where gays and lesbians speak to and for lesbians and gays only. Then, other displaced political entities can be enriched by understanding the experience of different sexualities.[4] Thus, a study of the interface between sexuality and ethnicity or culture can be a significant step towards a new cultural gravity, in which the center is implicitly inclusive. For Said (quoted in Fuss, 1989, p. 115) identity politics is dangerous and misleading if it is based on "exclusions that stipulate, for instance, only women can understand feminine experience, only Jews can understand Jewish suffering, only former colonial subjects can understand colonial experience."

The conceptual framework for such analysis is opened up by the proposition that, "part of the project of queer is to resist definition" (Morgan, 1995, p. 30). Queer theory rests on destabilizing fixed identities. Indeed, the whole notion and need for identity is questioned. Because queer theory has brought into focus the fluidity of sexuality, boundaries have vaporized and the parameters of meaning and significance have altered. Wayne Morgan (1995, p. 31) writes that the concept of identity has, "perhaps, never been under such sustained attack." Sneja Gunew (1993, p. 10) writes: "In the past few decades there has been an unprecedented assault on the concept of this fixed subject by all those women, minorities, non-Westerners who realized they were excluded . . ." In the context of sexuality and culture another Australian commentator writes, "There needs to be a greater awareness, acknowledgment and negotiation of differences and multiple subjectivities, the interweaving of multicultural and multisexual lived realities; lives lived on crossing borders and blurred boundaries" (Pallotta-Chiarolli, 1996, p. 99). This is where the indivisibility of identity construction and its manifestations are situated, on the edge, on borders, in the in-between. We are arguing, therefore, that gay, lesbian, transgendered or ethnic identities are not important by themselves, but important because of their connections. Said (1993, p. 408) has helped place this argument in focus when he observes, "Survival in fact is about the connections between things." Identities are by their very nature contesting the socio-cultural and political field for recognition. We are arguing here that multicultural and multisexual identities are connected by their pursuit of survival.

BUDDHIST THOUGHT AND QUEER THEORY

Perhaps this has a resonance with David J. Tacey (1995, p. 204) when he says, "We are at the edge of a new experience of the sacred." If we take sacred here to mean having a sense of purpose or wholeness, we can relate it to the understanding of the "connections between things." Approaching subjects in this way is to emphasize empathy. In this context it is useful to take a cursory look at the position of Buddhism. As Buddhist scholars have responded to contemporary issues, a nexus between Buddhist thought and postmodern thought has been realized. Where Buddhist thought and postmodernism are at their closest is when they assert the autonomy of the individual and subvert the authority of static, fixed identities.[5] Buddhist thought has much to offer the postmodernist in terms of bridging the hiatus between the unfixed identity and social or political activism (see Inada, 1990; Murti, 1980; Conze, 1983).

As uncertainty is a chief characteristic of postmodern societies like Australia (Bauman, 1992), it is not unusual to find that the interrogation of sexual and ethnic identity is studied through many windows of the "other." In other words, the Buddhist perspective allows one who is caught up in postmodernity to better understand and live through the shifting, undoing, and remaking of identities. The Eskimo's ability to view life without despair, aware of contradictions and tensions, is also testimony to the fact that there are many ways to respond to uncertainty, ambiguity, and fragmentation. Madan Sarup (1996, p. xvi) in his work on identity and the postmodern world argues that "we do not have a homogenous identity but that instead we have several contradictory selves." As postmodernity pulls apart and qualifies identity, philosophies like Buddhism and non-Western cultural perspectives will assist in creating new ways of mapping culture and self, allowing greater reflection and possibilities for insight.

In Buddhism, understanding the "connections between things" leads to empathy which in turn leads to compassion. Queer theory attempts to understand the full ambience of a subject, just as Buddhist thought appeals to the "fact that one's experience must always be open to the total ambience of any momentary situation" (Inada, 1990, p. 99). Thus, the individual who understands the "connections between things" opens up, "new possibilities for the construction of self and the assertion of agency" (hooks, 1990, p. 28). This may be a part of the new experience of the sacred.

Interestingly enough, Cornel West (1993, p. 204) agrees with the Buddhist viewpoint when he writes:

> the new cultural politics of difference consists of creative responses to the precise circumstances of our present moment–especially those of marginalized First World agents who shun degraded self-representations, articulating instead their sense of the flow of history in the light of the contemporary terrors, anxieties, and fears of highly commercialized North Atlantic capitalist cultures (with their escalating xenophobias against people of color, Jews, women, gays, lesbians, and the elderly).

This perspective is transformative, but how can it be situated in a context in which the "interaction with legal culture, gay liberation legal rights reforms depend upon concepts of fixed identity?" (Morgan, 1995, p. 33). This is an important question that reminds us that there is an unresolved tension in the dialectics of identity. If deconstruction unfixes the stasis of identity, what reference can then be used to secure a place in a polity? Is that necessary? From a Buddhist perspective the polity is subservient to the individual. Take away the reference (constructed identity) and you gain totality.[6] In a Western legal discourse this means nothing. There is a fundamental difference in viewpoint here. What lies beyond deconstruction for the Buddhist is transformation and freedom (Kalupahana, 1986; Murti, 1980). In comparison, unlike Buddhism, deconstruction has been described as an "analytic tool not a synthesizing one" (Morgan, 1995, p. 39). However, perhaps this misses the point. Deconstruction adds to the depth and density of the socio-cultural landscape. It adds to the ambience of identities. The emergent visibility of the cultural edge, border crossing and the unfixed subject brings with it a more complete understanding of society and culture. The gravity of identity is shifting in these terms towards a less stereotyped, more ambiguous and complex configuration of power and relations. The problem that arises then has been voiced by Ken Wilber (1996, p. 325) in the following terms, "the greater the depth of transcendence, the greater the burden of inclusion." In this sense, destabilized identities bring about a politics of difference as well as a politics of inclusion. Thus, identity politics is subsumed by new approaches and possibilities, where ambience as a paradigm is more important than any reductionist paradigm. Perhaps the best way to describe this new paradigm is by referring to it as the politics of connections.

THE INTERFACE
BETWEEN THE MULTISEXUAL AND MULTICULTURAL BEING

Australian commentator and social critic Phillip Adams (see Park, 1995, p. 5) writes in the foreword to a multicultural coffee table photobook called *Beyond Black and White: The Many Faces of Australia*, "This book vividly records our differences, the way we are striving to build a new kind of nation, one that feels invigorated by diversity rather than threatened by it." In the book's introduction by Andy Park (1995, p. 15) we read, "To really see . . . is to understand collaboration. Between text and image; between condition and context; between art and craft; between people." It is interesting to note that what this book attempts to do is portray the cultural diversity of Australians by seeing connections. It blends images of the Hmong community from Laos now living in Hobart with Japanese tourist surfers at Bondi Beach in Sydney and a Latvian migrant standing next to a Hill's Hoist rotary clothesline in a suburban backyard.[7] The photographs in this book depict migrant life by fusing cultural or geographic references together with both obvious and obscure representations of ethnic difference. The purpose of this portraiture is to accent difference as well as subvert stereotypical representations.

Among the numerous representations of ethnic people and communities, which Park (1995, p. 15) says "testify to that critical interstice between blindness and insight," there are several pages which depict gay men and lesbians at the annual Sydney Gay and Lesbian Mardi Gras parade. Yet, despite the inclusion of these representations, it must be observed that the photographs locate gays, lesbians and transgendered people in a familiar and stereotypical setting with imagery that is immediately recognizable as Sydney's inner-urban queer ghetto. The purpose of this appears to be the wish to include sexually diverse representations of Australians. However, there is a contradiction in showing ethnic identities in a multiplicity of representations and gays and lesbians in a singular, unambiguous, non-blurred, identifiable once-a-year event rather than conducting their everyday lives in everyday places. Is this an example of tokenism or a misplaced gesture of inclusiveness?

Unlike the early 1990s Australian film *The Sum of Us*, in which the working-class gay male lead character problematizes the stereotype of the laconic, Aussie male (thus infusing a degree of otherness or difference into a familiar cultural image of masculinity and blurring categories), Park's book does not liberate gay representation from its fixed moorings. Arguably, the book does just the opposite and re-inforces rigid and fixed ideas about gay, lesbian and transgendered people. This is a pity given the nature of this book's overall intention to depart from stereotypical perceptions of Australians from all backgrounds.

This example illustrates the difficulties of representation in both the old socio-cultural, political and legal context which is reductive and in the new pluralist density in which representations are burdened by inclusion. Within this matrix of representation the issue of identity is very much alive. The old yardstick of the Anglo-Celtic male–the bushman, the digger[8] or Paul Hogan as "Crocodile Dundee"–is increasingly destabilized by the multicultural and multisexual presence. Books like *Beyond Black and White: The Many Faces of Australia* reflect Australia's transformation from a monocultural society. On the face of it, Australia has undergone an enormous shift in national identity in recent decades. The book highlights, however, the continuing problem of how identities of difference are situated in this new and still emerging multicultural, multiracial, multi-religious, multisexual landscape that is Australia in the last moments of the twentieth century.

In fact, in Australia it can now be proper, politically upright and "contemporary" to have respect for another's cultural and sexual integrity. It can be a matter of pride in the late 1990s to admit being part Maori, Aboriginal, Greek or whatever. It can be "mature" to admit being a multilayered individual. It can be "modern" to accept diverse sexual experience. It can be acceptable to celebrate the diversity of the individual and society. But the problem remains of having a voice in the Australian polity. Is there a fundamental flaw in *becoming* gay or lesbian or black in the search for political equality? Does *becoming* this or that imply a loss of the shifting, heterogeneous self? Does that mean a split between the inside and the outside as Johnson (1987, pp. 174-5) suggests?

Gordon Matthews in his autobiography, *An Australian Son* (1996), traces his self-discovery of different identities, along the way *becoming* Aboriginal, *becoming* Sri Lankan, perhaps finally *becoming* Australian. Matthews' confusion about his origins led him to mistakenly embrace the Aboriginal race and community as his own. Reflecting on this, he wonders, "if it is better to have belonged and been wrong than never to have belonged at all? The answer to that is an unequivocal yes. The identity which I acquired conferred a great deal that was positive and that will remain with me forever: friends, community and culture. Aboriginal Australia will forever own a place in my heart" (Matthews, 1996, p. 228). Matthews' search for identity has given him an insight into the texture of multiple identities. *Becoming* in this sense led to new possibilities, depths as well as angst. Matthews' voice in the Australian polity reflects a maturation and appreciation of pluralism and multiplicity. In Matthews' case, his voice in that polity represents a new energy, one that is critiquing essentialism, while in the words of hooks (1990, p. 29), "emphasizing the significance of the 'authority of experience.'"

DIFFERENT SOCIAL REALITIES

According to some scholars the problem of having a voice in the Australian polity lies in the deeply embedded resistance to diversity from the core institutions of Australian society. In this sense there are two distinct social realities, "the social reality experienced by people in the course of their everyday life; and the one authoritatively defined by the people who are part of the dominant power structure" (Jamrozik et al., 1995, p. 4). Such critics argue that the core institutions remain monocultural and, "This monoculture, being the dominant culture, acts as a formidable force of stability and resistance to outside influence"(Jamrozik et al., 1995, p. 8).

Here, then, the same dilemma is perceived between the fixed and the unfixed identity. Institutions and the professions are culturally conservative.[9] They are the "vehicles of continuity, and, as such, they function on principles of stability and predicability, not change" (Jamrozik et al., p. 181). Jamrozik et al. argue that because of these two social realities, the result is a dichotomy "of cultural transformation from 'below' and monocultural continuity 'above'" (Jamrozik et al., 1995, p. 178). Important implications as to how the multicultural and multisexual communities are situated are thus framed by this dichotomy. How deep does cultural pluralism go? For most Anglo-Australian middle-class people, cultural transformation is "limited to the acceptance of pleasures in new food, drink, entertainment, style of living and travel, and an occasional 'ethnic' film on SBS[10] television" (Jamrozik et al., 1995, p. 177). The corollary for the homosexual subject is that he or she is experienced through such iconic events as the annual Sydney Gay and Lesbian Mardi Gras or in cafes or venues along Oxford Street, the heart of Sydney's queer quarter. For the multisexual, multicultural subject the dichotomy of social realities is clear and explicated in these examples.

One further illustration underscores this issue of social contradictions. On the historic night of 2 March 1996 Australian Federal elections were held simultaneously with the Sydney Gay and Lesbian Mardi Gras parade. That night saw an overwhelming win for the conservative Liberal-National Party coalition after 13 years of Labor Party government, and a record 650,000 people attending the largest Mardi Gras parade ever. These contradictory images of a conservative political landslide occurring simultaneously with the country's largest ever celebration of sexual diversity represented two social realities. It was one Australia, and yet there were two.

CONCLUSION: IDENTITY AS UNFIXED AND CONNECTED

This discussion has raised some of the central conceptual problems and issues associated with contemporary ideas regarding identity, sexuality, race and culture. We have argued that the queering of identity has produced a subject which has no reference, that is, unfixed in a fixated world. What we have also pointed out is that coeval with the emergence of this unfixed subject is the question of how the new cultural paradigm is situated in the Australian polity. We have claimed that being in the in-between border re-gions, being on the edge, implies a suspension of reference. That suspension blurs the nature and characteristics of identity. In relation to the dichotomy of social reality that exists, the unfixed subject is perceived to be ambiguous, subversive and non-political. The new cultural density aids in making these matters more complex. Although hierarchical models of identity are sub-sumed by this explosion of inclusion, the very essence of concern now lies in explicating every aspect of Australian culture. As we said earlier, transgend-ered, gay, lesbian, Aboriginal, Greek, Jewish, Anglo-Celtic or other ethnic identities are not important by themselves, but important because of their connections. Surely, that is the basis of a new political response.

It is, for example, the reason why it is important to say that no reference to Australian national identity can be made without including the Aboriginal, the indigenous Australian. The significance of explicating every socio-cultur-al aspect of Australia is that it breathes life into cultural transformation and makes it a dynamic interaction of participants. The terms "gay" and "les-bian," "black" and "white" (Johnson, 1987, p. 183) continue to define and "fix" matters but the uncertainty caused by the breakdown of stereotypes, multiple representations, multiple voices, is creating a new dynamic of rela-tions just a cooee[11] away from full participation in the community and na-tional polity (Yeatman, 1993, p. 243). Said (1994, p. 52) has commented that, "Every human being is held in by a society, no matter how free and open the society, no matter how bohemian the individual." The importance of this statement cannot be overestimated in the context of this paper. There can be suspension of reference, identity be unfixated, but participation is mandatory and impossible to ignore while there is always relational activity. From our perspective, such participation without a fixed identity, engenders insight, collaboration and the understanding of the importance of connections between things. Australian national identity is in the process of being entirely reconfigured. This may be in some small measure what is meant by the phrase that we are in Australia, "on the edge of the sacred" (Tacey, 1995). Identity is now adrift in a configuration of power and relations which has yet to reach its greatest density. The interface between multiculturalism and sexuality offers a discourse in which that fecund density can be realized.

AUTHOR NOTE

The authors are grateful to Heather Wearne for her comments on earlier versions of this article.

NOTES

1. The term sexuality is used here instead of sexual orientation because it implies autonomy and fluidity rather than being oriented towards one sex (Calhoun, 1994, p. 16).

2. This question is most important as it brings into focus the whole nuance of identity. What we are dealing with is the abstraction of self, that is, what is it that leads an individual human being to represent a certain quality. C. J. F. Williams (1989, p. 154), from a strictly philosophical angle, states that, "identity . . . is a non empirical-concept." This suggests that rooted in the whole notion of identity is the problem of abstraction. Applied to sexuality or race, in this instance, the individual abstracts the role and then performs through that role. Abstracted performance is what is codified. The difficulty for any study of identity is that, precisely because of its abstract nature, it is highly convoluted.

3. A recent example of this is the clearly articulated stance taken by Amnesty International (AI) since 1991. In consolidating a gay, lesbian or transgendered subject within the framework of international law and human rights, an official AI document states that "Sexual orientation is an integral part of a person's identity . . . " (AI, 1994, p. 19).

4. The onus on the gay and lesbian theorist is to represent the full depth of their work. Edward Said (1994, p. 13) writes: "The central fact for me, is, I think, that the intellectual is an individual endowed with a faculty for representing, embodying, articulating a message, a view, an attitude, philosophy or opinion to, as well as for, a public."

5. Kenneth K. Inada has explored the nexus between Buddhism and postmodernism. He contends that, like Buddhism, postmodern thought is an attempt to give attention to the "total experiential nature of things" (1990, p. 95).

6. In Buddhist thought, what is compounded must be uncompounded. The self is transient, temporal and constructed. Nirvana, or total freedom, is the extinguishment of the self.

7. The Hill's Hoist rotary clothes line is widely seen as an iconic symbol of Australian suburbia and the "Aussie backyard."

8. Bushman–a farm labourer. Digger–An Australian or New Zealand soldier or war veteran.

9. Jamrozik et al. (1995, p. 180) observe that "Resistance to cultural transformation is particularly evident in the professions, such as medicine, teaching, social work and the law."

10. The Special Broadcasting Service (SBS) is Australia's federally funded national multicultural television and radio network, broadcasting programs in a wide variety of community languages.

11. Just a cooee away–Australian idiom for "not far away," "near."

REFERENCES

Amnesty International. (1994). *Breaking the silence: Human rights violations based on sexual orientation*, New York: Amnesty International USA.

Bauman, Zygmunt. (1992). *Intimations of postmodernity*. London: Routledge.

Calhoun, Craig. (1994). Social theory and the politics of identity. In Craig Calhoun (Ed.) *Social theory and the politics of identity* (pp. 9-36). Cambridge, MA: Blackwell.

Conze, Edward. (1983). *Buddhist thought in India*. London: Allen and Unwin.

Fuss, Diana. (1989). *Essentially speaking*. New York: Routledge.

Gunew, Sneja. (1993). Feminism and the politics of irreducible differences: Multiculturalism/ethnicity/race. In S. Gunew and A. Yeatman (Eds.), *Feminism and the politics of difference* (pp. 1-19). Sydney: Allen and Unwin.

Hoeg, Peter. (1993). *Miss Smilla's feeling for snow.* London: Harvill.

hooks, bell. (1990). *Yearning: race, gender, and cultural politics*. Boston: South End Press.

Inada, Kenneth. (1990). A Buddhist response to the nature of human rights. In Charles Welch and Virginia Leary (Eds.), *Asian perspectives on human rights* (pp. 91-103). Boulder: Westview Press.

Jamrozik, A., Boland, C., & Urquhart, R. (1995). *Social change and cultural transformation in Australia*. Cambridge: Cambridge University Press.

Johnson, Barbara. (1987). *A world of difference*. Baltimore and London: Johns Hopkins University Press.

Kalupahana, David, J. (1986). *Nagarjuna: The philosophy of the middle way*. New York: State University of New York Press.

Matthews, Gordon. (1996). *An Australian son*. Port Melbourne: William Heinemann.

Morgan, Wayne. (1995). Queer law: Identity, culture, diversity, law. *Australasian Gay and Lesbian Law Journal, 5,* 1-41.

Murti, T.R.V. (1980). *The central philosophy of Buddhism*. London: Unwin.

Palotta-Chiarolli, Maria. (1996, May). Only your labels split the confusion: Of impurity and unclassifiability. *Critical inQueries, 1*(2), 97-118.

Park, Andy. (1995). *Beyond black and white: The many faces of Australia*. Melbourne: Portside Editions.

Said, Edward. (1993). *Culture and imperialism*. London: Vintage.

Said, Edward. (1995). *Representations of the intellectual*. London: Vintage.

Tacey, David. (1995). *Edge of the sacred*. North Blackburn, Victoria: Harper Collins.

West, Cornel. (1993). The new cultural politics of difference. In Simon During (Ed.), *The cultural studies reader* (pp. 203-217). London: Routledge.

Wilber, Ken. (1996). *A brief history of everything*. Melbourne: Hill of Content Publishing.

Williams, C.J.F. (1989). *What is Identity?* Oxford: Clarendon Press.

Yeatman, Anna. (1993). Voices and representation in the politics of difference. In S. Gunew and A. Yeatman (Eds.), *Feminism and the politics of difference* (pp. 228-245). Sydney: Allen and Unwin.

Young, Iris Marion. (1990). *Justice and the politics of difference*. New Jersey: Princeton University Press.

Index

Aboriginal and Torres Strait Islander
Commission (ATSIC),
154,173
Aboriginals
assimilationist policy towards, 8
civil rights of, 7
definition of, 23-24n
genocide of, 6
Kooris, 173-174,175
Kukuyalina, 172
land rights of, 7,154,155
as lesbians, 173-174,177,180
Murris, 172,173,182n
national identity of, 217
Nyoongah, 139,141
as percentage of Australian
population, 6
racism towards, 6,63,154,174
welfare programs for, 10
Adams, Phillip, 214
Adelaide, Australia, demographics of,
6
African Americans, as movie
characters, 103-104
Africans, Australian immigration
policy towards, 8
AIDS Council(s), 91
AIDS Council of New South Wales,
81,176
Asian outreach program, 36
AIDS Council of Victoria, 48
AIDS epidemic. *See also* HIV/AIDS
effect on gay and lesbian studies,
3-4
Aleph, 146,176
American Psychiatric Association, 3
Americans. *See also* United States
Australian criticism of, 20
Amnesty International, 218n
Anderson, Jamie, 175

Anglo-Celtic, definition of, 23n
Anglo Celts, as percentage of
Australian population,
24-25n
anti-discrimination legislation, 16-17,
139
anti-Semitism, 19-20
in Catholic schools, 148
forced confrontation of, 139-140
internalized, 140-141
Jewish community's response to,
137-138
of lesbian community, 139-140,
141,145-146,147-150
of Nazi Party, 137,138
"Are Jewish Lesbians Kosher?"
forum, 146
Ashkenazi Jews, 150
Asian(s)
as Australian immigrants, 7-9,
13,14,15
negative attitudes towards, 93
as overseas students, 24n,52,53,193
as percentage of Australian
population, 9,18,71-72
as percentage of U.S. population,
71-72
self-esteem of, 71-73
self-identification by, 14-15
stereotypes of, 72
Asian and Friends social group, 39-40
Asian homosexuals
cinematic representation of, 19,
99-112
The Buddha of Surburbia, 101
Chinese Characters, 102
Desperate Remedies, 100
Fresh Kill, 102
Khush, 102,107
The Last Emperor, 101

Haworth
DOCUMENT DELIVERY
SERVICE

This valuable service provides a single-article order form for any article from a Haworth journal.

- *Time Saving:* No running around from library to library to find a specific article.
- *Cost Effective:* All costs are kept down to a minimum.
- *Fast Delivery:* Choose from several options, including same-day FAX.
- *No Copyright Hassles:* You will be supplied by the original publisher.
- *Easy Payment:* Choose from several easy payment methods.

Open Accounts Welcome for ...
- Library Interlibrary Loan Departments
- Library Network/Consortia Wishing to Provide Single-Article Services
- Indexing/Abstracting Services with Single Article Provision Services
- Document Provision Brokers and Freelance Information Service Providers

---

MAIL or *FAX* THIS ENTIRE ORDER FORM TO:

Haworth Document Delivery Service
The Haworth Press, Inc.
10 Alice Street
Binghamton, NY 13904-1580

or FAX: 1-800-895-0582
or CALL: 1-800-429-6784
9am-5pm EST

PLEASE SEND ME PHOTOCOPIES OF THE FOLLOWING SINGLE ARTICLES:

1) Journal Title: _____

   Vol/Issue/Year: _____ Starting & Ending Pages: _____

   Article Title: _____

---

2) Journal Title: _____

   Vol/Issue/Year: _____ Starting & Ending Pages: _____

   Article Title: _____

---

3) Journal Title: _____

   Vol/Issue/Year: _____ Starting & Ending Pages: _____

   Article Title: _____

---

4) Journal Title: _____

   Vol/Issue/Year: _____ Starting & Ending Pages: _____

   Article Title: _____

(See other side for Costs and Payment Information)

COSTS: Please figure your cost to order quality copies of an article.

1. Set-up charge per article: $8.00

($8.00 × number of separate articles) _____

2. Photocopying charge for each article:

1-10 pages: $1.00 _____

11-19 pages: $3.00 _____

20-29 pages: $5.00 _____

30+ pages: $2.00/10 pages _____

3. Flexicover (optional): $2.00/article _____

4. Postage & Handling: US: $1.00 for the first article/

$.50 each additional article _____

Federal Express: $25.00 _____

Outside US: $2.00 for first article/

$.50 each additional article_____

5. Same-day FAX service: $.50 per page _____

GRAND TOTAL: _____

METHOD OF PAYMENT: (please check one)

❏ Check enclosed   ❏ Please ship and bill. PO # _____

(sorry we can ship and bill to bookstores only! All others must pre-pay)

❏ Charge to my credit card: ❏ Visa;   ❏ MasterCard;   ❏ Discover;
❏ American Express;

Account Number:_____ Expiration date:_____

Signature: ✗ _____

Name: _____ Institution: _____

Address: _____

_____

City: _____ State:_____ Zip:_____

Phone Number: _____ FAX Number: _____

MAIL or *FAX* THIS ENTIRE ORDER FORM TO:

Haworth Document Delivery Service	**or FAX:** 1-800-895-0582
The Haworth Press, Inc.	**or CALL:** 1-800-429-6784
10 Alice Street	(9am-5pm EST)
Binghamton, NY 13904-1580	